P9-AOW-178

# CORONATION OF THE POET

*Joachim Du Bellay's Debt to the Trivium*

# CORONATION OF THE POET

## *Joachim Du Bellay's Debt to the Trivium*

BY

ROBERT GRIFFIN

UNIVERSITY OF CALIFORNIA PRESS
BERKELEY AND LOS ANGELES
1969

UNIVERSITY OF CALIFORNIA PUBLICATIONS IN MODERN PHILOLOGY
Volume 96
Approved for publication December 17, 1968
Issued August 29, 1969
Price, $5.50

UNIVERSITY OF CALIFORNIA PRESS
BERKELEY AND LOS ANGELES
CALIFORNIA

UNIVERSITY OF CALIFORNIA PRESS, LTD.
LONDON, ENGLAND

LIBRARY OF CONGRESS CATALOG CARD NO.: 74-626075


PRINTED IN THE UNITED STATES OF AMERICA

To Leslie

# CONTENTS

Introduction . . . . . . . . . . . . . . . . . . . 1

Part One

I. Logic and Renaissance Poetics . . . . . . . . . . . . 7

II. Rhetoric and Renaissance Poetics

The Rhetorical Tradition . . . . . . . . . . . . . 25

Invention . . . . . . . . . . . . . . . . . 33

Disposition . . . . . . . . . . . . . . . . 37

Style . . . . . . . . . . . . . . . . . . 40

Part Two

III. From Poetic Theory to Practice

Art and Nature . . . . . . . . . . . . . . . . 67

Variety and Imitation: Theory . . . . . . . . . . . 77

Variety and Imitation: Practice . . . . . . . . . . . 79

Du Bellay's Translations of the *Aeneid* . . . . . . . . . 84

*L'Olive* . . . . . . . . . . . . . . . . . 96

Part Three

IV. *Les Antiquitez de Rome*. . . . . . . . . . . . . . 115

V. *Les Regrets*

Fortune's Wheel . . . . . . . . . . . . . . 138

The Satiric Reaction . . . . . . . . . . . . . 141

Rhetoric and Satire . . . . . . . . . . . . . . 148

The Lesson of Satire . . . . . . . . . . . . . 164

Conclusion . . . . . . . . . . . . . . . . . . 167

Bibliography . . . . . . . . . . . . . . . . . . 173

Glossary . . . . . . . . . . . . . . . . . . . 180

Index . . . . . . . . . . . . . . . . . . . . 183

# INTRODUCTION

STUDIES OF, notably, pre-Romantic literature are open to possible misinterpretation if no account is taken of evolution in aesthetic principles and critical terminology Some of the blame and praise bestowed on Renaissance poetry by modern critics, based on post-Freudian analysis, imagistic evaluation and Marxist ideology[1] would certainly bewilder poets and critics of that earlier period. Critical and poetic conceptions, such as pure poetry, art-for-art's-sake, imagery as the private, unordered, irrational domain of the poet, have few—if any—accurate reference points in the sixteenth century. Poets are now applauded for "imaginative invention" and damned for excessive rhetoric, as if rhetoric betokened images without substance and rehearsed emotions. Gourmont's tendentious definition of rhetoric as "l'art d'écrire sans don naturel" sums up the modern view.[2]

Yet the European Renaissance was suspicious of unguided imagination, that mistress of error, and invention had a drastically different connotation than it has today. An even greater error is the casual dismissal of rhetoric, since rhetoric, along with logic, was the handmaiden, if not the prerequisite, of poetic composition and understanding. In fact, throughout the sixteenth century poetry was inseparably joined to grammar, rhetoric and moral philosophy in the *studia humanitatis*. In recent years, Renaissance scholars have become increasingly aware of the importance of traditional rhetoric in Renaissance education, in influencing thought process and composition and in shaping the poetry of that period. But to date the most extended treatment of the relation between the arts of the Trivium and poetry has focused on national literatures and individual figures outside of France, or else, when dealing with French writers, it has singularly avoided the Renaissance.[3]

Joachim Du Bellay, as a poet and would-be revolutionary, occupies a significant and not fully explored position in the debate between the spontaneous overflow of powerful feeling and emotion methodically

[1] See, for instance, G. Vipper, "La Poésie de Joachim du Bellay et sa portée historique," *Beitäge zur romanischen Philologie*, II (1963), 77–95.

[2] Cf. "Du style ou de l'écriture," *La Culture des idées* (1964), pp. 13–39.

[3] Among a few other notable exceptions, see I. D. McFarlane's introduction to his edition of *The "Délie" of Maurice Scève* (1966), pp. 55–92, and Richard Griffiths' "The Influence of Formulary Rhetoric upon French Renaissance Tragedy," *Modern Language Review*, LIX (1964), 201–208. In his introduction to *Les Regrets* (1966) M. A. Screech notes that "Il nous manque une étude de la rhétorique chez Du Bellay," p. 23.

recollected in tranquility. On the one hand, critics have praised Du Bellay through the centuries—often to the exclusion of other Pléiade poets—for his continuing modernity.[4] His poetry has reflected a different image to distant generations; while Verdun Saulnier viewed it as the truest Renaissance spirit, Du Bellay's contemporary François Olivier found his appeal fluid and unsusceptible to facile generalization: "Quamquam sunt in iis nonnulla quae me fugiunt, quod scilicet res ipsas non capio."[5] His poetry is (wrongly) seen in the modern sense as a purely spontaneous and original reaction to external phenomena, and his critical theory in its historical context makes him (but with reservations) a prophet of Romanticism.[6] But one of the charms of history is its ironies. The nineteenth-century generations that "discovered" and labeled the Renaissance judged it by such Romantic canons as sincerity, radical individuality and the sanctity of artistic creation, which, although similar, are not always congruent with criteria held three centuries earlier. These Romantic standards, modified by accretions of later theory, have generally continued as the criteria for evaluating Du Bellay's poetic production, often to his detriment. The greatest Du Bellay scholar, Henri Chamard, censures him for not having lived the feelings he sings in *L'Olive* and elsewhere criticizes the *Vers lyriques* for their "rhétorique, insincérité,"[7] as though the two terms were synonymous. Chamard's equation has been the keynote for divers Du Bellay critics who have also attempted, as Verlaine put it, to wring the neck of rhetorical eloquence. For Joseph Vianey, Du Bellay's rhetoric is "creuse," Marcel Raymond couples it with platitude and Frank McMinn Chambers reproves the poet's model for its "artificial rhetoric,"[8] a reproach that might have struck any Renaissance poet as praise. Rhetoric is considered as being either antithetical to poetic creation or else as a lower form of composition; W. F. Patterson speaks of rising from rhetoric to the level of poetry, while Henri Weber insists that, were it not for its rhetorical character, the "Complainte

[4] E. G., Anon., *Mémoires pour servir à l'histoire des hommes illustres dans la république des lettres* (1727–1745), XVI, 398; C. A. Sainte-Beuve, *La Poésie française au XVI<sup>e</sup> siècle* (1843), p. 334.

[5] *Du Bellay* (1963), pp. 95, 171.

[6] Francis Ambrière, *Joachim du Bellay* (1930), p. 64; Frédéric Boyer, *Joachim du Bellay* (1958), p. 96.

[7] *Joachim du Bellay* (1900), p. 199; *Histoire de la Pléiade* (1961–1963), I, 288; see also Henri Peyre, *Literature and Sincerity* (1963), pp. 20–21.

[8] Vianey, *Le Pétrarquisme en France au XVI<sup>e</sup> siècle* (1909), p. 165; Raymond, *L'Influence de Ronsard sur la poésie française (1550–1585)* (1927), I, 109, 121; Chambers, "Lucan and the *Antiquitez de Rome*," *PMLA*, LX (1945), 946; see also Guido Saba, *La Poesia di Joachim du Bellay* (1962), p. 68.

du désespéré" might attain the periodic movement of Chateaubriand.[9] To be sure, these last two critics represent a modified and demonstrable view, if only for the relationship they allow between rhetoric and poetry.

The following chapters will attempt to elucidate this relationship and show that the study and application of grammar and especially logic and rhetoric form the groundwork of Du Bellay's poetic theory and practice, just as they did in varying measure for other poets in Renaissance Italy and England. The chronology of a poet's work often forbids the smooth curve of artistic evolution that biographers and critics like to imagine. This is the case with Du Bellay whose *Discours,* for instance, largely postdate the superior *Regrets.* Without undue concern for chronology, then, I have ordered my material in a sequence that affords the reader a necessary background in the Trivium, an eye to the ways theory and practice either agree or disagree, and an appreciation of the Trivium's function in Du Bellays' finest sonnet collections. Remarks on grammar, the initial, most minor and least constant art of the Trivium, will be incorporated into separate chapters and in close analysis of poetry. Inasmuch as classical learning was secondary to and subsumed under the rhetorical ideals of Renaissance literature and the best means of attaining poetic eloquence was by imitating classical authors,[10] some attention will be paid to identifying previously unknown classical sources of Du Bellay's poetic theory and practice while much attention will be directed to the function of these sources in his poetry.

The first part will outline the basic precepts of Renaissance logic and indicate their importance to rhetorical thought and composition. After defining the evolution of the rhetorical tradition prior to and during Du Bellay's formative years at the Collège de Coqueret, the *Deffence et Illustration* will be placed within that tradition and his understanding and application of the steps of rhetoric will be studied.

The second part will discuss some of the basic tenets of Renaissance poetics and their relation to the Trivium. Since the fundamental conceptions of imitation and translation are more often separately clarified in theory than in practice where they coalesce—not to mention the half-dozen ancillary terms that compound the confusion—a section of this chapter on Du Bellay's failures and successes as a translator of Vergil follows the remarks on the *Deffence et Illustration.* Scrutiny of *L'Olive*

---

[9] Patterson, *Three Centuries of French Poetic Theory (1328–1630)* (1966), I, 91; Weber, *La Création poétique au XVI*e *siècle en France* (1956), p. 410.

[10] For the development of this idea in a much broader context, see Paul Oskar Kristeller, *Renaissance Thought* (1961), pp. 98–99 and 153, n. 1.

reveals the variable alliance of translation and imitation with creation in Du Bellay's first poetic effort.

Finally, with this background Du Bellay's complementary sonnet collections, *Les Antiquitez de Rome* and *Les Regrets,* will be successively analyzed in order to describe the function of their rhetorical content and to trace the evolution of his poetic experience. Because the *Jeux rustiques* lack the structural integrity of these three collections, comments on these poems will also be incorporated in various chapters. Wherever possible, I have contrasted or likened Du Bellay's theory and practice to that of other poets of the European Renaissance and especially to that of Ronsard, not for an odious comparison, but rather to indicate what is unique or common in Du Bellay's poetry. For the sake of brevity—the cardinal value of classical rhetoric—I have limited comparisons with the Pléiade to Ronsard.

I wish to express my gratitude to the National Foundation for the Arts and the Humanities and to the University of California for fellowships which facilitated this study. For many thoughtful suggestions and helpful criticism of my book manuscript, I am personally indebted to my colleagues Jean-Pierre Barricelli and William Mead. To Mrs. Susan Luca go my thanks for her painstaking efforts in preparing my manuscript for publication. No expression of gratitude can do justice to my wife who bore with this book over the years and whose patience is worthy of a far better book.

# PART ONE

CHAPTER I

# LOGIC AND RENAISSANCE POETICS

THE EDUCATION of the young Brigade at the Collège de Coqueret differed in quality and degree, not in kind, from the standard collegial curriculum of the time, and ran the gamut from grammar to rhetoric. Jean Dorat's favored method of comparing the syntax, metrics and idiom of Latin and Greek introduced his students not only to the Pantheon of antiquity, but to the conception of creative imitation as well. This studied mastery of poetry and eloquence relied on imitation of classical authors; extending back through the late Middle Ages to classical antiquity, excellence in the study of classical poets coupled with original poetic composition often led to the Coronation of the poet.[1]

In the desire of the students to embrace all of antiquity, they measured the conceptual and stylistic debt of Vergil to the Homeric poems, of Ciceronian eloquence to Demosthenes. The study of comparative grammar was therefore a method of passing beyond the purely grammatical level to a more extended and elaborated understanding of classical—and, inevitably, French—letters. Dorat's catholic interests exposed the future Pléiade to the diminished Hellenism of the Alexandrian poets and his excursions into a medieval glossing of texts risked repeating the excesses of previous centuries. But his search for arcane symbols in classical myth and his revelation of allegorical significance and moral depth in the *Odyssey* opened to the Pléiade the conception of poetry as a spiritual adventure and the relationship between the single word and its larger meaning; the allegorized autobiography of Ronsard's "Hymne de l'autonne,"[2] for instance, and the Pléiade's cultivation of "motz signifians" are not unrelated to this desire for extended meaning.

The study of rhetoric at Coqueret, which we will examine in the next chapter, seems to have been more methodical, judicious and relatively exclusive. For this generation that deferred so much to classical tradition, the models for the study of the scope, precepts and procedures of rhetoric were Cicero, the greatest rhetorician of Rome and the most widely discussed paragon of Latinity, Quintilian who codified and

[1] See Henri Chamard, *Histoire de la Pléiade* (1961), I, ch. 2, and Ernest H. Wilkins, "The Coronation of Petrarch," *Speculum,* XVIII (1943), 158–162.

[2] Cf. Donald Stone, Jr., "The Sense and Significance of Ronsard's Seasonal Hymns," *Symposium,* XVIII (1964), 321–331, and Pierre de Nolhac, *Ronsard et l'humanisme* (1966), pp. 73 and 80, n. 3.

catalogued the elements of oratory, and Horace whom the Renaissance increasingly viewed as a prime theoretician of rhetoric. Renaissance belletrists of all magnitudes were capable of tirelessly discussing the Horatian marriage of "things" and "words." The enthusiasm and sense of urgency in these discussions arose from a belief that the *res-verba* coupling surpassed its original stature as a grammatical conception and lay at the very base of verbal creation. From the point of view of the poet addressing himself to the poem under consideration, the conception and mental investigation of the poetic problem, or "invention," and the verisimilar relationship between poem and nature are included under the heading of "things," along with the implication and employment of useful moral precepts. This general attitude receives particular expression through "words," which includes such considerations as appropriate diction, elegance and "sweetness." From a reversed point of view the dichotomy assumed the relationship between the art of the poem and its persuasive effectiveness on the audience.

The *res-verba* configuration became a primary tool of aesthetic analysis in the Renaissance. Francesco Berni chides the Petrarchan poets for their inattention to invention, "Ei (Michelangelo) dice cose e voi dite parole," while Montaigne extends the parallel to include human conduct, slighting Athenian rhetoric and logic because they "s'embesongnoient après les parolles," whereas the Spartan is praised for busying himself "après les choses."[3] There is a tacit understanding that the development involving words, things and nature, however that formula be construed and phrased, should be indissoluble and organic. Jules-César Scaliger, in concert with other Renaissance authors of poetic treatises, insists that poetic images forming the "word-thing" diad be grounded in a universally apprehensible logic.[4]

In the French Renaissance collège the study of logic included the two steps that had been traditional since classical antiquity: invention and judgment. Invention was the procedure that examined the merits, truths and falsity of an idea or proposition. Rather than creating *ex nihilo,* one simply discovered material that pre-existed in nature. Inven-

[3] Berni, *Rime, poesie latine* (1885), p. 124; *Oeuvres complètes de Montaigne* (1962), I, 25, p. 142.

[4] "Quum re & verbo omnis constet oratio, & figura in utroque reperiatur: ab universali definitione iacienda fundamenta primum, et eius essentiam agnoscamus . . . luculentis exemplis notiores faciemus," *Poetices libri septem,* fifth edition (1617), ch. 28, "Figura," p. 275. See p. 270 for the triple requirement of correctness in grammar, logic and rhetoric. Cf. Marcel Raymond, *Baroque et renaissance poétique* (1955), p. 130, and C. F. Lenient, *De ciceroniano bello apud recentiores* (1885), p. 50.

tion was both the faculty of discovery and the discovery itself. On a linguistic level this procedure comprised the consideration of the individual terms of a concept, or "reason" or "argument" as it was variously called. The second step in the logical process was judgment or disposition which established the methods for ordering single words into simple propositions, propositions were expanded into deductive or inductive arguments and ultimately into complete discourses. Thus, logic's dual function permitted the transition from a dimly glimpsed thought, passing through a methodical examination and arrangement of proofs, into an elaborated and forceful presentation of that thought. Ideally, the system represented the normal function of the mind in its passage from impression to expression.[5]

Although the content of logical prepositions varied within the whole range of two millennia of human interests, the variations in form and function were slight. From Aristotle's *Topics* through Cicero's parallel treatise which condensed them, invention was considerably more elaborated than judgment; the peripatician devoted seven books out of eight to it, while the Roman orator's *De inventione* implies judgment more than it treats it. Through the Middle Ages to the Renaissance major works like Boethius' *De differentiis topicis* and Rudolph Agricola's *De inventione dialectica* recognize the traditional division of logic and the preference for a more extended and methodical treatment of invention.

The period surrounding Du Bellay's formative years at Coqueret witnessed a renovation in the scope and method of logic. This renewal was spurred by the publication of Pierre de la Ramée's contentious master's thesis (1536) which rejected the authority of Aristotle and later by the first publication of Ramée's *Dialectique* (1555). The advent of Peter Ramus is not surprising in a period that sought to unearth and equal the treasures of classical antiquity and that strove for linguistic expansion, concision and logical articulation, for "plus de nerfs et moins de chair," as Pasquier put it. The exact relationship between the Pléiade and Ramus is conjectural. We know that he was forbidden to teach logic at the University of Paris around the time when the future Pléiade began studying together, and so he sought examples of natural logic in the works of poets and orators. Dorat wrote scabrous epigrams about him after 1556, but the others seem to have been on

[5] Cf. Montaigne's "Nature luy a donné, comme à tous, assez de matiere sienne pour son utilité, et de subjects siens assez où inventer et juger," III, 3, p. 797, and Charles Arnaud, *Quid de pueris instituendis senserit Ludovicus Vives* (1887).

better terms with him and contributed translations of classical poets with which he illustrated his editions of the *Dialectique,* such as Du Bellay's *Aeneid* translations. Du Bellay himself gave considerable space to the dispute between Peter Galland and Ramus in his "Petromachie."[6] But whether or not they subscribed to any or all of his system, they could not have been immune to its effects. As the most controversial and influential dialectician of his time, and perhaps the most original, his thought colored other logical—which is to say, pedagogical—systems and exerted a formative influence on Elizabethan rhetoricians—which is to say, critics of poetic language—of the next half century. His terminology, albeit Aristotelian in origin, became a recognizable jargon and implied an influence on thought patterns in poetry as well as prose. Although the Pléiade probably knew other dialectical systems, they show a preference for some basically Ramist terms and, more important, an awareness of kindred logical procedure and its implications.[7]

Although Ramus added nothing to Aristotelian logic and used the same nomenclature, he intelligibly ordered the three arts of the Trivium which a century of schoolmen had interchanged and confused. More an organizer and simplifier of Aristotelianism than its actual enemy, he opposed the unnatural and contrived organization of scholasticism, and made logic the foundation not only of all systematic and rational knowledge but of all intelligible discourse as well. Aristotle had distinguished, at least in theory, between logic, the science of rigid demonstration, and dialectic, the reasoning from probabilities, which included generally accepted opinions. Such a distinction would classify Cicero's

[6] *Joachim du Bellay, Oeuvres poetiques,* ed. Chamard (1908–1961), V, 240. Henceforth, the Chamard edition of Du Bellay's poetry will be indicated in the text by volume and page. Chamard's 1961 edition of the *Deffence et Illustration* will be indicated by page or chapter number alone. On Ramus and the Pléiade, see Michel Dassonville, "La Collaboration de la Pléiade à la *Dialectique* de Pierre de la Ramée," *BHRen,* XXV (1963), 337–348; Gilbert Gadoffre, *Ronsard par lui-même* (1960), p. 25, and "L'Université collégiale et la Pléiade," *French Studies,* XI (1957), 297; A. Maurat-Ballange, "Ramus et Dorat," *Extrait du bulletin de la société archéologique du Limousin,* LXIII (1913), 5–27; Nolhac, pp. 167–169; Walter J. Ong, *Ramus and Talon Inventory* (1958), p. 517; Ronsard, *Oeuvres complètes,* ed. Paul Laumonier (1914–1960), X, 380.

[7] Of course, they knew and appreciated other preceptors like Muret, Le Roy and Lambin who joined eloquence and philosophy, but from an altered point of view. Muret, for instance, held that philosophy allows *res* and *verba* to come together logically, "distincte et ordinate," but unlike Ramus, he did not hold to the overall primacy of dialectic. Like Le Roy, he appealed to Cicero's and Quintilian's broad moral philosophies as a requisite to general understanding—an appeal that is entirely foreign to Ramus. Cf. Muret's *De philosophiae et eloquentiae conjunctione oratio* IV (1557) and Ramus' *Rhetoricae distinctiones in Quintilianum: oratio ejusdem de studiis philosophiae et eloquentiae conjugendis* (1549).

*Topica* as dialectic rather than logic, and would tend to align rhetoric with dialectic, since rhetoric is synthetic and a means of concrete communication, whereas strict logic is analytic and a means of abstract study. Scholastic logicians confused this distinction, at best adhered to in the areas of application rather than in the internal method of the disciplines, and Ramus insisted that no such distinction existed at all by saying simply that "Dialectique ou Logique, est une mesme doctrine pour apercevoir toutes choses."[8] Ramus continued and expanded the Aristotelian notion that logic is a science by extending it to the Quadrivium, and echoed the advice of Cicero, Agricola and Sturm that exposition be adapted to one's audience. But he brought together rigid theory and fluid practice by holding that mathematician and poet have equal access to the comprehensive truths of nature provided they both apply the correct method, or conversely, that examples of the exercise of natural reason could be found among the best poets and orators. Dialectic, then, became an analysis of the instinctive procedures of the mind. In the long line of humanists from Petrarch, Valla, Lefèvre d'Etaples and others, Ramus is the most adamantly vocal in uniting philosophy and eloquence, and therefore we may take him as a convenient exemplar. His favored procedure for literary textual examination involved ferreting out grammatical usage, rhetorical figures and natural dialectical method.[9]

In scholastic logic that method consisted of first recalling and integrating into one's mental activity the precepts and examples that had been institutionalized by traditional logic. One found his subject matter by examining what were called the "places" of systematic inquiry. Ramus, borrowing Aristotelian terminology but strongly objecting to the fundamental inapplicability of the *Organon* and of the welter of accretions imposed upon it by schoolmen, reduced the places of argument to two basic types. Intrinsic, or "artficial," arguments are those which are inherent in the object under consideration and which are always manifest to any alert observer. For instance, in Ramus' "grammar of logic" the statement "fire burns" establishes a relationship between an antecedent and its consequence, whereas, from another point of view, heat is seen as the effect of its cause, fire; both relationships depend on primary sensations, on the objects themselves, and

[8] See Perry Miller, *The New England Mind: The Seventeenth Century* (1961), pp. 320–321; Ong, *Ramus, Method and the Decay of Dialogue* (1958), p. 56; *La Dialectique (1555)* (1964), p. 62.

[9] Cf. *P. Rami, professoris regii et Audomari Talaei collectaneae praefationes, epistolae, orationes* (1577), pp. 304–305, 327, 356.

neither needs a footnote of authoritative explanation. Less compelling are the extrinsic, "inartificial," places that rely on testimony of authority, and the analogies of moral philosophy, proverbs and ancient wisdom. The crossing of the Rubicon and even the greatness of Caesar's Rome are problematical to the extent that they are received at second hand, "ex fabrica rei." Since inartificial arguments are seen through another man's eyes or through the collective conscience of a whole culture removed in space and time from the Renaissance, they appeal to the imagination rather than to reason and trigger emotions not controlled by primary experience.[10]

Ramus differed from contemporary logicians such as Philipp Melanchthon by reducing the ten places to four basic types from which one could derive the other categories, such as etymology, nominal definition, morphology and so on.[11] In Ramist handbooks the whole system is laid out for the visual imagination, as a diagrammatic scheme resembling a family tree, into groups of related dialectical principles. In descending order of perfection they are (1) cause and effect, (2) subject and adjunct, (3) opposites, and (4) comparison of quality and quantity. In the octave of a sonnet to Jeanne d'Albret, Du Bellay illustrates the process of invention by which the truth and falsity of a given proposition are examined:

Le seul penser me sembloit un vray songe,
Et en l'oyant le trouvois incroyable:
Ores voyant chose tant admirable,
L'effect certain m'est presque une mensonge:
Car tout esprit se travaille & se ronge
Pour mettre en oeuvre un escript recevable,
Et s'il le veult faire à jamais durable,
Fault qu'un long temps en pensee il se plonge. (II, 226)

Cause, in its turn, is subdivided into the time-honored and comprehensive quartet of efficient, material, formal and final causes. Aristotle and Cicero recognized the importance of cause, since a subject is perfectly known if its cause is understood. In works like Erasmus' *De copia,* the Renaissance generally upheld this recognition, although, as with

[10] Cf. Miller, *The New England Mind: From Colony to Province* (1953), p. 12, and Montaigne: "Les sens sont nos propres et premiers juges, qui n'apperçoivent les choses que par les accidents externes," III, 8, p. 908.

[11] See Neal Gilbert, *Renaissance Concepts of Method* (1960), p. 126; *La Dialectique,* p. 29. Rather than illustrating them all, some of the minor ones being derivative, I will confine my remarks to the primary places to show how they affected the conception of poetic method, and to give an idea of the interrelatedness and extensive divisibility of Renaissance logic.

Scaliger, the terms are sometimes interchanged.[12] In his criticism of the *Deffence et Illustration* the Quintil Horatien, Barthélemy Aneau, justly attacks Du Bellay's argument by etymology for having neither "methode didascalique, ne les lieux d'icelle . . . definition, division ou partition, causes, effectz, affins, contraires" (p. 21).

The efficient cause is the motivating force by which anything comes into existence and for Ramus is the source of all good and evil, as it was for his elders.[13] Early in the *Illustrations de Gaulle et singularitez de Troye* Jean Lemaire has Mercury prepare the logic of tragedy by addressing Paris in these words: "selon lordonnance que tu en prononceras . . . ie feray delivrance de la pomme aureine (qui est cause motive de leur different) à la plus belle des trois." The passage begins with the significant preface, replete with major rhetorical conceptions, "L'eloquence artificielle de dame Venus, ses paroles delicates, et sa douce persuasion causerent telle efficace et telle emotion au coeur du ieune adolescent Paris, que encores en pourra il maudire les rhetoriques couleurs, qui luy seront retorquees en douleurs," indicating the immediate relationship between rhetoric and logic.[14] The efficient cause is further trifurcated into art, nature and the accidents of Fortune, three of the most important forces in the Renaissance mind, which may intermix and progress logically to the final cause.

---

[12] For excellent presentations of European historical background on this point, see Bernard Weinberg, *A History of Literary Criticism in the Italian Renaissance* (1961), I, 48–49, and William Crane, *Wit and Rhetoric in the Renaissance* (1964), pp. 57–58. Of course, medieval rhetoricians also recognized an argument from cause and effect not only as intellectually perfect but aesthetically pleasing as well. Cf. Geoffroi de Vinsauf's *Poetria nova* (1210) (from Edmond Faral, *Les Arts poétiques*):

> Dulcescitque magis meliusque saporat in aure
> Quando quod effectus sibi vendicat applico causae. (vv. 976–77)

Montaigne represents an extreme position in his opposition to a commonly held view: "Es choses naturelles, les effects ne raportent qu'à demy leurs causes" (II, 12, p. 512), but in numerous instances he either treats cause and effect together (I, 7, p. 32; III, 5, pp. 821 and 839; 10, p. 1001; 11, p. 1006; 12, p. 1035) or separately (III, 2, p. 793; 5, pp. 843 and 849; 6, p. 876; 8, p. 902; 9, p. 929; 10, pp. 994–995; 11, pp. 1003–1004 and 1009). Cf. Quintilian, *Instituto oratorio,* V, x, 80; and George Gascoigne's "plain and perfect proof" which he discovers by repeatedly examining the "cause" of his misfortune ("Dan Bartholmew's Dolorous Discourses," v. 174).

[13] *La Dialectique,* p. 70. Cf. Jean Bouchet, "le moien et la cause motive / Dont justice est dicte distributive," *Epistres morales et familieres du traverseur* (1545), II, v, 10; Béroalde de Verville, "Ceux qui n'avoyent cogneu l'efficient premier / De la necessité de cest heureux brasier (l'amour)," *Le Cabinet de Minerve* (1601), p. 61; "La source premiere, cause motive et origine de toute la sédition," *Variétés historiques et littéraires, recueil de pièces volantes et curieuses* (1855–1863), VI, 195.

[14] *Oeuvres* (1882), I, xxxii, 249.

For instance, in the realm of art, one could advance from the poet as prime cause, through the creation of verse by imitation, to the final cause of instructing and pleasing; the efficient cause, or reason for writing which the poet finds, preconditions the choice of material, its arrangement and intent.[15] Or one could equally posit divine inspiration as the efficient cause, poetry's persuasive power as the material cause, persuasion veiled in allegory as the formal cause and the ennobling of mankind as the final cause. Within the neo-Platonic nature of things, one would descend from the efficient cause or conception of the Idea in God's mind to its material imitation in nature; drawing on his memory and imagination, the artist or poet would form and express the figured archetype as the coordination of multiple experience and progress to things and finally rise toward the Idea.[16] For Marsilio Ficino, the words of poetry speak directly to the mind, and through this special "effect" can lead the audience to a direct acquaintance with the Divine Mind.[17] One might exemplify the commonplace Chain of Being by positing God as the first cause of creation and, proceeding through the other causes, establish man's rational soul as his formal cause, that which gives him his name and being, and finally show that nature is made for man, man for God.

Du Bellay's translation of *Urania,* I, xx on the beneficent relationship of heaven and earth, "Causant divers effectz" (VI, 405), is stronger and more schematic than Pontano's "varios rerum parientia casus" from which it is adapted and indicates the extent of his concern for this system. Schematization, however, did not force the Pléiade into rigid and unrelenting confines of thought. Etienne Jodelle might choose to accentuate the unified link between Creator and creature, "Et de tous ses effects la cause plantureuse," while Ronsard might praise God "Pour la variété de ses effaits divers." Moreover, one might also wish to emphasize the possiblities of misfortune inherent in the logical chain, as in "Dieu commanda lors a la seconde cause / Te infortuner ains que tu fusses né."[18]

[15] See Rosemond Tuve, *Elizabethan and Metaphysical Imagery* (1965)), p. 390, and Montaigne, I, 39, p. 238. Without a knowledge of poetic cause, a poet could not conjoin *res* and *verba.* Cf. Cicero's *De oratore,* I, vi, 20 and I, xxii, 103.

[16] See *Les Tragiques,* I, 1243; John Rainolds, *Oratio in laudem artis poeticae 1572* (1940), p. 11; and Giordano Bruno, *Opera latine* (1879–1891), II, part 3, 89–102.

[17] *Opera omnia* (1561), p. 614.

[18] *Les Oeuvres et meslanges poetiques d'Estienne Jodelle* (1870), II, 26; Ronsard, ed. Laumonier, X, 102; Michel d'Amboise, *Les Complainctes de l'esclave fortuné* (1529), 91$^{vo}$.

The tricks of fortune and their disregard for virtue held a special fascination for Du Bellay, after the high optimism and determination of the *Deffence et Illustration,* especially in his later poetry; we shall presently see how they inform the theme and structure of many of the sonnets in the Roman collections and we will hear the poet's complaint against the breach between virtue and fortune as in the last lines of "France, mere des arts." For the time being we shall simply examine some of the implications it had in logical development, choosing poems from three distinctly different but roughly contemporaneous collections.

He begins the "Elegie amoureuse" of the *Jeux rustiques* by praising the "parfaict jugement" and divine origin and nature of his anonymous beloved's discourse. Her perfect understanding allows him to dispense with choosing and exploring the argument of sublunary mutability (since the conception was part of the normal intellectual baggage of the period) and with dwelling "Sur le pouvoir, sur la cause & nature, / Sur les effects, & la diverse fin" of human and divine love. Heaven has destined him to sing "sans art & fiction" the cause of his love, her manifest perfection, and in the second half of the poem he invites her to judge the subject and object of his love to determine its veracity. Again, at the midpoint of his "Discours au roy sur la trefve de l'an MDLV" he outlines the role of the Goddess Fortuna in human affairs: "Ceste dame Fortune, à qui pour sa puissance, / Dont les divers effects nous donnent cognoissance, / Sans en sçavoir la cause . . . ." He goes on to eulogize the virtuous deeds of Henri II where "Le hazard n'a que voir, ny la Fortune aussi" (VI, 10) and grandiloquently points to posterity's favorable judgment of the king's actions. To be sure, such analysis brutalizes the full poetic context, and Du Bellay would certainly concede this, for it paraphrases and condenses the imagery and its development which flesh out the poem's driving logic, "beautify" his cause and fittingly incarnate his intention; but the logical chain of development is no less evident for all that. Even in the short compass of a quatrain, of sonnet 155 toward the end of the *Regrets,* the logical seams are apparent. After praising Pontus de Tyard's first *Discours philosophiques* for their macrocosmic expansiveness, and before inviting him in the tercets to look earthward for fear of stubbing his toe, Du Bellay prepares his conclusion with

> Qui n'admire du ciel la belle architecture,
> Et de tout ce qu'on void les causes & l'effect,
> Celuy vrayement doit estre un homme contrefait,
> Lequel n'a rien d'humain, que la seule figure.

In the second verse quoted the poet mentions what happen to be the primary places of dialectical invention, after which he gives a perfect example of what Ramus called the "Enonciation relative d'essence," an axiom which unites disparate thought fragments on the way to a logical conclusion: "Par ceste mesme cause le vray jugement de la relative demande la relation estre vraye."[19]

The point is that the Renaissance poetic and critical eye was far more concerned than the modern to establish and judge the discursive ligatures in any poetic or prose composition, especially in those cases where argument is based on a sequential reference to the basic places of cause, effect, subject and adjunct. In a distich such as "Bien infortuné devoit estre / L'astre soubz qui tu vins à naitre" the modern critic might tend to decry a lack of original imagery and imagination. But instead Aneau censures only the weakness of the argument and its "improprieté de la cause à l'effet" (I, 130), since, as any Renaissance schoolboy knew, the unmoving stars determine the capricious destinies of men; if imagination is here subject to censure it would be accused of violating a generally assumed relationship. These terms provided standard vehicles for determining and expressing Renaissance thought of all kinds and came naturally to writers of the period. Ronsard speaks of the bucolic relationship of a hunter teaching his dog obedience as one involving invention and judgment.[20] Montaigne used the system, representing his own education, as a negative contrast to his ideal education; he can only "tirer quelque matiere de propos universel, sur quoy j'examine son (his student's) jugement naturel. . . . Mes conceptions et mon jugement ne marche qu'à tastons."[21] Across the channel some fifty years later we find Polonius defining true madness by means of logical figures where the comic effect resides largely in his choplogic and in the utter failure of his judgment:

> That we find out the cause of this effect;
> Or rather say the cause of this defect,
> For this effect defective comes by cause. (*Hamlet,* II, ii)

Ramus would have laughed at Polonius along with the Elizabethan audience, for in his conclusion to the *Dialectique* he insists that the use

[19] *La Dialectique,* p. 119. Du Bellay uses the same kind of logical connective in *Regrets* 42 which repeats a theme (v. 8) from his "Satyre de maistre Cuignet" (V, 249) where Ramus appears.

[20] Ed. Laumonier, VI, 239. Cf. the first two paragraphs of Montaigne's essay "Que le goust des bien et des maux depend en bonne partie de l'opinion que nous en avons," I, 14, pp. 49–50.

[21] I, 26, pp. 144–145. Cf. Francis Bacon, *Works* (1863), IX, bk. V, ch. 5, p. 105.

of natural reason and judgment, not a display of knowledgeable procedure, is the end of dialectic: "l'exercice monstroit le fruict de l'art, ainsi nous fault icy penser que non par l'art seullet mais beaucoup plus l'exercice d'icelluy et la practique faict l'artisant." Montaigne a generation later will echo the same criticism of pedants who have "la souvenance assez pleine, mais le jugement entierement creux."[22] The ordering of words into sentences and then, by analysis or synthesis, into a complex proof, should be easily absorbed into any argument, scientific or poetic. In the "Elegie d'amour" of the *Jeux rustiques* Du Bellay resumes his lady's argument that she should not "juger du cueur par le visage" and that "il fault premier cognoistre que d'aymer." Although her "argumens sont fort à redoubter," she can be dissuaded since she has the two requisite parts of systematic thought, "un bon esprit & jugement solide," for distinguishing truth from falsity. After appealing to arguments by analogy and formal cause, he gives his alternatives:

> J'ay plusieurs poincts, que je pourois induire
> A ce propos, si je voulois deduire
> Ce fait au long, & demonstrer comment
> L'amour s'engendre en nous premierement,
> Quelle est sa fin, son essence & nature, . . .

If the line of argument smacks of love casuistry and if its bald terminology does not sufficiently distinguish itself from Polonius' wordy plea for brevity, it still shows the need poets felt for an underlying logical argument. The deduction and induction offered by the poet roughly resemble the last two steps in Ramus' *Dialectique*.[23] For drawing a particular conclusion from an axiomatic statement Ramus explored a wide variety of syllogisms that differ in complexity and in the disposition of premises and conclusion.[24] As did Aristotle, Ramus referred the poet to the enthymeme which seeks concrete proof in human affairs drawn from such probable arguments as are available in the matter under discussion.

One is hard pressed to find the Renaissance poet who is averse to syllogistic argumentation, except when the syllogism itself is faulty.[25]

[22] *La Dialectique*, p. 153; Montaigne, I, 25, p. 138.

[23] But is not exclusively Ramist. Cf. Rabelais' "Par le blanc, à mesmes induction de nature, tout le monde a entendu joye," I, 10; Thomas Sebillet's "Trouve donc le poëte avant toute autre chose, qui'il puisse proprement dire et commodément adapter au sujet qu'il veut deduire de son poéme," *Art poétique* (1932), I, 3; Descartes, *Discours de la methode* (1962), p. 453.

[24] *La Dialectique*, p. 143.

[25] Lawrence Harvey in *The Aesthetics of the Renaissance Love Sonnet* (1962) mentions the "syllogistic reasoning" of Louise Labé's sonnets 2 and 10, and Marcel

Aneau reproves not Du Bellay's use of syllogistic method, but rather the wide sweep he allows to a syllogism whose terms do not correspond from major premise to conclusion: "tu ratiocines ainsi: Barbare est qui prononce mal la langue, ou Latine, ou la sienne propre. Or les François ont esté & sont autant civils en moeurs & loix, courageux en faitz & gestes, que les Grecs & Rommains. Donc la langue Françoise n'est point barbare" (p. 22). One of the principal differences between the Aristotelian and Ramist syllogism is the latter's preference for disjunction rather than resemblance, where variety and degrees of the problem's diversity are stressed. We have noted Raymond's aesthetic cavil with the syllogistic reasoning of Du Bellay's satirical sonnets. But the paramount attention accorded by Ramists to distinctions of diversity in controversial issues[26] and their interest in discovering the properties a subject both possessed and lacked lent themselves naturally to satire; for this genre aims at establishing a disparity between what conditions actually are and what they should be ideally, and preaches, or at least implies, a moral conclusion. But this syllogistic "figure of difference" extended beyond satire and was universally applicable, witness a tercet from Ronsard's *L'Amour de Cassandre:*

> La rose & moy differons d'une chose,
> Un Soleil voit naistre & mourir la rose,
> Mille Soleils ont veu naistre l'amour . . .[27]

Renaissance poets from Ronsard to Marvell invariably couch the "carpe diem" theme, innately one of persuasion, in the language and form of the syllogism. The universally anthologized ode "A Cassandre," with its three distinct movements, falls unfailingly into this pattern and shows how dialectic can weld together a delicate but forceful poetic argument. In the first stanza, the closely balanced identification of the

---

Raymond seems not to like "la netteté du syllogisme" in Du Bellay's most satirical *Regrets* where the poet draws moral lessons from "Tout ce qu'on void de bien & de mal en ce monde" (*L'Influence de Ronsard sur la poésie française* (*1550–1585*), I, 123). Nor is the poetic syllogism, whether Ramist or Aristotelian, limited to France; in 1579 Antonio Riccoboni insisted that the poetic argument needed syllogism in addition to character, harmony, etc. (quoted by Weinberg, I, 583). Cf. Donald Lemen Clark, *Rhetoric and Poetry in the Renaissance* (1963), p. 135. The verbal expression of this type of reasoning was considered by some classical rhetoricians as a rhetorical figure (see Quintilian, IX, ii, 106).

[26] See Tuve, *Elizabethan and Metaphysical Imagery,* p. 350.

[27] Ed. Laumonier, XV, 205. Of course, the syllogism may serve—or even constitute—any type of Renaissance poem. Cf. George Turberville's "Of a Rich Miser": "A miser's mind thou hast, / thou hast a prince's pelf: / Which makes thee wealthy to thine heir, / a beggar to thyself," *Epigrams, Songs, and Sonnets* (1869).

folds of Mignonne's dress with the petals of the rose implicitly establishes the major premise that she is like the rose:

> Mignonne, allon voir si la rose
> Qui ce matin avoit declose
> Sa robe de pourpre au soleil,
> A point perdu, cette vesprée,
> Les plis de sa robe pourprée,
> Et son teint au vostre pareil.[28]

The rapid opposition between the exhortation of the first verse, "allon voir si la rose," and the shock of the past indefinite "A point perdu, cette vesprée" prepares the second movement in the following stanza where the minor premise is made explicit, "roses die": "Las, voiés comme en peu d'espace. . . ." The concluding stanza, initiated by its logically rigorous "Donc, si vous me croiés, mignonne," tells the listener that, like the rose, her beauty too will fade, and extends the pressing and reasoned invitation to gather rosebuds while she may. The argumentation differs from Polonius' speech in that Ronsard has "beautified" his cause by ingenious juxtaposition of key words, skillful use of rhyme and moving orchestration of colors, rather than by erudite embroidery. But the reasoning underlying his plea is fundamentally similar. It recalls Ramus' earlier injunction of the *Partitiones* to conjure up "une image de la nature" by a methodical ordering of thought that will permit the poet to embrace "toute la question en descendant de l'idée la plus générale aux espèces et aux cas particuliers."[29]

Once the syllogism has determined the truth or falsity of an argument by relating it to an axiom, one can move on to method which, as Ramus has it, "est de nature ou de prudence,"[30] the dialectical analogues of the rhetorical procedures of natural order and artificial order. Natural method was intended for a learned audience and organized its inquiry into any subject in a progressively descending order of generality. It began by defining and dividing wholes into parts, parts into yet smaller parts until the subject was fully understood. The "méthode de prudence" allows the poet, through induction, to lead a recalcitrant or unenlightened audience to a desired conclusion and permits him a wide latitude in disposing the components of his argument. Even a later Aristotelian like Scaliger will link poetic insight with consistent discernment (*prudentia*) before going on to style. The dialectic chain of

[28] Ed. Laumonier, V. 196. Cf. Descartes, p. 183.
[29] *La Dialectique,* p. 25.
[30] Ibid., p. 145.

the natural method, no less open to poets, is more rigorous in its attempt to relate particular and derivative truths to universals; as with Descartes, one advances from the simple and familiar to the complex and difficult until the whole conception is formed and judged: "Tota methodus consistit in ordine & dispositione eorum ad quae mentis acies est convertenda, ut aliquam veritatem inveniamus."[31]

It is often difficult in a poetic context, even erroneous, to identify the general movement of natural method simply as Ramist, to the complete exclusion of classical philosophers and rhetoricians; for the genius of Renaissance thought is its ability to synthesize the similar and antithetical thought systems with which it became charged. In the "Discours au Roy sur la poésie" (VI, 161) Du Bellay follows the Horatian mixture of usefulness and pleasure by a contrast—which Horace's famous Epistle to the Pisos disallows—between history and poetry. Amidst numerous rhetorical figures he says "Je ne veux pas icy par le menu deduire / Plusieurs autres raisons que je pourrois induire / Pour monstrer ce qui est semblable en ces deux" (vv. 97–99).[32] History is limited to natural order, while the freer poetry, "plus hardy, d'un art non limité / Sous mille fictions cache la verité" (vv. 87–88). He goes on to illustrate this Platonic assertion by means of a rhetorical device, *pragmatographia* (vv. 89–92), which here is probably based on an extrapolated understanding of the often-misquoted Horatian dictum "ut pictura poesis."

Differences are occasionally more of terminology than of substance. For instance, Ramus contended that natural method should be based on "definition, distribution" and likened these to the rhetorical and poetic procedures of statement of facts, proof and conclusion. These three steps correspond to the important procedures codified by Quintilian for determining the main issues and principal character of any question: the *status coniecturalis* for determining whether a thing was or was not the case; the *status definitivus* for defining the issues; the *status generalis* for the interpretation of admitted facts and definitions.[33] Judging an idea from each or every *status* led to pedantic excess

[31] *Regulae ad directionem ingenii* (1966), V. See *La Dialectique,* pp. 41 and 145, along with Montaigne, III, 8, p. 904.

[32] Jean de la Taille uses the same expression, "deduire par le menu ce propos," in establishing the relation between history and dramatic poetry, *De l'art de la tragédie* (1939), p. 28.

[33] *La Dialectique,* pp. 124 and 147; Quintilian, III, vi, 80 and xi, 11. Cf. Jean Lemaire, "vostre jugement ha lieu et vostre conjecture est veritable," "La Couronne Margaritique," IV, 57; Scève's prolix "Parlant le definit divisant l'argument / Par ses universels pronts à definitive / De ses predicaments suivant la divisive. / Genre, espece, differe au propre, et accident . . ." of "Microcosme," *Oeuvres poétique complètes de Maurice Scève* (1927), p. 238.

where intense analysis of the conception overshadowed its aesthetic expression, that is, where *res* was disjoined from *verba.* The idea thus became a fitting subject of satire. Such a wordsmith as Rabelais could realize this potential by having Epistemon specify "Conjecturallement je refererois cestuy heur de jugement en l'aspect benevole des cieulx et faveur des Intelligences motrices . . ." and pursue the sentence with more than two hundred words that "clarify" the logical predicables and predicaments (III, 44). But Ramus' special service to dialectic was the refashioning of the miasma of subtle distinctions and sophistic labels that plague the works of Buridan, Dulard, Tartaret and Peter of Spain by substituting the simple terms "argument" and "raisons." Thus, the logic in Ronsard's instructions to the painter Janet need not obtrude and permits a delicacy equal to the portrait he has just commissioned:

> Mais si l'on peut juger par conjecture,
> Persuadé de raisons, je m'asseure
> Que la beauté qui s'aparoist doit
> Du tout respondre à celle que l'on voit.[34]

The probable reminiscence of Ariosto's famous portrait of Alcina (*Orlando Furioso,* VII, 14–15) and the implied Platonic perfection are not clouded by specious reasoning, but rather appear clearly and embellish Ronsard's argument.

Daniel Mornet's passing comment on the "confusion de la littérature et de la pensée du XVI$^{e}$ siécle,"[35] despite its pejorative implication in context, should be at once underscored and placed in perspective. The observation suggests that it would be incorrect to superimpose on Renaissance poetry the modern notion of a separation between poetry and discursive reasoning, just as it would be wrong laconically to distinguish rhetoric from poetry; Renaissance distinctions hold rather between good and bad grammar, logic, rhetoric and poetry. Whenever such a separation exists in Renaissance discussions, it is found on a theoretical, not on a functional, level. From Aristotle, Cicero, Quintilian and Horace, through the Middle Ages to the Renaissance, logic was differentiated from rhetoric and poetry—at their widest points of divergence—in that the movement of the former was primarily intellectual, a logically determined progress from idea to idea, while the

---

[34] Ed. Laumonier, VI, 157. Cf. XII, 168. vv. 97–99. The *genera judicalia* and *rationalia* are here alligned with the *status coniecturalis* to determine the veracity of an idea. In eulogy, until the *status coniecturae* is clarified, the qualities of the object considered cannot be determined. Cf. Quintilian, III, vi, 5, *Ad Herennium,* I, xvii, 27, and Antoine de Harsy's marginal notation on *raison* and *cause* in *Les Oeuvres françoises de Joachim du Bellay* (1575), p. 534.

[35] *Histoire de la clarté française* (1929), p. 20.

movement of the latter was primarily imaginative, an emotionally determined progress from image to image. But in school exercises, in prose composition and in poetry alike, the distinction was often radically blurred or simply dismissed. According to Montaigne, "le dialecticien se rapporte au grammairien de la signification des mots; le rhetoricien emprunte du dialecticien les lieux des arguments; le poëte . . ." (II, 12, p. 522). The divorce in the Ramist system where invention and disposition became the two steps of logic, while rhetoric was reduced to style, merely underlined the need for a logical basis of rhetoric and poetic composition; in practice they were organically united in a refashioning of Cicero's injunction to prove, please and move (*Orator,* 69–70). As Ramus put it, the poet "est souvent en toutes parties de Logique excellent."[36] Ramist handbooks of rhetoric speak of embellishing arguments to make them convincing by hammering them out with logic and embossing them with rhetoric.

It is difficult to separate the frequent insistence that poetic proof be based on simile and example[37] from the Pléiade's extreme care in establishing a base of multiple comparisons in poems of all kinds. Whether they be Ronsard's likening the battle between Pollux and Amycus consecutively to the firmness of a rock, angered waves, smashing hammers, and theatrical acoustics or Du Bellay's introductory comparison of Pope Paul IV to the Triumph of the traveler over the storm, Peace over Mars, spring over winter (V, 342), the focus is on the unity of disparate experience and an overriding conclusion developed from a pleasing variety of particular images. In epic contexts poets often take pains to establish exact equivalences of experience, as in Du Bellay's comparison of David taking the measure of Goliath to the preparative destruction of a tower (IV, 128), by means of the formulary "Comme . . . non autrement . . . ." This does not mean that a poetic argument is legitimate when the bones of its logical structure protrude and are evident to the eye, nor that statement can or should be empirically verifiable; all theoreticians of rhetoric and *arts poétiques* are clear on this point. It does mean that poets are bade to weigh the truth, full implications and relatedness of their poetic conception to other conceptions and to examine the functional—which can also mean decorative—link between individual images, word patterns and the total meaning of the poem. By shaping logic as an instrument of demonstration instead of its former role as a science of abstract reasoning, poetry was construed as a means of delightful, friendly persuasion to a point of view, mood,

[36] *La Dialectique,* p. 150.

[37] Cf. Tasso's *Discorsi del poema heroico* (*1594*) quoted in Weinberg, I, 33, and Quintilian, V, xi, 5–6, 23; IX, ii, 100.

emotion, idea. Forceful argument depends not on the choice of imposing words read in isolation, but rather on the effectiveness of those words in forwarding the truth the poet has found and judged. Part of the genius of "Mignonne, allon voir" is its simple economy and the inevitability of its progression from polite invitation to consider a natural phenomenon to the final imperative and the personal reference to a general truth in the simile "Comme à cette fleur, la vieillesse / Fera ternir vôtre beauté."

The outgrowth of poetry from the Trivium tends to make Renaissance poetic inclusive, not exclusive, in the sense that thought and intention, eloquence and imagery, feeling and meaning, mental concept and spatial construct are all creatively linked. The importance of this interrelationship to the finished poem and our understanding of it can scarcely be overstated. From antiquity the human brain had been thought to house three distinct cavities: the frontal held the imagination, the central contained the judging faculty, while memory was located in the posterior cavity. Rabelais' Doctor Rondibilis describes this arrangement in detail without a trace of irony (III, 31). Like a mirror, the mind assumed and reflected the physical and spatial characteristics of the objects before the eye, "the window of the soul." The Renaissance tendency to view the mind as a compartmentalized region housing these various intellectual faculties supported the metaphorical imagery of the "seats of argument" from which invention was derived.

Invention was considered figuratively as a spatial movement involving the discovery of ideas that were housed in "seats" of the mind, *sedes argumentorum,* and entailed the object-like movement of these ideas from the copybook to the mind to their final garnished arrangement on paper. The writer is often compared to the hunter tracking his prey through the mental region.[38] In the "Elegie d'amour" discussed earlier Du Bellay has his lady plod through the labyrinthine human heart in her search for truth, successfully guided by her commendable invention, and he pursues this spatial coefficient of thought to the last line of the poem. Throughout the *Essais,* that thesaurus of Renaissance psychology, Montaigne speaks of the firm or shaky seat of his judgment, describes his active judgment as moving from place to place, from subject to subject, and by continually applying his judgment through emendations of his text, creates the spatial impression of thought evolving on the printed page. Ramist logic itself is initially a series of

[38] See Sister Joan Marie Lechner, *Renaissance Concepts of the Commonplaces* (1962), p. 144. Cf. Montaigne's "le magasin de la memoire est volontiers plus fourny de matiere que n'est celuy de l'invention (I, 9, p. 35), "siege de sa raison" (I, 12, p. 48), the literal "memoire suffisamment informée" (III, 6, p. 878) and the "belles instructions et louables du magasin de leur memoire" (III, 8, p. 909).

relationships established between words as objects before it relates thoughts. And as it progresses it points to the symmetrical arrangement of axioms and the figurative arrangement of syllogisms, just as rhetorics like Foclin's and Scaliger's stress the spatial arrangement of figures involving repetition and transformation, and define figures of style by the "contours" which words design. Its description of dialectic as "imago et pictura naturae" is therefore a figure of speech on the most literal level. According to Ramist Alexander Richardson of Cambridge, "When we define, do we not lay the thing out?"[39]

So when we relate Ramist dialectic, taken as the exemplary foundation for the study of verbal communication, to the domain of poetry—as Ramus insisted it must be related—we find the poet in the role of a quasi-allegorist who begins with a significant conception half-glimpsed in the raw material of experience and who seeks out words and figures of words to embody and clarify that conception, as opposed to, say, the symbolist who would begin with images of things and relate them to ever-elusive conceptions. This embodying of thought appears to involve physical arrangement of words where juxtaposition is related to meaning, where images are used to define and where each word is ideally a logical part of the argument. At the hands of poetic theorists the function of images often becomes axiomatic if not doctrinaire; Scaliger begins his chapter on the definition of poetic figures in Book III by stating that "Figura est notionum, quae in mente sunt." At the hands of the poet the formal design of imagery is as subtle as his talents allow, but still often implies the same basic premise that images body forth spatially arranged thought and that their selection and arrangement should be apportionate and not random.

The following chapters will examine in Du Bellay's poetic theory and verse some of the implications of *faconde,* the Renaissance rhetorical equivalence of thought and eloquence, and will explore the ways in which message and mode, emotion, psychology, logic and rhetoric come together and evolve in his poetry. The Renaissance mind saw the human and natural world as a system of interlocking analogies of humors and elements, as a process encompassing the decline of civilizations and the survival of their spirit. Ramus' credo that "la nature de toutes choses s'entretient et s'entresuyt"[40] is repeated in Du Bellay's major collections where perception is inseparable from judging, imaging from conceiving, the particular from the universal.

[39] Quoted by Miller, *The New England Mind: The Seventeenth Century,* p. 147. See Frances Yates, *The Art of Memory* (1966). Michel Foucault, *Les Mots et les choses* (1966), p. 33, and Albert Thibaudet's note in *Montaigne* (1963), p. 494.

[40] *La Dialectique,* p. 100.

## CHAPTER II

# RHETORIC AND RENAISSANCE POETICS

### THE RHETORICAL TRADITION

RENAISSANCE writers of varying conditions uniformly define grammar as the art of speaking correctly, logic as the art of arguing well, while rhetoric retains the title bestowed on it since antiquity of *ars bene dicendi.* Throughout the *Deffence et Illustration* Du Bellay refers variously to "l'art de bien dire" and "dire meilleur." "Le bien dire" appears to occupy the midground between a myopic attention to versifying and the lyric abandon of poetic fury. Ronsard stipulates basic differences between the many "Qui les vers par leur nombre arrengent & disposent," a euphemistic allusion to the *grands rhétoriqueurs,* and the handful who "Sont remplis de frayeur & de divinité." Between these two callings, he goes on to say, one finds the commendable poets associated with "les mieux disans."[1]

Unlike the Ramist tendency to simplify and erase distinctions among areas of communication, treatises on rhetoric during the several generations preceding the *Deffence et Illustration* distinguish between poetry and prose, form and content. W. F. Patterson carefully differentiated between the Art de Première Rhétorique, based on the traditional procedures of prose composition, and Seconde Rhétorique, which is essentially a pedestrian manual of versification; these come together to form a Pleine Rhétorique. He further identifies the common manuals of themes, myths and decorative allusions that could be adapted to verse or otherwise incorporated into the body of a poem. These Poétries, not to be confused with *poésies,* are also distinct in matter and in manner from Arts Poétiques—the *Deffence et Illustration* being the most notable sixteenth-century French example of the latter—which are of more inclusive scope, more aesthetically oriented and deal with questions ranging from inspiration to translation.[2]

While Patterson's distinctions are helpful, they would have been even more so had they suggested the proximity and interrelations among the various types of treatises; for although the Art Poétique grew out of the medieval systems of rhetoric, it never fully outgrew them. Students in the Collèges continued to learn the precepts of rhetoric by a carefully

---

[1] Ed. Laumonier, XIV, 195–197.

[2] *Three Centuries of French Poetic Theory* (1966), I. Cf. F. Buisson, *Répertoire des ouvrages pédagogiques du XVI*^e^ *siècle* (1886), p. 727. Late medieval humanists often referred to their field of study as poetry because the eloquence they sought was based on the imitation of classical poets.

reasoned analysis of model authors and imitated these precepts in their compositions and numerous poetic exercises. Patterson's criticism of Antoine Foclin for not distinguishing adequately between poetry and rhetoric reflects a modern, not a Renaissance, prejudice.[3] Indeed, just as a late medieval theoretician such as Jacques Legrand would say that "poetrie, a mon advis, est subalterne de rethorique (sic)," Renaissance poets uphold the natural and beneficial tie between rhetoric and poetry to the point that they are occasionally indistinguishable.[4] The association does not enjoin a cold forensic atmosphere, inflexible rules or formal strictures on poetry. Ronsard concludes a formally irregular and epicurean poem to Jamyn with "C'est trop presché," intimating that he has resorted to arts of persuasion his friend would recognize.[5]

Midcentury theorists and educators assume the association as a basic premise. Foclin's *Rhetorique francoise* (1555) used snippets from the Pléiade poets to illustrate effective rhetorical procedures, much as his friend Ramus did that same year in demonstrating the uses of natural reason. Early in his *Art poétique françoys* Sebillet insisted on the near-identification of poetry and rhetoric, differing only in metrics, "Et sont l'orateur & le poëte tant proches & conjoinz, que semblables & égauz en plusieurs choses, différent principalement en ce que l'un est plus contraint de nombres que l'autre" (I, iii). In his view, "la Rhétorique est autant bien espandue par tout le pöéme, comme par toute l'oraison," rhetoric is systematically and structurally contributory to the creation and formation of poetry. In the *Deffence et Illustration,* and in Aneau's tormenting commentaries as well, the reflex conjoining of poet and orator follows hard upon praise of "l'art de bien dire" (pp. 58, 81, 117, 150). Du Bellay satirized the educations of Peter Galland and the "Abbé Bonnet" for not having, among other things, a sympathetic grasp of "poëtes & orateurs" (V, 112, 240).[6] This simultaneous or successive grasp of poetry and rhetoric will inform the poet's understanding of his models and the use he makes of them. The undisputed assumption that Du Bellay composed *L'Olive* on Petrarch's model and patterned the *Regrets* after Ovid's exile poetry means that he followed

[3] P. 389. Cf. C. S. Baldwin, *Renaissance Literary Theory and Practice* (1949).

[4] Quoted in *Recueil d'arts de seconde rhétorique,* ed. Ernest Langlois (1902), p. viii. See Bernard Weinberg, *A History of Literary Criticism in the Italian Renaissance* (1961), II, 721–724, 737 and 748, for similar views in Daniello, one of *L'Olive's* models, and in such contemporaries of Du Bellay as Minturno and Scaliger.

[5] Ed. Laumonier, XV 83.

[6] This is perhaps in answer to Galland's cavalier objection to the trinity of rhetoric, poetry and philosophy in *P. Gallandii . . . contra novam academiam P. Rami oratio* (Paris, 1551), f° 22: "pravarum opinionum levitatisque magistris poetis et oratoribus."

the footsteps of poets who consciously and successfully transposed rhetoric into poetry. In an epistle to Salanus, his preceptor of rhetoric, Ovid maintains that rhetoric is the skeleton of his poetry (*Ex ponto,* II, 5), and in the *Tristia* he raises the basic rhetorical conventions of the Augustan period into the realm of fine art. So we must follow with caution Chamard's argument that Du Bellay's "ancienne manière" of rhetoric was infelicitous and limited to the early days of Coqueret.[7] The composition of his *Discours*—which Chamard elsewhere extols to the detriment of Ronsard's "Remonstrance au peuple de France"[8]—meshes chronologically with that of the *Regrets,* continued into Du Bellay's last year and is a paradigm of conventional rhetoric.

Nor does it ever strike these poets that rhetoric of itself is ever infelicitous or that it should be shunned.[9] Rather, we find theoreticians before and after the *Deffence et Illustration* making the same distinctions that dialectic established between effective and unsuccessful usage. What changes in their attitude toward rhetoric is a reapportionment and shift of interest, which can be sketched with representative examples in a highly synoptic manner. The *Instructif de la seconde rhétorique* (1501), probably authored by Regnaud Le Queux and reprinted several times before Du Bellay's manifesto, lays down laws of poetry for disposition of rhymes, false proportion, improper consonance and fitting neologisms to which the successful versifier must adhere.[10] This treatise differs from later ones by its almost exclusive emphasis on rhyme systems and rhythm. Pierre Fabri's popular *L'Art de rithmer,* for instance, still within the Seconde Rhétorique tradition, begins to strive for stylistic economy and to exorcise the cherished *rimes équivoquées* of his predecessors. In Guillaume des Autelz' *Réplique aux furieuses défenses de Louis Meigret* (1550) we perceive a clear shift in emphasis from elegant disposition and quality of rhyme to the rhetorical persuasion that comes from a knowledge and application of functional rhetorical figures. He enjoins modern poets to observe medieval genres and "sus tout à mouvoir les affections, et illustrerons frequemment noz propos de sentences populaires . . . imaginations et appréhensions ingénieuses, inventions divines, propres et poétiques descriptions, haultesse de style, gravité de sentences, magnificence de mots innovez et translatez." In his *Art poétique* Peletier allowed for the

[7] *Joachim du Bellay* (1900), p. 296.

[8] *Histoire de la Pléiade* (1961–1963), I, 203.

[9] Northrop Frye makes the telling point that the notion of a "verbal structure free of rhetorical elements is an illusion," *Anatomy of Criticism* (1966), p. 350.

[10] See Patterson, I, 151–153.

kind of merger between appropriate rhetorical eloquence and rigorous and guarded use of rhyme that the mature Pléiade consciously sought: "an Poësie, il faut fere tous les deus, e bien dire e bien rimer."[11] The shift holds true in Italy as well where Tasso in 1565 praises "the choice of words and of sententiae, the novelty of the figures and especially of the metaphors"[12] that are instrumental in forwarding concepts. Despite the significant revaluation of poetic, now seen more in terms of style than of rhyme disposition, and despite the concomitant fall from grace of Seconde Rhétorique, rhetoric remains a building block and companion of poetry. In the section of his Art Poétique (*Poetices libri septem,* 1561) dealing with the ideas of poetry, Scaliger, unaware of a difference between poetry and rhetoric, simply establishes different ways of *bene dicendi.*[13] And in "Contre les envieux poetes," an ode containing standard logical arguments and rhetorical topics, Du Bellay disdains the "facheux sons" of the *rhétoriqueurs* (IV, 52), but elsewhere enthusiastically sings the honors of the Parlement of Paris, the successors of Cicero and Demosthenes, where "Bruit l'eloquence, & tout ce qui honnore / Un orateur disertement loyal" (II, 274–275).

Most commentaries on the *Deffence et Illustration* stress that its original contribution resides in its enthusiastic rejection of the *rhétoriqueurs* and Marotic poetry and in its revolutionary sense of mission toward language and poetic expression. Critics go on to point out that Du Bellay's substantive comments are a pastiche and mélange of classical and contemporary treatises.[14] But the same could be said of many other works of the period, for Renaissance poetic is remarkably consistent and disagrees on points of emphasis rather than on basic tenets. Since most manuals are instructional or polemical and not fundamentally philosophical, differences occur in the attitude the writer entertains about the audience he is addressing;[15] otherwise, there is a feeling of sameness and *déjà vu* in reading treatise after treatise. In essence, Pierre Villey is correct in asserting the decisiveness of Italy in shaping Du Bellay's poetic ideas.[16] His massive borrowings from Sperone Speroni's seventh dialogue, the *Dialogo delle lingue,* argues for

[11] Des Autelz quoted by Patterson, pp. 362–363; Peletier du Mans, (1930), p. 150.

[12] Quoted by Weinberg, I, 176.

[13] Fifth edition, p. 323.

[14] Cf. Verdun Saulnier, *Du Bellay* (1963), p. 49.

[15] Cf. Michel Dassonville, "De l'unité de la *Deffence et Illustration de la langue francoyse,*" *BHRen,* XXVII (1965), 96–107.

[16] *Les Sources italiennes de la "Deffence et Illustration de la Langue française"* (1908), p. 78.

a community of spirit, and the same would apply to the eighth dialogue which dealt with rhetoric and which Du Bellay undoubtedly knew. The Janus-like figures of Sebillet and Peletier, both by their recognition of merit in the Marotic poets and tolerance of equivocal rhyme and by their desire to elevate and expand the conception of poetry, preclude any absolute divorce between Arts Poétiques and the rhetorical treatises that precede them. This is especially true of Peletier's two major treatises, the *Art poétique d'Horace* (1544) and the *Art poétique* (1555) which surround the *Deffence et Illustration.*

So any contradiction is more apparent than real between Donald Lemen Clark's assertion that Du Bellay promulgates the medieval tradition and Joel Elias Spingarn's passing counter-assertion that he signaled the introduction of classical ideas of poetry and reform of rhetoric.[17] The elaborate dedication of the *Deffence et Illustration* (pp. 5–7) is interchangeable with the exordium of Jean Molinet's *L'Art de rhétorique.*[18] And Du Bellay's inspection of his predecessors and catalogue of suitable genres is altogether traditional. Although their applications to the vernacular were woefully inadequate, medieval rhetoricians wrote more explicitly and more extensively on the kinds of neologisms Du Bellay advocated. But young poetic schools axiomatically seek their place in history by dismissing the older generation—a dismissal less total than the tone of their poetic manifestos implies. Like Boileau's *Art poétique* or the *Préface de Cromwell,* the *Deffence et Illustration,* although less balanced, unjustly maligns its predecessors. In 1674, however, Boileau was writing a résumé of an established fact, while the contradictions of the *Deffence et Illustration* arose partly from a still unsettled, contentious question involving the nature and use of poetic language. The Pléiade's formal rejection of the

[17] Clark, *Rhetoric and Poetry in the Renaissance* (1963), p. 78; Spingarn, *A History of Literary Criticism in the Renaissance* (1949), pp. 173, 177. We should emphasize reform over introduction. Edmond Faral has shown that such great source books of rhetoric as Cicero's *De inventione,* the *Rhetorica ad Herennium* and Horace's *Ars poetica* were used by medieval poets and theoreticians but with a more mechanical application and limited understanding, *Les Arts poétiques du XII$^{e}$ et du XIII$^{e}$ siècles* (1958), pp. 61, 99.

[18] "Certes, très honnouré seigneur, ce tant pou que n'en ay en teste ne vous y puet gaires ou pou aidier; vous en avez plus en la bouche que n'en sçay mettre par escript; ne la chalemele de Pan, qui abusa le roy Midas; ne la fleute du dieu Mercure, qui endormi le cler Argus; ne la viele d'Amphion, qui répara les murs de Thebes; ne aussi la harpe d'Orpheus, qui ouvri les portes d'enfer, n'eurent ensemble tele armonie ne si joyeuse resonance que vous, très honnouré seigneur, avez en bouche et en faconde." Quoted by Langlois, *Recueil d'arts,* p. 214.

*rhétoriqueurs* assumed a modification far more than a rejection of rhetoric per se, just as Hugo's "escalier / dérobé" modified but did not jettison the alexandrine. They objected to the *rhétoriqueurs'* intense, seemingly demented stress on disposition of rhyme and poetic diction viewed largely as ultra-richness of rhyme, and in this limited sense we may speak of the Pléiade's inclusion of classical ideas.

From Cicero's time through Tacitus up to the education of the early Church Fathers classical rhetoric under the instruction of the *declamatores* declined throughout the Mediterranean to the point where poetry not only blended with rhetoric but became subservient to it as well. Instead of finding and examining suitable matter drawn from experience, imaginary situations were conceived simply for the stylistic virtuosity they afforded. Flashes of ingenious stylistic display were preferred to consistency of thought and form. The Pléiade's quarrel with the *rhétoriqueurs* was directed against this kind of imbalance and they attacked the preference for *disposicion* and vacuous mechanics of composition which led to more decorative than functional expression, or a blend of both—an expression that focused more on the poet's ingenious rhyming than on the poetic conception and the style that crystallized it. Although the *Abrégé de l'art poétique* places disposition on an equal footing with invention, style and pronunciation, Ronsard strongly dissuades his reader from becoming a mere versifier. Du Bellay is even more adamant in reducing what the *rhétoriqueurs* had emphasized, as he presents and modifies the full Ciceronian system:

> Et premier, c'est une chose accordée entre tous les meilleurs aucteurs de rethorique, qu'il y a cinq parties de bien dire, l'invention, l'eloquution, la disposition, la memoire & la pronuntiation . . . pour autant aussi que la disposition gist plus en la discretion & bon jugement de l'orateur qu'en certaines reigles & preceptes . . . je me contenteray de parler des deux premieres, scavoir de l'invention & de l'eloquution. (pp. 32–33)

The clear preference for poetry based on knowledge and experience, not just rigid rules of versification and disposition of rhymes, coupled with a judicious and lofty style[19] characterizes the young Pléiade's conception of their calling and explains away some of the inconsistencies in Du Bellay's treatise. For one thing, the faulty Greek etymology of *Barbare* that Chamard criticizes in Du Bellay's clumsy attempt to establish a link between customs and verbal expression (p. 16) seems

[19] This preference with its attendant distinctions makes it difficult to justify Patterson's observation on Pléiade poetic that "The Greeks and Latins are valuable chiefly for the study of literary invention and disposition, in short, of style," p. 411. Cf. *Quintilian,* IX, ii, 77.

actually to be a reference to the rhetorical concept *barbaros lexis*. Scoring the older generation for barbarous language, he is at the same time exhorting the young poets to observe classical standards of expression and to avoid coarse and unpolished conditions of language. Quintilian long before had discussed the concept as a racial characteristic of expression and after him Du Bartas referred to the need for violating decorum through barbaric language to express violence, "Je souille mon discours, veu qu'en cest argument / Il faut, pour bien parler, parler barbarement," while Boileau demurred: "Mon esprit n'admet point un pompeux barbarisme."[20]

Du Bellay's "Metamorphose d'une rose" (V, 183) alludes to Aphthonius, whose rhetoric was a prime source of *declamatio* in sixteenth-century France and Italy, who was studied on an equal basis with Hermogenes and Longinus and who probably left his mark on such disparate works as Marot's "Estrenne" II and Ronsard's "Exhortation pour la paix." But he follows Turnèbe in equating empty and sycophantic versifying with the *declamatores* (VI, 119). The rhymed banter and doggerel of the Marotic poets with their stress on witty ornamentation should give way to a more deeply emotional and humanizing knowledge, a suasive energizing of experience. Despite the belated influence of Aristotle's *Rhetoric* and his observations on the means of persuasion, the injunction to teach, please and move—the threefold aim of oratory—was available to the midcentury poets through numerous derivative sources.[21] Fabri's second book of *L'Art de rithmer* counsels the traditional divisions of an oration and concludes that "rethorique est la royne de la pensee des hommes, qui tourne les couraiges, suadant et dissuadant en tel fin qu'il plait." Du Bellay is even more specific in advocating that poets be steeped in examples of rhetorical persuasion,

> quand aux figures des sentences & des motz, & toutes les autres parties de l'eloquution, les lieux de commiseration, de joye, de tristesse, d'ire, d'admiration, & toutes autres commotions de l'ame: je n'en parle point apres si grand nombre d'excellens phylosophes & orateurs qui en ont traicté, que jeveux avoir eté bien leuz & releuz de nostre poëte, premier qu'il entreprenne quelque hault & excellent ouvraige. (pp. 159–160)

[20] Quintilian, I, v, 8; Du Bartas, *Works* (1935–1940), III, 193; Boileau *L'Art poétique*, I, 159, p. 15. Cf. Montaigne, II, 17, p. 622, and Du Bellay's "Patriae desiderium," *Poésies françaises et latines de Joachim du Bellay*, ed. Ernest Courbet (1931), I, 447. *Barbare* is allied to the *scientia recte loquendi* which is fundamental to the existence and purpose of rhetoric (Quintilian, II, xiv, 5).

[21] See Clark, p. 138, for the rhetorical example as the instrument of poetry elsewhere in Renaissance Europe.

and, as Miss Tuve points out, his later repudiation of the older poets is followed by a description of poetic persuasion of an implied audience based on Cicero's *De oratore* and Quintilian's *Institutio oratoria:*[22]

Je pense bien qu'en parlant ainsi de notz rymeurs, je sembleray à beaucoup trop mordant & satyrique, mais veritable à ceux qui ont scavoir & jugement . . . Pour conclure ce propos, saiches, Lecteur, que celuy sera veritablement le poëte que je cherche en nostre Langue, qui me fera indigner, apayser, ejouyr, douloir, aymer, hayr, admirer, etonner, bref, qui tiendra la bride de mes affections, me tournant ça & la à son plaisir. Voyla la vraye pierre de touche, ou il fault que tu epreuves tous poëmes, & en toutes Langues. (pp. 179–180)

Early in the *Deffence* he invoked Pythia, Goddess of Persuasion (p. 28), and he never stopped singing paeans to her. In "A Jacques Gohory parisien sur la poursuite d'Amadis," a piece that Foclin's *Rhetorique* cites as a model of rhetorical form, Du Bellay worships at the altar of poetry, the muses and Pythia (V, 253–261). He extends the divine gift as a compliment to Lansac: "Ils (les Dieux) t'ont donné le pouvoir / D'emouvoir" (V, 322). So the modern abhorrence of poetry as an instrument of rhetorical persuasion seems to have little place among Renaissance canons, and when it does, close analysis discerns a discrepancy between lofty appeal to poetic fury or kindred conceptions and the profane reality of poetry as a practiced métier. Divine madness is present as an attractive theme but is absent on the level of praxis. When in the *Deffence* Du Bellay speaks of "faulse persuasion" (p. 73) he is referring not to a procedure which he disallows, but rather to the conception—the inferior status of the French language—expressed by that procedure; or when he disclaims any intention of persuading his beloved to grant love's favors (and yet tells us parenthetically that he rightly deserves them), he does so simply to convince her of his basic worthiness to love her (V, 135). The strongest disclaimer of rhetoric is issued by Ronsard in the "Response aux injures," a poem grounded in such classical and contemporary rhetorical examples as the Horatian dictum "ars est celare artem":

En l'art de Poësie, un art il ne faut pas
Tel qu'ont les Predicans, qui suivent pas à pas

[22] *Elizabethan and Metaphysical Imagery* (1965) p. 181. Rather than loading notation with analogies and actual sources drawn from classical and medieval rhetorics and poetics, Quintilian's great compendium of Ciceronianism on which Du Bellay relied so heavily will usually be cited for representative convenience. Cf. Olivier de Magny's "Se sont tous arguments fort communs à nostre age," *Les Souspirs* (1874), p. 9.

> Leur sermon sceu par cueur, ou tel qu'il faut en prose,
> Où toujours l'Orateur suit le fil d'une chose.
> Les Poëtes gaillards ont artifice à part,
> Ils ont un art caché qui ne semble pas art
> Aux versificateurs, d'autant qu'il se promeine
> D'une libre contrainte, où la Muse le meine.[23]

Moreover, his allusion to "Predicans" is so colored by invective against Calvinists as to eschew any precise reference to rhetorical training per se.

So finely attuned was the critical eye to rhetorical persuasion that Du Bellay's editor felt compelled to identify the verse "O trois-fois malheureux & quatre fois, celuy," a rhetorical figure of amplification which here introduces a description of a traveler's return to misfortune, as a poetic figure "en faveur des pauvres gentilshommes contre les plaideurs et usuriers" (VI, 210).[24] Whether attacking the forces of ignorance with his "Lire menaçante," praising the king in the extended sweep of a *discours,* defending Jean Du Bellay's honor within the rigid confines of a sonnet, or simply conveying an elegiac mood, Du Bellay evinces a thorough knowledge and sophisticated employment of the accepted instruments of Renaissance poetic. With recognition, then, of the extent to which rhetoric penetrated his conception of poetry, we may proceed closer to the fabric of his poetry with a description of the systematic function of rhetoric.

## Invention

As we have suggested, logic and rhetoric relied on essentially the same methods of investigation, had recourse to interchangeable terminology, and therefore we can reasonably expect them to share and attain similar goals. Indeed, rhetorical figures are often either developed from dialectical places or, especially when they involve amplification or comparison, are identical with dialectical investigation; both contribute to, but do not fully constitute, poetry. Sebillet does not separate the first step of speculative thinking from that of rhetoric as the dual preparation for poetic activity, "Le surplus de l'invention qui consiste en l'art, prendra le pöëte des Philosophes et Rheteurs qui en ont escrit livres propres et particuliers," and he does not fail to couple invention and judgment.[25] It will be remembered that Ramus' reduction of rhetoric

[23] Ed. Laumonier, XI, 160. Cf. Henri Weber, *La Création poétique au XVIe siècle,* p. 566, n. 2.

[24] For an example of the rhetorical *pour et contre* in Ronsard, see ed. Laumonier, IX, x, and in Rabelais, see *Pantagruel,* ch. 18.

[25] *Art poétique françoys* (1932), pp. 27 ff. Cf. Montaigne, III, 9, p. 967.

to style entailed dismissing the last two forensic steps of memory and delivery, and replacing the first two with dialectic. Like the pattern of logical progression, rhetorical composition should mirror natural thought process as it passes from conception to expression, or as the Pléiade would put it, from invention to style in the *ordo naturalis*.

Despite the convenient divisions of invention, disposition and elocution, practicing poets insist on the organic function of these faculties. In the hyperbolic conclusion to his "Tumbeau de Henri II," perhaps his last poetic effort, Du Bellay urges French poets to immortalize the late king's honors: "Et vous soit ce subject un commun argument" (VI, 91). In the adjoining Latin version the poet equates *argument* with *seges*, implying that invention is a seed from which the finished poem naturally matures. As to the discovery of a subject or poetic "cause" by means of invention, Du Bellay follows Quintilian's advice that one should transcend isolated words and observe the movement from judgment to arrangement of components to the emotionally persuasive value of varied figures (X, ii, 27); in short, too many poets divorce *res* from *verba*, "sans penetrer aux plus cachées & interieures parties de l'aucteur qu'ilz se sont proposé, s'adaptent seulement au premier regard, & s'amusant à la beauté des motz, perdent la force des choses" (p. 46). Chamard seems to neglect semantic gradations when he dismisses as "une redondance oratoire" Du Bellay's imperative that the poet who wishes to undertake a great work should "inventer, adopter & composer" (p. 137). This appears to be a reference to the widely held steps of Renaissance psychology whereby invention, assisted by a controlled imagination, refracts the "discovered" conception into images and passes them on to judgment which evaluates, emends and arranges imagery for our better understanding.[26] Ronsard elaborates this counsel in his *Abrégé:* "L'invention n'est autre chose que le bon naturel d'une imagination concevant les Idées & formes de toutes choses qui se peuvent imaginer tant celestes que terrestres, animées ou inanimes (sic), pour apres les representer, descrire & imiter . . . (tes inventions) seront bien ordonnées & disposées: & bien qu'elles semblent passer celles du vulgaire, elles seront toutesfois telles qu'elles pourront estre facilement conceues & entendues d'un chascun."[27]

The critic must therefore be wary of examining individual images

[26] Cf. Grahame Castor *Pléiade Poetics* (1964), ch. 16, and Quintilian, VIII, iii, 88: "φαντασία in concipiendis visionibus." A similar evolution in meaning appears to obtain in Aneau's belief that the orateur should "adrécer, ordonner & conjoindre" (p. 26). For a view completely opposed to my own, see Yves Le Hir, *Rhétorique et stylistique de la pléiade au parnasse* (1960), pp. 115–116.

[27] Ed. Laumonier, XIV, 13.

out of context and separated from their intended function, that is, he should hesitate to divorce invention from elocution. To the extent that this study discusses individual images out of context, it too will be arbitrary. The love of detail and the plastic contours of images with which Pléiade poets are often credited go beyond sensuousness in order to convey a conception the poet has in mind, witness Du Bellay's passage on invention and his attempt to relate individual components to a general idea in the "Chant de l'amour et du primtemps":

> De quelle riche couleur
> Peindray-je ma poësie
> Pour descrire la valeur
> Que j'ay sur toutes choisie?
> Tous les verds tresors des cieux,
> Riche ornement de la plaine,
> Representent à mes yeux
> L'object de ma doulce peine. (V, 41–42)

The poet's question is rhetorical only in the sense that it reflects a commonly-shared attitude toward rhetorical method. We find it recast in the formulaic complaint that the poet, faced with a noble subject, is overwhelmed by an abundance of material. The question is a standard deliberative element of forensic discourse (*genus deliberativum:* Quintilian, IX, ii, 19). In the "Ode au prince de Melphe" Du Bellay criticizes those (Ronsard?) who falsely praise dignitaries in fixed Pindaric fashion, but he himself goes on to find Caracciol's virtues so manifest that he does not know where to begin his poem (V, 351). In turn, Ronsard precedes an amplified eulogy with the same *embarras de richesses,* "Ainsi voulant Turnebe r'animer, / Je suis vaincu ayant trop de matiere."[28]

It is true, of course, that the Pléiade did value variety, if not for its own sake, in concert with Cicero's advice to gain expertise in all things human (*De oratore,* I, xvi), Quintilian's (X, i, 69) and Horace's (*Ars poetica,* vv. 309–322) admiration of rich invention and their own enthusiastic discovery of a spatially and temporally expanding universe. Just as Ramus dwelled on invention, the Pléiade increasingly expanded and elevated poetic contemplation, preparatory to arrangement of material and stylistic garnishing, in conjunction with their desire to rise above the petty fascinations of an earlier generation. Du Bellay sarcastically railed against the excesses of the Petrarchistic poets and their automatic selection of sensual details to illustrate a time-worn conception, "Je choisiray cent mille nouveautez, / Dont je

[28] Ibid., XIII, 195.

peindray voz plus grandes beautez / Sur la plus belle Idee" (V, 77), and in the epic invocation of his "Monomachie" he rhymed his "maitiere choizie" with "saincte fantaizie" in implicit opposition to the worn-out sounds of the *rhétoriqueurs* (IV, 129). Ronsard's genealogy of poetry at the beginning of his *Abrégé* is no less clear in expounding an enlarged invention based as much on the poet's intrinsic worth as on the extrinsic authority of classical poets: "Car le principal poinct est l'invention, laquelle vient tant de la bonne nature, que par la leçon des bons & anciens autheurs."[29]

The reestablishment of the Muse on Parnassus and the appeal to poetic fury as a means of dignifying the poet's station did not preclude a learned poetry based on reason and systematic composition. Heightening can occur by the very combination of verbal and rational activities. Du Bellay's *vers rapportés* develop variations on this theme: "Plume, langue, entendement, / Qui fait que si hautement / J'escry, je parle & raisonne" (V, 310). Within the basic unity of Renaissance thought, logic and rhetoric are organically united just as individually both systems are organically pursued. The triad of *docendi, movendi, delectandi* was variously interpreted and differently construed, as for instance, in d'Aubigné's announcement around the end of the century that poetry should teach a sterner lesson and move its audience to more serious contemplation by means of a violent, and often violated, subject and syntax, for "Ce siecle, autre en ses moeurs, demande un autre style" (*Les Tragiques,* II, 77); but poets resisted separating proving from pleasing. In satire as in praise Du Bellay assumed an instrumental beauty, "Voz beautez donq' leur servent d'argumens, / Et ne leur fault de meilleurs instrumens" (V, 72), or an identification of proof with pleasure: "Pour argument une beauté choisie" (II, 238). The result of this unity is that while poetic arguments are sometimes identified as being *feinct* (II, 216), criticized for being *foible* (II, 225), are subtle or blatant, inartificial or artificial as Quintilian had allowed,[30] poetry is never censured simply for having a persuasive argument. Argument and invention are congruent in the discovery and selection they effect (V, 134) and in their natural desire to embrace a wide spectrum of experience:

> SIRE, si vostre loz d'une *Iliade* entiere
> Ne donnoit à chascun assez ample matiere,
> Sans d'autres argumens son poëme allonger,
> J'irois avec Ascree en Parnase songer
> Cent mille inventions pour blasmer la Discorde, (VI, 13)

[29] Ibid., XIV, 5–6.
[30] V, x, 11; cf. Aristotle, *Rhetoric* III, xiii, 1414a.

The principle of wide selectivity applies to imitation where, as Bernard Weinberg says about Tasso, imitating a model implies espousing an example and arguing in its behalf, however subtle and disguised that argument might be.[31] In a well-known passage Du Bellay esteems the procedure of Cicero and Vergil with no reservations: "Immitant les meilleurs aucteurs Grecz, se transformant en eux, les devorant, & apres les avoir bien digerez, les convertissant en sang & nouriture, se proposant, chacun selon son naturel & l'argument qu'il vouloit elire, le meilleur aucteur, dont ilz observoint diligemment toutes les plus rares & exquises vertuz" (p. 42).

### Disposition

Emphasis on the continuousness of poetic creation, on the unified and successful translation of human experience into meaningful, persuasive and pleasurable patterns of expression—or the reverse where the reader passes from particulars, word by word and line by line, to a general and inclusive understanding—makes it difficult or even unfeasible precisely to discern the passage from invention to disposition, disposition to style. But this does not mean that theory fails to accord with practice, that the steps of thought are inexistent in the poet's mind or that there is no equivalence between the stages of thought and the verbal trajectory of the poem. It means, rather, as in the second step, that in the multiple arrangement of lines into rhyme groups and stanzas, stanzas into sections until the poem is completed, the poetic conception will be concurrently and progressively expressed. It also means that in a successful and confined verse form, such as an epigram or a sonnet, the link will tend to be imperceptible between an assertive proposition and verbal structure—and therefore worthy of critical attention. Accordingly, it is in the longer poems, such as the *discours,* that the outlines of disposition are the boldest and the most easily distinguishable from style as that term was then understood. Later chapters will treat the implications and possibilities of thought structure, inevitably along with idea and style, in Du Bellay's sonnet form. For the moment, we are attempting to put a single poetic method into perspective by varied examples drawn from the entire corpus of his poetry.

In his digest of the whole of classical rhetoric, Quintilian established the sequential steps of discourse as exordium, proposition, narration, confirmation, refutation and peroration. From Aristotle (*Rhetoric,* III, xiii–xvii) on, rhetoricians were allowed to combine these comple-

[31] I, 213.

mentary components, for instance confirmation with refutation, according to the needs of the subject. Du Bellay, like many other literati of his time, adheres to the classical disposition and function of these components of *ordo naturalis* in various types of longer poems. In the "Discours sur le sacre du treschrestien Roy François II" he observes the exordium's standard purpose of putting his audience in the proper frame of mind and mood of receptivity; adhering to the structure of Michel de l'Hospital's "De sacra Francisci II," Du Bellay detaches this initial step in epigrammatic form (VI, 169–170). Even in "La Vieille Courtisanne," not a *discours* in the usual understanding of that term (although its meaning was extremely inclusive), his brief introduction moves clearly and easily to the narration, which in rhetoric means the skillful exposition of the particulars that would be treated: "Donques, à fin de mieulx faire cognoistre / Tout mon malheur..." (V, 149). When, as in the "Entreprise du Roy-Daulphin pour le tournoy," he consciously leaves and resumes his plotted line (VI, 48–49, vv. 183–220), "Mais reprenant nostre premier propos," his digression coincides with Quintilian's prescribed technique for adding charm and elegance to the main subject (IV, iii, 15; IX, iv, 27); as a means of ennobling the itinerary to the tournament in Paris, Du Bellay describes the mythological, albeit spurious, founding of Orléans through the love of Bacchus and Aurelia.[32]

The most obvious example of this system at work—and therefore not necessarily the most successful—is the "Hymne au Roy sur la prinse de Callais," a poem which Du Bellay scholars have generally admired. Each movement is carefully punctuated by an apostrophe to Henri II, a somewhat mechanical procedure which in terms of Renaissance aesthetics would draw too much attention to the poet's method if the steps were not integrated.[33] By clearly controlling here the various movements of his thought and carefully directing it to a premeditated end, Du Bellay atones for the earlier weakness Aneau had drawn to his attention in the *Deffence*: "sans but final avisé, sans continuelle poursuite & sans consequence, tant en l'oeuvre universel que en chacune partie" (p. 22).

The emotional tone is set in the exordium where a summary of Augustus' peace-making efforts and the implied parallel with Henri II are built into an elaborated asyndeton. Considering his argument

[32] Cf. Ronsard, ed. Laumonier, I, 48, for an obvious reference to the techniques of digression.

[33] Or to use the common formula, although discourse requires an argument as a body requires nerves, the nerves, bones and veins should not protrude. Cf. Rudolph Agricola, *De inventione dialectica* (1534), p. 487, and "De l'institution des enfants," "il ne faut qu'on y puisse compter les os et les veines," I, 26, p. 171.

legitimate, he uses the Direct Approach (*principium*), and in the proposition the comparison is made specific, "SIRE, vous avez faict comme cét empereur" (v. 15). Du Bellay states his case that, while Fortune is the cause of such human misfortunes as the loss of a besieged city, the king's manifest Virtue ultimately prevailed, "Et avez nostre espoir devancé par l'effect" (v. 36). This case draws on the same recommended commonplaces (*honestum, utile, facile*) that Ronsard relies on in his "Exhortation pour la paix."[34] The narration links the commonplace theme of Virtue and Fortune with historical facts, "Vous avez prins CALLAIS deux cens ans imprenable, / Montrant qu'à Vertu rien n'est inexpugnable" (vv. 37–38), as he couches Henri's long-awaited project in various allegories. The following section, beginning with "Mais à qui fault il, SIRE, attribuer l'honneur" (v. 71), combines confirmation with refutation. Du Bellay refutes the king's counsellors who opposed the move on Callais and who were unaware of Henri's "fortune heureuse" and "vertu valeureuse," and he continues on through a series of proofs that Quintilian advised in his book on confirmation. Proceeding by means of deduction (v. 103: Quintilian, V, i, 1), he states that "si lon juge bien" the reader will see an extended parallel between the king's actions and Caesar's (V, xi, 15), and appeals successively to common argument (V, xiii, 29), "Mais ce discours la, SIRE, est un discours commun, / Et qui, sans que j'en parle, est notoire à chacun" (vv. 111–112), and to vivid portraiture, "Ici je vous supply mettre devant voz yeulx" (v. 123: V, xiii, 56–57). A succession of "Je voy" leads up to the peroration, "SIRE, parmy le bruit & publique allegresse / Du peuple vous loüant, j'ay prins la hardiesse / De vous offrir ces Vers . . ." (vv. 145–147) in which he apologizes for not having polished them and says to Henri, in effect, "Te Deum laudamus."[35]

If modern critics find reason to admire this work from the poet's twilight years, his watchdog commentator, Aneau, was not so charitable with the young Du Bellay of the *Deffence*. When the Quintil correctly says "tu es ainsi inconsequent, les chapitres & propos ne dependant

[34] Ed. Laumonier, IX, 15. Melanchthon classifies this series of arguments as one of cause and effect, *Elementa rhetorices* in *Opera omnia* (1834–1860), XIII, col. 450.

[35] Just as he should in accordance with such classical models as Lucian's *Encomium of Demosthenes* and Claudian's *Panegyricus Probini et Olybrii* and such Renaissance examples, no matter the subject, as Henri Estienne's *Francofordiensis emporii encomium,* Melanchthon's *Oratio in laudem novae scholae,* Marot's "Au Roy, du temps de son exil à Ferrare" and Ronsard's "Exhortation pour la paix," all of which end with this type of prayer. See also the marginal notation, "la priere que lon faisoit anciennement en faveur des Empereurs," at the end of the "Discours sur les Quatre Etats," *Oeuvres francoises,* ed. de Harsy, p. 540.

l'un de l'autre, mais ainsi mis comme ils venoient de la pensée en la plume, & de la plume au papier: tellement que tout l'oeuvre est sans propos & certaine consistence, sans theme proposé & certain, sans ordre methodique, sans oeconomie" (p. 22), he is neither arguing against a composition that mirrors thought nor for an atrophied arrangement of parts. The last word in his castigation is transliterated from the Greek rhetorical term οἰκονομία which referred to the reciprocal arrangement of the parts of an intellectual whole.[36] In other words, his composition should reflect at once the rational and natural movement of thought; in a poetic framework the term would require logical method in his divine madness. Du Bellay himself implicitly argues against a rigidly uniform understanding of this middle step when he praised the radically different styles of Aristotle and Plato which arise as individual responses from their disposition: "La vérité si bien par eux cherchée, la disposition & l'ordre des choses, la sentencieuse breveté de l'un & la divine copie de l'autre est propre à eux" (pp. 71–72). But earlier in the *Deffence* he had tied disposition to decorum and judgment of a prior poetic conception in all its multiplicity: "la disposition gist plus en la discretion & bon jugement de l'orateur qu'en certaines reigles & preceptes: veu que les evenementz du tens, la circunstance des lieux, la condition des personnes & la diversité des occasions . . ." (p. 33),[37] and elsewhere he discusses the arrangement of individual poems within a collection, concluding that he must "disposer en meilleur ordre que devant: les comprenant, chacun selon son argument" (VI, 253). In a reader-oriented literature, such as the Pléiade's with its driving preoccupation with reputation and immortality, the disposition of the poetic argument will be considered, finally, for its corresponding effect on the reader; the discussion of the Horatian mixture of usefulness and pleasure in the first book of Scaliger's *Poetices* also turns on the effect of poetic action on the mental disposition of the reader and on his ability to distinguish good from evil.

## Style

Elocution, affirms Du Bellay in the *Deffence,* is the "partie certes la plus difficule, & sans la quelle toutes autres choses restent comme inutiles" (p. 34). Style is not only the most difficult part of composition, but, through its complexities, is the most susceptible of graduation and varieties of expression and the surest means of attaining a lasting

[36] Thomas Sebillet's *Art poétique Françoys* (1932), speaks of "locupléter et l'invention et l'économie," p. 28.

[37] Cf. Ramus, *La Dialectique,* p. 150.

reputation as well. His statement derives from Quintilian's introductory remarks on style (VIII, pr. 13), in which the Roman preceptor reduces eloquent expression to the ornate and the appropriate, both of which were key conceptions for the Pléiade poets and relate to the evolution of their styles.

Rhetorical systems of all periods legislate on matters of appropriateness, or decorum, which trifurcate poetry into high, middle and low levels of address. From Cicero through Horace to the medieval scheme of "Vergil's Wheel"[38] the separation of levels progressively crystallized, involved the poet's task of moving, teaching, pleasing, or all of these, and determined his choice of sublime, middling or low characters and genres and of style ranging from the pleasingly negligent to the elevated and highly ornate. To be sure, the principle of decorum always entails teaching and pleasing, no matter what the level of reference or the emphasis of the poet; whether it be a narrative in the grand style, elegy or satire in the low style, the audience learns the manner of address and conduct appropriate to a particular social station and derives pleasure from the harmony of poetic components. Aristotle implies this unity in his long analysis of emotions and traits corresponding to social rank (*Rhetoric,* II, ii–xi), and Quintilian explicitly links apt characters, emotional appeal, fitting style and derived lesson: "in rebus spiritus et in verbis sublimitas et in affectibus motus omnis et in personis decor petitur" (X, i, 27).

In practice and when not making self-conscious pronouncements, the Pléiade's stylistic range is mobile and seems at times to heed Cicero's invitation to combine styles simultaneously or successively (*Orator,* 100–109). If the judgment of Nicolas Edoard, the 1588 editor of the "Vieille Courtisanne," is an index of consensus opinion, Du Bellay covered the full range in a single poem, delighting and sternly admonishing, in a varied style: "la nayve grace des vers propres elegans, gravement sonnans, & neantmoins doux-coulans" (V, 181). The Pléiade's general evolution down from a high-flown style in their early years to a more moderate one, "ny trop haut, ny trop bas," is amply described in the posthumous preface to the *Franciade.* When he is writing about choice of style at a given moment, Ronsard obeys Horace's injunction to acknowledge and separate modes of expression and also

[38] Cf. Faral, pp. 86–89. In his commentary on Ronsard's "Elegie à son livre" at the beginning of the second book of the *Amours* Belleau concludes "Doncques s'accommodant à l'esprit de sa seconde maistresse . . . il suit un nouveau style," *Les Oeuvres de P. de Ronsard,* ed. Marc-Antoine Muret (1584), p. 119. There seems to have been little real connection between these levels and the Pléiade's notion of the four stages of divine fury.

recognize the need for variety of expression: "Et qui voudra bien plaire, il faut / Ne chanter pas tousjours le haut."[39] Even the categorizing Scaliger was obliged to suggest that a pure style does not fully exist,[40] but theorists and poets alike agreed that some sort of stylistic distinctions were good, necessary and related rationally to other choices incumbent on the poet. Thus, whenever manuals comment on subject matter to be included in a poem, they do so in terms of its appropriateness to the intent, means and tone of the poem. Decorum becomes one of the common denominators of literary expression, and whether it be a discussion with Grévin in 1561 on tragedy, "D'Athenes, Troye, Argos, de Thebes & Mycenes / Sont pris les argumens qui conviennent aux scenes," or statements on lyric poetry in the posthumous preface of the *Odes,* 1587, "toute sorte de Poësie a l'argument propre & convenable à son subject," Ronsard and others viewed the basic questions—here invention—in a similar way. And the question of decorum weighs heavily in further considerations, especially of style, up to the completion of the work. Scaliger holds that stylistic figures should be appropriate to the argument, "argumentis convenire," and in the second preface of the *Franciade* Ronsard continues: "Quant aux comparaisons . . . Il faut les bien mettre & les bien arranger aux lieux propres de ta Poesie: car ce sont les nerfs & tendons des Muses, quand elles sont placees bien à propos, & servantes à la matiere: sinon, elles sont du tout ridicules & dignes du foüet."[41]

The whipping for indecorous figures to which Ronsard alludes was liberally and pedantically applied to Du Bellay by the Quintil Horatian, but—within aesthetic canons of the time—not always without justification. A glance at such ill-fitting stylistic figures as, for instance, improper metaphors and similes, is as instructive as the study of often exaggerated praise for decorous ones. Aneau takes Du Bellay to task for his "translation vicieuse & inconsequente," referring to the trope *translatio* which alters the meaning of a word by its unusual association with another word or idea and thereby suggests a multiplicity of ideas as in Shakespeare's "strong toil." In a short space Du Bellay used the

[39] Ed. Laumonier, VI, 93.

[40] IV, xiii ("Puritas"), p. 427.

[41] Ronsard, ed. Laumonier, XIV, 198; I, 59; XVI, 342–343; *Poetices,* IV, xxxviii, p. 467. Cf. Des Autelz' defense of Saint-Gelais and Pernette du Guillet in his *Replique* where pleasure and the successful use of the rhetorical figures of *prosopopoeia* and *enargia* both derive from appropriate selection: "sont vrayment oeuvres poëtiques, bien ornees de figures convenantes à leur subjet: & que plus m'y plait, en l'une je voy une prosopopee, mouvant jusques à tout l'affection de misericorde: en l'autre une evidence & vive representation des choses y narees" (p. 116).

verbs *planter, manger* and *bastir* to describe how Roman authors enriched their language through imitation. Aneau does not criticize Du Bellay's otherwise legitimate use of mixed metaphor as such, but rather attacks his desire to use it "ou il n'est besoing, & appliquer figures ou proprieté seroit mieux convenante, estimans l'oraison par tout figurée estre plus belle que la simple & egale & rarement entremeslée de telz ornemens" (p. 43), after which Aneau himself finishes in a flourish of ornamental figures.

Although the Quintil's theory belies his practice, it consistently reflects a widely held belief that expository style should be more moderate. He judiciously charges Du Bellay with "superflue transnomination" for his reference to Horace as "le Pindare Latin," because such periphrasis "ne convient pas à la prose didascalique." In the same breath, he carefully disallows the allegorical dedication of the *Deffence et Illustration,* since, as an extended metaphor, the low position of an actor fails to correspond to Jean Du Bellay's high station and since the terms of reference do not remain consistent throughout the development (pp. 3–4). If the schoolmasterly Aneau's denigrating attitude toward an over-eager student suggests the rule-minded Polonius, his extreme concern for effective form and style bespeaks the same care the subtler minds of the Pléiade were later to realize in their poetry. At times it appears that the Quintil has learned his lesson not too wisely but too well; when Du Bellay compares thought devoid of style to a sword concealed in its sheath, Aneau rejoins with "impropre similitude" (p. 34), painfully demonstrates why the figure is illogical and in the process unwittingly overthrows Quintilian's identical image on which Du Bellay's comparison is founded (VIII, pr. 15). But in the "Anterotique," after passing in silence over the poet's extended, traditional and justifiable use of *tapinosis* for derision, he succinctly inveighs against the verse "Vieille doncq' plus que toy vilaine" first for its illogical base and then for not being a rhetorical figure appropriate to the context, "Affectée comparaison du plus à soy, qui ne peult estre, & ne tombe en figure par laquelle se puisse excuser" (I, 129).

While the Pléiade would undoubtedly have benefited from an understanding of the Aristotelian notions of necessity and probability in justifying the poet's role as an imitator of reality and in their ideas on poetic unity, and while they misconstrued some Horatian aphorisms on the purpose of poetry, their working grasp of decorum held them in good stead. The poet's temperament, as it were the muse he invokes, should determine the level of address, and the speech of his characters should corroborate their status: "l'audace / Ne convient à la chose basse / . . . Et Achille entre les pucelles / Convenoit mal avecques elles" (V, 64–65). The mixture of style in the "Vieille Courtisanne," however, praised at length by Edoard, does not contravene decorum in a bittersweet poem describing a base profession and leading to an elevated moral lesson. The poetic voice, then, is "accommodée à toutes les affections que tu voudras exprimer en tes vers" (p. 167). In prosopopoeia involving several voices as in the "Monomachie," where the importance of the characters derives from the moral attitude they represent, David employs a psalmodic style in keeping with his holy mission, "le boucler de ma ferme esperance" (v. 164), while Goliath's obsession and bumptiousness force his thought into a low language and a repetitive and unrhythmic cadence:

> Si quelqu'ung donq' en la vertu se bagne, . . .
> C'est là, c'est là que ma vertu notoire
> Se deust baigner: non point en cete fange. (vv. 111, 157–158)

The low voice is employed not only to describe pastoral scenes and to personify morally repugnant characters, but also to guide and comment upon the narrative voice itself. Du Bellay uses it as a tactic to praise himself with faint damning, as in the "Discours au Roy sur la trefve de l'an MDLV," a poem laced with a variety of rhetorical figures, when he says "Je ne veulx point icy, pour mon hymne borner, / D'art plus elabouré voz louanges orner" (VI, 15). After issuing this disclaimer, he strikes a pose of humility and leaves to those more knowledgeable than he the attempt to capture Henri's greatness in their verse; since such a great undertaking would break his back, the narrator defers to the image used so well in the *Antiquitez de Rome* 30 of the simple gleaner collecting random kernels in the harvester's path. Again, at the end of his "Ode au seigneur des Essars" (IV, 177–178), anterior to the *Regrets,* he contrasts the "harpe Ronsardine" with his slight "papiers," just as he will do in the first sonnet of his great Roman collection where he damns the ambitious Vendômois with faint praise and thus sets the tone for the following sonnets.

Despite this recurrence of the same voice in a similar context, Du Bellay is not inconvenienced by the tripartite dictates of decorum, but rather makes them serve his ends. His letter to Jean Morel on the "Tumbeau de Henry II" leaves no doubt about the freedom he feels: "Je l'eusse bien peu enrichir si j'eusse voulu (& l'oeuvre en estoit bien capable, comme vous pouvez penser) de figures & inventions poëtiques d'avantage qu'il n'est, & qu'il semblera peult estre à quelques admirateurs de l'antique poësie, que je le devois faire: mais il m'a semblé que pour la dignité du subjet, & pour rendre l'oeuvre de plus grande majesté & durée, un ouvrage Dorique, c'est à dire plein & solide, estoit beaucoup plus convenable qu'un Corinthien, ou autre de moindre estoffe, mais plus elabouré d'artifice & invention d'architecture... jamais proposé autre but ny utilité à mes estudes, que l'heur de pouvoir faire chose qui luy feust aggreable."[42] The unadorned "doric" style and his professed Horatian aim of mixing usefulness and pleasure comply perfectly with the conception he entertains about Henri II's features and unassuming habits:

> Son parler fut naïf, non poly d'artifice,
> Mais sentant son grand Roy, qui fait autre exercice,
> Son visage estoit doulx, meslé de gravité, ... (VI, 83)

Moreover, the terminology of the adjoining Latin translation could have been drawn from any statement on decorum from the time of Horace to the Renaissance: "*Sermo* fuit *simplex,* nimiaque haud arte politus, / Sed qualem magni Principis esse *decet.*"

This allusion to the king's unassuming manners is high praise indeed, but usually the grand style was considered appropriate for praising nobility and its attendant honors. An elevated (but not recondite) address befitted the Pléiade's early ambitions, polemical mood and hatred of the *profanum vulgus* they saw in their elders. The "vestige de rare & antique erudition" recommended by the *Illustration* is associated in descending order with "les louanges des Dieux & des hommes vertueux, le discours fatal des choses mondaines..." (p. 113), and in the form of archaisms this erudition, confirmed in theory by Minturno and in practice by Spenser, is applauded as belonging to the high style. High style can therefore include a "docte stile" leading at once to refined pleasure, instruction and moral elevation;[43] those poets given to "L'utile et doulce escriture" and of whom "Les Roys sont les argumens" show us "Le beau, l'honneste, l'utile, / Avec' ung plus docte

[42] *Lettres de Joachim du Bellay,* ed. Pierre de Nolhac (1883), pp. 36–37. In his 1603 preface to *The Barons Wars* Michael Drayton rejects the seven-line stanza because it "softened the verse more than the Majestie of the subject (Queen Isabella) would permit." The eight-line stanza, having the majesty, perfection and solidity of a Tuscan pillar, is preferred (*Works* [1931–1941], vol. II). Montaigne, on the other hand, attacks the indecorous description of "les chetives pieces de la porte de ma cuisine" by means of "ces gros mots de pilastres, architraves, corniches, d'ouvrage Corinthien . . . ," "De la vanité des paroles," I, 51, p. 294. Cf. Quintilian, VIII, vi, 55.

[43] Cf. Robert J. Clements, *Critical Theory and Practice of the Pléiade* (1942), p. 130; Du Bellay, V, 205.

stile" (IV, 174). The young Du Bellay is fully within the *rhétoriqueur* tradition of badinage when he compares Bertrand Berger to a shepherd composing pastoral odes in the manner of Theocritus or the bucolic Vergil, but at the end of the poem he points to a higher calling: "ores il te fault / Avec ung style plus hault / Poulser la royale plaincte" (IV, 188). When the Angevin himself remains on a lower level in a poem dealing with praise of the Gods and virtuous men, it is simply *faute de mieux* since his "Muse est trop basse" to sing "Si hault & brave argument"; he leaves to others who have "le stile assez hault" the task of praising Marguerite de Valois and her niece, and encourages them accordingly: "Sus donc, ô François espris" (IV, 159).

The precepts and rationale of decorum, then, elicited from the Pléiade an attitude of unconstraining obedience. While recognizing its basic distinctions and the interrelationship of genre, character, style and intent, they also increasingly recognized their own resourceful command of language in turning traditional themes and doctrine to advantage. For all its inconsistencies and structural weaknesses, the *Deffence et Illustration* never loses sight of its central purpose: "l'amplification de nostre Langue (qui est ce que je traite)" (p. 104), "Le principal but ou je vise, c'est la deffence de notre Langue, l'ornement & amplification d'icelle" (p. 182). Amplification of a subject is a function of language, since style varies as intent varies, and this amplification was open to the talents of the poet. Its province extends to imitation, as Du Bellay tells us in his chapter "D'amplifier la Langue Francoyse par l'immitation des anciens Aucteurs Grecz & Romains" (p. 45), where the poet may focus on a detail, image or idea in his model and heighten his borrowing by carefully refracting it in his own poem. In this sense, Joseph Vianey is correct in speaking of certain *Antiquitez* as amplifications of Horace.[44] Imitation, grounded in judgment, can entail amplifying an argument explicitly, "Et sa vertu à ses enfans sera / De l'imiter un argument plus ample" (VI, 55), or implicitly, as in Ronsard's "Hymne de l'or" or in the praise of Turnèbe mentioned earlier: "Je suis vaincu ayant trop de matiere. / Comme la Mer sa louange est sans rive, / Sans bord son los, qui luit comme un flambeau . . . ."[45]

[44] *Le Pétrarquisme en France au XVI^e^ siècle* (1909), p. 324.

[45] Ed. Laumonier, XIII, 195. I am forced here to disagree with Saulnier's suggested limitation of amplification to epideictic, although it is certainly less successful and therefore more obvious in Du Bellay's occasional poetry: "Introduction à l'étude de Joachim du Bellay," *L'Information littéraire* (1950), 6; *Du Bellay,* p. 104. Cf. VI, 229–230.

But amplifying an argument did not necessarily constitute a commentary on the subject's social standing or inherent beauty; rather, it represented the poet's attempt to strengthen and draw attention to anything he considered remarkable or noteworthy irrespective of the expansiveness or concision, hyperbole or litotes, required to do so and of the disgust or admiration that attention might inspire. Rhetoric is conditioned by the poem's argument and by its own function of indicating the subject's proper value. The "Anterotique de la vieille et de la ieune amye" presents two examples of hyperbolic amplification through the same image where the intent is to heighten first ugliness, then beauty. The old woman is so hideous "Que mesmes le Soleil se cache / De peur d'y prendre quelque tache" (vv. 33–34), whereas the young girls' locks are "si crespes & blonds, / Qu'ilz font honte au beau Soleil mesme" (vv. 98–99). The similarly described sun—in itself the source of light and life, as well as a symbol of earthly aspiration—is not only the extreme reference point successively for perverse ugliness and surpassing beauty, but within the total context points succinctly to the poem's intent of contrasting the hag with the maiden. The same technique recurs in the "Prosphonematique" where the frightful sound of cannon and thunder are "Moindre pourtant que le bruit de ton (Henri II's) nom" (III, 66). This concept and use of amplification falls more within Cicero's belief that we amplify matter and manner concurrently (*De oratore,* III, xiv, 53) and especially Quintilian's ideas of "signifying more than we say, that is emphasis" (IX, ii, 3) and "passing beyond the highest degree" (VIII, iv, 6), rather than within the Longinian association with purely extensive quantity and cumulative abundance.[46] Longinus' correlative separation of oratorical and poetic amplification is rejected out of hand by Du Bellay at the end of the *Deffence:* "Il est tens de clore ce pas, afin de toucher particulierement les principaux poinctz de l'amplification & ornement de notre Langue" (p. 85); although they are similar, he goes on to say, he will treat only poetic amplification just to avoid duplicating Etienne Dolet's *Orateur Francoys.*

Ornaments, here associated with amplification, were the substance of style. Vianey may have had this in mind in his enigmatic reference to the *Deffence et Illustration* where Du Bellay "prodigue les ornements

[46] *On the Sublime,* XII. This amplification by intensifying instead of extending the poetic argument represents a breach with medieval practice (see Faral, p. 61, and George J. Englehardt, "Medieval Vestiges in the Rhetoric of Erasmus," *PMLA,* LXIII [1948], 739–744). Cf. George Gascoigne's "Gascoigne's Good Morrow," and Henry Howard, Earl of Surrey's "Give Place, Ye Lovers."

poétiques. Ce qu'il entend par là, on le devine,"[47] for in truth we can only speculate as to the word's full range of meaning. In his lengthy discussion on style Quintilian interchanges *ornaments* with the terms *flowers* and *colors* (VIII, iii), and the Pléiade makes the same equation. If Binet can be taken as a reliable aesthetician, then for Ronsard "La prose peut bien exprimer les ornemens de poësie et les vestir modestement: mais la poësie doit estre toute revelée en bosses et fleurs apparoissantes."[48] Such associations are not superficially metaphoric. Du Bellay's allusion to *colori* involves an actual association with painting (VI, 70), and in numerous instances the meaning of *ornament* extends to enhanced personal qualities and thought itself.[49] Ronsard describes himself as "l'ornement du langage François," while Du Bellay more modestly assigns to Antoine Minard the role of ornament, the *pars magna,* of the Senate.[50] Even more widely linked with ornament was the word *figure;* true eloquence, we are told in the *Deffence,* consists of a judicious use of "metaphores, alegories, comparaisons, similitudes, energies, & tant d'autres figures & ornemens, sans les quelz tout oraison & poëme sont nudz" (pp. 35–36). A figure is integrated into the same complex of meaning as ornament, flower and color. It is an image in the sense that it is likened at once to the spatial icon of the painter, crystalline form of the sculptor, components of architectural style as we saw earlier and to the verbal correlative of thought. As Du Bartas put it, ". . . le langage / N'est rien que de l'esprit un resonant image."[51] Similar tercets of *L'Olive* and "Les Amours" hold that the image of the poet's beloved is so engraved in his heart that a diamond would sooner take another shape than "Le vray protraict, en autre se transforme" (I, 57), "Se transformer en une autre figure" (II, 249). Ronsard's "Noz imagers ont la gloire en tout lieu, / Pour figurer soit un homme ou un Dieu, / De si tres pres imitans la nature"[52] is anticipated by the *Illustration* where the "figure de poëte" leads Du Bellay to dismiss Cicero's belief that a

[47] *Le Pétrarquisme,* p. 112. Cf. Ernst Robert Curtius, *European Literature and the Latin Middle Ages* (1963), p. 71.

[48] Paul Laumonier, *"La Vie de P. de Ronsard" de Claude Binet* (1910), p. 40. Seneca the Elder's *Controversiae* associate descriptive amplification specifically with *colores.* The attitude remains consistent from the Pléiade until at least the end of the century. Pierre de Laudun's *Art poétique françois* (1598) recommends for poetic amplification all of the rhetorical tropes and figures discussed later in this chapter.

[49] Cf. *Deffence et Illustration,* p. 29; V, 44; VI, 214, 228, 231; Ronsard, ed. Laumonier, III, 160.

[50] Ed. Laumonier, XII, 258; Du Bellay, VI, 106–107. *Pars magna* is the expression Quintilian uses to describe the role of ornaments and figures: X, ii, 1.

[51] *Works,* III, 130. Cf. Quintilian, IX, i, 10.

[52] Ed. Laumonier, I, 32–33.

copy (*imago*) cannot equal its model since the mind's idea is not manifest to the senses (p. 89).

The supremacy of style within the Pléiade's matrix of values is incessantly contrasted in the *Deffence et Illustration* with a shocking "nudity" of poetic language prior to 1549: "nostre Langue si pauvre & nue, qu'elle a besoing des ornementz" (p. 23), "leurs conceptions avecques paroles nues, sans art & ornement" (p. 49), "tant denué de tous ces delices & ornementz poëtiques" (p. 95). But these and many other descriptions of style as clothing have nothing to do with purely ornamental figures. Rev. Walter J. Ong has explained that *ornamentum* signified "equipment or accoutrements, which the 'naked causes' of dialectic like naked persons, would need rather more than pretty clothing to get along in this world."[53] As the visual expression of thought, figures, however variously they are labeled, must be carefully weighed and selected. To this end, the Pléiade heeds Quintilian's stress on decorum in choosing figures and Cicero's *electio* and *compositio* (*De oratore,* III, xxxviii–liv). Half of the *Abrégé*'s section on style is given to the choice of words and design of sentence: "Elocution n'est autre chose qu'une propriété & splendeur de paroles bien choisies & ornées de graves & courtes sentences, qui font reluyre les vers comme les pierres precieuses bien enchassées les doigts de quelque grand Seigneur. Soubs l'Elocution se comprend l'election des paroles . . . tu tireras au vif les plus parfaictz lineamens de ton tableau."[54] Remembering that a poetic argument is at once an idea and its verbal expression, the choice and physical arrangement of words can be no less important than the idea to which they are wedded and of which they are, ideally, the fitting manifestation. And most of Scaliger's books III and IV are devoted to the relationship of poetic constructs, their creation of new ones and the desire to name—which is to say, understand—them.[55]

Concern for the organic relationship and metamorphosis of poetic ornaments and for naming them implies that the rhetorician's skill lies in combining constructs for a varied poetic affect that one can roughly identify, not just in ornamenting verse at random or in having static embellishments. At times, overlapping or multiplicity of functions occasions the minor problem of finding names for particular poetic constructs, just as it is often impossible to separate teaching, moving and

[53] *Ramus, Method and the Decay of Dialogue* (1958), p. 277. Scaliger, for his part, insists on correct grammar and logic in style, "Efficacia," p. 270. Cf. Quintilian, IX, i, 8.

[54] Ed. Laumonier, XIV, 15.

[55] "Ubi vero partes orationis certo ordine disponuntur, ita aliquibus aliquae reddantur, ut aliam formam, ita aliud nomen invenere," p. 467.

pleasing or to fragmentize grammar, logic and rhetoric. The problem is compounded by the many identifiable constructs which are given now a Latinized name, now a Hellenized name, or both at the same time. If the terminology seems cumbersome to the modern reader who is unfamiliar with the full spread of the Trivium, we must remember that it once passed for a commonly understood shorthand that avoided vague responses to poetic configurations. At the most general level the problem is reduced and poets speak with unanimity about the trinity "Figures, Schemes, Tropes."[56] Ronsard here aligns the terms from the most comprehensive to the least, although each one, like the places of invention, is subject to numerous subdivisions.

A trope alters the customary meaning of a word. Foclin and Ramist rhetoricians like Talon, following Quintilian, classify metaphor, synecdoche, metonymy and simple or continued irony under this heading. Metaphor, in turn, breaks down into catachresis, hyperbole (neither of which Aneau liked, as we have seen), enigma and allegory. Du Bellay's insistence that metaphoric epithets be chosen with variety and decorum in mind points to an enriched pleasure derived from seeing a lively and logical relatedness, transmuted by the cool heat of the imagination, between a particular referent and a more general one (pp. 114, 162). He experimented once with the medieval enigma which Rabelais criticized as a genre and which the Pléiade rejected for its obscurity.[57] But he stands on common Renaissance ground through his tendency to view allegory simply as an extended metaphor and to cultivate the clarities of that metaphor by establishing a perceptible identification between something fairly well known and something of greater value but less clearly known.[58] "France, mere des arts," for instance, insensibly transfers simile, "Ores, comme un aigneau," into metaphor and takes on allegorical proportions and personae as the metaphor is pursued. In the process, the relationship is established and heightened between the individual case of Du Bellay in exile and the general and more naturalistic image of the wandering sheep; the metaphor gains a mythic dimension owing to the Petrarchan and Vergilian models on which the poem is based and which are inevitably conjured up.

The poet's free use of synecdoche adheres to Quintilian's description (VIII, vi, 19) where, as throughout classical rhetoric, it is valued for

[56] Posthumous preface to the *Franciade,* XVI, 332.

[57] The "Epitaphe d'un flambeau" has inspired as much conjecture among major Du Bellay critics as Rabelais' enigmas. Chamard viewed it as an allusion to Calvinistic heresy, V, 123, and Saulnier as a reference to prostitution, *Divers jeux rustiques,* ed. Verdun Saulnier (1965), p. xlvii. Cf. Quintilian, VIII, vi, 52.

[58] *Lettres,* ed. Pierre de Nolhac, p. 47.

the variety it affords. He uses it in all shapes and forms, substituting a part for the whole, "Et pour avoir souillé d'une tache eternelle / Leur sang & leur maison, par la mort paternelle" (VI, 157), or "Et toy Carie honnorable" (III, 90), where Caria's national honor (the whole) is really that of its king (the part) Mausolus. Too often the Pléiade heeds Du Bellay's suggested frequent use of antonomasia (p. 161), related by Quintilian to synecdoche (VIII, vi, 28), because it usually degenerates into no more than deployed erudition, "Neveu d'Atlas" (III, 138), or sends the reader farther back into the footnotes of mythological handbooks, "Fille du neveu d'Atlas."[59] In the same way, periphrasis fills out a line without justifying the expenditure of space, "le feu, l'onde, la terre, / Et cest autre element qui nous faict respirer" (VI, 13). It tends to arrest thought in a convoluted allusion to what might otherwise be a moving description of the loss of British naval hegemony: "ceulx qui le Soleil voïent cacher en l'onde, / Qui or' plus que jamais sont separez du Monde" (VI, 28). But this variety is generally discriminate and tight-fitting. For Foclin, metonymy—just one step away from synecdoche—is essentially a grammatical procedure where an effect is implied from its cause or a cause from its effect and where subject and adjunct are thus related. Its rigor, however, does not constrain the good poet whose ingenuity enables him to weave various types of metaphor into the structure of his poetry and into the Renaissance cultural and historical fabric. In the Hymnes des Estoilles" Ronsard comments on Coligny's death in particular and man's fate in general:

> Ce guerrier qui tantost
> Terre & mer d'un grand Ost
> Couvroit de tant de voiles,
> Court de teste & de nom
> Pendille à Mont-faucon:
> Ainsi vous plaist, Estoilles."[60]

The background for his observation is set in the previous stanza by the upward and corresponding downward movement of Fortunes' familiar wheel. A similar cause-effect condition underlies the movement of these verses where the epic synecdoche of sails substituted for ships gives way to a shallow irony based on Coligny's name and a deeper irony based on the contrast between the full outline of sails and banners and the specter of the gallows. The whole is metonymic according to Foclin's

[59] Ed. Laumonier, I, 88. Cf. Quintilian, VIII, vi, 61.

[60] Ed. Laumonier, XVII, 42. Examples of synecdoche and metonymy combined are frequent. Cf. Du Bellay's "Lors il voyra combien un coeur vaillant / . . . Si bravement sa couronne servie" (II, 295), and Quintilian, VIII, vi, 49.

description of giving a circumstance (Coligny's nemesis) in place of the subject (the stars' control of man's destiny).

As a special use of language, tropes are essentially grammatical distinctions and may be incorporated in the broader rhetorical distinction of schemes, which arrange words in striking configurations for a special effect. Taken together, they comprise what was known variously as figures of words, of diction or of speech. Since a scheme could be classified as a figure of words, the two terms are often interchangeable. Finally, figures of words build figures of sentence or thought which detail the manner and substance of an idea or feeling ranging from simple exclamations and *sententiae* to an elaborated structure that explores all of the complexities and possibilities of disposition. A full analysis of these figures at work in any poet would rival the length of his complete works. But a random selection of schemata and figures can be representative if it suggests the effect of individual figures, describes the functional relationship among them and reveals the vast range of stylistic devices available to the poet.

Frequently, classification as trope or figure of diction rests upon fine distinctions. Although *paronomasia* (*adnominatio*) involves the changing meaning of words, it does so by juxtaposing homonyms, as in Scève's "Calamyte a mes calamitez" (*Délie* 190). Therefore, Foclin classifies it as a figure of diction—rather than simply as a trope—based on no certain word order since the juxaposition may be random or implied. Quintilian holds that paronomasia attracts the ear of the audience and arouses attention (IX, iii, 66). Indeed it does attract the ear, but under Du Bellay's pen any significant attention aroused by that attraction is conjectural, and examples of its successful use are rare. The rise and fall in his alternated Latin pentameter-hexameter depends especially on sound and meaning shift and accords perfectly with the movement of imagery from illustrious pyramid to obscure tomb and with a poem whose theme resides in the last verse "Sed fortuna mihi sola negata fuit" (VI, 96): "Vel Croesus vel Crassus habebat opes, / Et Pharias Moles & Caria Mausolea." And the banter derived from a linguistic accident can be justified on a level of superficial satire: "Bref, ce Bonnet fut un Bonnet / Qui jamais ne porta bonnet" (V, 114). But usually this Marotic game belies the revolutionary spirit of the *Deffence et Illustration,* as with Du Bellay's "Epitaphe de Clement Marot" where the author of the *Epistres* is incongruously compared to the author of the *Aeneid:* "Qui de Maro avoit plus que le nom" (III, 54), which falls short of its beneficiary's wit. Or else the sonorous peculiarities tend to detract from the larger context of an amplified description of the Argonaut's heroic trek through the desert carrying the debilitated Argos; they "servoient de mer à leur mere affoiblie" (VI, 49).

On the other hand, the closely related figure *traductio*—the cumulative inflexion of a word—rarely fails to justify its employment in Ronsard's verse. At the end of the "Hymne de la Mort" the words *coulement, nouveau* and *change* are refashioned to dramatize the flux of sublunary existence, and are reinforced assonantally by the varying internal nasal rhymes and alliteratively by the insistent suggestiveness of *pressant-present* as well as the eternal present of "fut, se refaict":

> Mais tout ainsi que l'onde à-val des ruisseaux fuit
> Le pressant coulement de l'autre qui la suit,
> Ainsi le temps se coulle, & le present faict place
> Au futur importun qui les tallons luy trace:
> Ce qui fut, se refaict, tout coulle comme une eau,
> Et rien dessous le Ciel ne se void de nouveau:
> Mais la forme se change en une autre nouvelle,
> Et ce changement là, VIVRE au monde s'appelle,
> Et MOURIR, quand la forme en une autre s'en va.[61]

Thus, Ronsard skillfully integrates a figure of change with a theme of change and with similar figures. In the "Discours des miseres de ce temps" he uses *traductio* to modify Isaiah II, 4, and follows it with two hyperbatons involving inverted verb and predicate, the initial one for its arresting power and the final one for the literal descriptiveness occasioned by word arrangement. The reversal of word order coincides with the thematic *monde renversé:*

> Et l'acier de son *coultre* il change en *un couteau.*
> *Morte est l'autorité:* chacun vit à sa guise;
> Au vice desreiglé la licence est permise,
> Le desir, l'avarice & l'erreur incensé
> Ont sans-dessus-dessoubs *le monde renversé.*[62]

While paronomasia and *traductio* are classified as schemes or figures requiring no specific word order, other and more numerous schemes are defined according to the relative positioning of words and the effect they produce. Two such schemes are *articulus* (comma) and epizeuxis,

[61] Ed. Laumonier, VIII, 178. Cf. Weber's analysis, p. 513, and
> Ramon la nef dans les chams bienheureus,
> Au port heureus des Isles bienheurées. (ed. Laumonier, V, 181–182)

The persuasive insistence resulting from the repetition of similar verbal roots is akin to arguing from the place *etymology.* Cf. Nicholas Everhard's "Le Laborintus," *Loci argumentorum legales* (1591), and Quintilian, I, vi, 28.

[62] Ed. Laumonier, XI, 28–29.

which are also styled as figures of emotion. *Articulus* omits coordinating conjunctions to create an impression of haste or perturbation. While the grammatical omission in this scheme purports to condense expression, its effect depends on accumulation of similars and therefore tends to preclude combination with other figures: "L'orgueil, la vanité, le vice dereiglé, / La seule occasion de ce monstre aveuglé" (VI, 220).[63] On the other hand, epizeuxis, the emphatic repetition of one or several words, is often combined with apostrophe, as in Ronsard's address to Louis de Bourbon, "Ha Prince, c'est assés, c'est assés guerroyé,"[64] or is itself the apostrophe, as in "France, mere des arts" where the repetition creates the impression of the poet's rebounding voice and underlines his emotional isolation: "France, France, respons à ma triste querelle. / Mais nul, sinon Echo, ne respond à ma voix" (II, 59).

In the *Regrets* this emotional isolation is underscored by means of an extended enumeration that elegiacally or ironically detaches Du Bellay's point of view from that of the world around him. But the two schemes on which this vertical enumeration depends, *expeditio* (or the summary dismissal of several supposedly considered alternatives) and *praeteritio* (or mentioning subjects one does not wish to consider at all) are elsewhere employed in situations devoid of satire or irony.[65] Du Bellay uses *expeditio* to amplify drastically his subject either by an ordered dismissal, as in "La Musagnoeomachie" 's description of Ignorance where he introduces mythological animals all by *Ny* and concludes that they "furent moins contrefaictz / Que ce Monstre" (IV, 7). Or else he amplifies his subject by an unordered but sustained rejection as in "La Complainte du désespéré," again introduced by *Ny,* of the mysterious and troublesome forces that plague man, for they would equal "Le moindre de mes travaux" (IV, 96–97). Both of these figures are decorous since the military arrangement in the "Musagnoeomachie" corresponds to the poem's polemical rejection of the Pléiade's adversaries,

[63] Cf. Ronsard's "Il aura tout soudain toute chose à foison, / Champs, prez, vin, bois, valetz, tesmoings, amys, justice" (ed. Laumonier, VIII, 183) and "Ilz remuent de nuict bancz, tables et treteaux, / Clefz, huys, portes, buffetz, litz, chaires, escabeaux" (VIII, 128), in addition to Quintilian, IX, iv, 125–126.

[64] Ed. Laumonier, XI, 101. Cf. Ronsard, V, 177 and VII, 94, where *epizeuxis* combines with *traductio.* It bears repeating that this figure is native not only to the Pléiade but to any poet schooled in classical rhetoric and poetic: "me, me, adsum qui feci (Vergil, *Aeneid,* IX, 427), ('dì, dì se questo è vero" (Dante, *Purgatorio,* XXXI, 5), "Quittez, quittez, Madame, un dessein si tragique" (Corneille, *Polyeucte,* V, 5, 1719).

[65] *Expeditio* is one of the basic techniques used in "Amour de Francine" I, a book where Du Bellay figures prominently, *Euvres en rime de Ian Antoine de Baïf* (1881–1890), I, 97–100, 114–116, 118. Cf. Scève, *Délie,* 18; Ronsard, ed. Laumonier, V, 186; Quintilian, IX, ii, 47.

and in the "Complainte" the lack of order accords with the occult powers and emotional difficulties that beset the poet. *Praeteritio* also serves to amplify, by contrasting either similar or dissimilar subjects. At the end of the "Discours au roy sur la poesie" Du Bellay specifically describes the logical method and places of this figure and its rhetorical function: "Je ne veux pas icy par le menu deduire / Plusieurs autres raisons que je pourrois induire / Pour monstrer ce qui est de semblable en ces deux, / Et ce qui est aussi de difference entre eux" (VI, 165). In the "Combat d'Hercule et d'Acheloys" he introduces a lengthy series of mythological and fictional battles with "Ce n'est icy que je chante" and with the usual *Ny* until he arrives at the similar but now heightened encounter of Hercules and Achelous (V, 29). The "Chant de l'amour et du primtemps," on the other hand, begins with

> Icy je ne chante pas
> De Mars la guerriere troppe,
> Ny les horribles combats
> Des deux Seigneurs de l'Europe. (V, 37)

in order to contrast this chaos with the harmonious apparition of spring. He thus succeeds in describing a subject he professes not to treat. The figure would approach irony if Du Bellay were aware of his duplicity or if this harmless duplicity became apparent to the reader through exaggerated use, as in the "Ample discours au roy" where after discussing the requisite virtues of a king in nine instances he concludes laconically, "Je n'en dy rien icy" (VI, 233).

When similars or dissimilars are arranged horizontally in balanced clauses they tend to form the figure *compar* (or isocolon), which Du Bellay employed in contrasting and uniting the events leading to Henri II's unexpected death: "Les nopces de sa Soeur, & la fin de sa vie" (VI, 87). He recognized the importance of this rhythmical and physical balance as an ingredient of his idea, and in his translations from Latin he attempted to preserve the figure's integrity one way or another within the limitations of French syntax: "Externis charus, charus & ipse suis"—"Aimé des estrangers, aimé des siens il feut" (VI, 84–85).[66]

[66] Ronsard used the figure in all its variety by juxtaposing adverbs at the hemistich in order to stress continuity, "Avienne que tousjours tousjours je te r'encontre" (ed. Laumonier, VIII, 194); by grammatical repetition to stress varied unity, "Cela desplaist à Dieu, cela deplaist au Prince" (XI, 42), "Reluisoient en la ville & reluisoient aux champs" (XI, 171); by confining repetition to separate hemistichs to stress at once equilibrium and richness, "Les loix & le pays si riche & si puissant" (XI, 102); or by opposing a hallowed institution with its present degeneration and by developing the figure into a chiasmus as it proceeds to the next line, "Qui l'Eglise de Dieu d'ignorans farcissoit, / Qui de larrons privez les Pallais remplissoit" (XI, 83). Cf. Scève, *Délie,* 367 and Quintilian, IX, iii, 80.

When this balance assumes the more complex form of a reflexive interchange between hemistichs it becomes a chiasmus, and allows the poet to intensify the differences and similarities of one or two pairs of grammatical components: "Ny la guerre en la paix, ny la paix en la guerre" (VI, 171). As a figure usually requiring two lines, simple chiasmus can serve to indicate hypocritical behavior through reverse symmetry,

> Entre les Courtisans du sçavant tu feras,
> Et entre les sçavants courtisan tu seras. (VI, 135)[67]

while compound chiasmus amplifies emotion through inverted word order (hyperbaton) and a complex symmetry:

> De ceux qui *l'homicide* ont *justement commis.*
> *Justement* avoient ils *commis* cest *homicide,* (VI, 144)

Like any other scheme, chiasmus must be justified by the contextual idea and, because of the relationship between thought and spatial arrangement, configuration of words. After an expansively symmetrical octave where an anaphora places Greece and Rome side by side, the logic of destiny is explained by means of a compact chiasmus which Du Bellay sets off with internal rhymes:

> Si Troye eust deu par humaine proësse
> Contre les Grecs plus longuement durer,
> Contre les Grecs la pouvoit asseurer
> De son Hector la brave hardiesse.
> Si de Hedin la peu seure fortresse
> Contre Caesar eust deu rien esperer,
> Contre Caesar la pouvoit remparer
> Du preux Romain la vertueuse addresse.
> . . . . . . . . . . . .
> *Car vif Hector,* Troye estoit asseuree:
> *Horace mort,* Hedin devoit perir. (II, 291)

Often related to chiasmus, due to its balance, is the figure epanalepsis where the same word begins and ends a line. But while chiasmus focuses on the crossed arrangement and rapport of at least two words, epanalepsis stresses one doubled word and the way in which it bears on the

[67] Ronsard who as a poet was far more color conscious than Du Bellay puts the figure to good advantage in a poem that begins and ends with the rose and that blends objects (gold, Sun, Rosy-Fingered Dawn, etc.) close to the rose in color:

> Verson ces Roses prés ce vin,
> Prés ce vin verson ces Roses (ed. Laumonier, VII, 189)

Cf. Scève, *Délie,* 49 and 65.

words it encloses. The figure was grist for the mindless rhyming skills of the *rhétoriqueurs,*

> A l'assault, gallans, a l'assault!
> Armez vous tost, saillez armez.
> Charmez vous, soyez charmez.
> Briffault, allez devant, Briffault,

but it was preserved and accorded judicious and more imaginative attention during the Renaissance in France and England, owing partly to the prestige it enjoyed in classical poetry:

> "Heureuse en peuple, & en Princes heureuse"
> "Parfaitte autant comme l'autre est parfaitte"
> "Flambeau duquel Amour allume son flambeau"
> "Discoure sur Milan, qui vouldra discourir"
> "Ainsi vesquit Henry, Henry mourut ainsi"
> "Much must he be beloved, that loveth much,
> Feare many must he needs, whom many feare."[68]

If in the redoubling the last word of a line begins the following line the figure is styled as anadiplosis, and can serve a multitude of functions ranging from amplification of a subject to arranging thought spatially to driving home Du Bellay's satirical point of view. In the "Combat d'Hercule et d'Acheloys" the presentation of Achelous, delayed and heightened by an extended *praeteritio,* as we have seen, is also amplified by anadiplosis: "Des trois formes d'Acheloys: / D'Acheloys, ce brave fleuve" (V, 30). Similarly, delay occasioned by *reduplicatio*[69] leads to anadiplosis that graphically schematizes the idea of two-fold triumph, physical and mental: "Celuy vrayment, celuy est doublement vainqueur, / Vainqueur de son hayneux & de son propre cueur" (VI, 8). Within the confines of the sonnet Du Bellay uses the figure to create the impression of accumulation and to announce the twin theme, the incon-

[68] Patterson, p. 169; Ronsard, ed. Laumonier, I, 35, VI, 158; Baïf, p. 109; Du Bellay, VI, 12, 89, an extended adaptation of "Sic vixit, sic interiit"; George Puttenham, *The Arte of English Poesie* (1936), pp. 200, 331, probably adapted from Erasmus' *Adagia* or *Apopthegmata.* Scaliger emphasized the importance of this kind of figure because of its effect on the reader: "Maxima ea efficacia & quae auditorum aures expugnet," ch. xl, p. 284; cf. Quintilian, IX, iii, 34 and *Georgics,* III, 47, IV 306, *Aeneid,* III, 435, XI, 358.

[69] Redoubling for emphasis. Cf. "Ta main, pere, ta main ne fut si ocieuse, / Quand pour damner icy ceste ame vicieuse ..." (VI, 147) used to dramatize the cause-effect association between the physical and the spiritual; Ronsard, ed. Laumonier, V, 191; *Aeneid,* II, 602 and *Georgics,* IV, 358, 447; Quintilian, IX, iii 29.

venience of truth and goodness in Rome, that will be treated in the tercets:

> Tu t'abuses (Belleau) si pour estre sçavant,
> Sçavant & vertueux, tu penses qu'on te prise: (II, 168)[70]

Continued on into subsequent lines as a chain sequence, Renaissance rhetoricians identify the figure not as anadiplosis but rather as *gradatio.* Paul Laumonier probably had this figure in mind when he accurately assessed the Pléiade's attitude as "guerre à toute contrainte provenant de la répétition d'un vers, ou d'un mot, ou d'un son à la rime, de strophe à strophe à une place fixe, ou d'un enchaînement de strophes qui eût diminué par trop l'autonomie verbale de chacune d'elles et gêné leur liberté d'expression à la rime; guerre à tout mécanisme formel qui eût forcé le poète à sacrifier la raison à la rime, à introduire sa pensée coûte que coûte dans un cadre étroit et rigide, ou à n'y mettre que des platitudes et des fadaises,"[71] but this does not mean that the Pléiade cast gradation aside as being unfit for their muse. Instead, they redefined it by divesting its rigidity and pretensions, and in so doing heeded Quintilian's plea for limited application and internal logic (IX, iii, 54–55). Deschamps' "Art de dictier," for example, uses gradation as an extensive and rigid "équivoque rétrograde" where the dissimilar or oppositional meanings of the rhyme words tend to vitiate the figure's driving force:

> Lasse, lasse, malheureuse et dolente!
> Lente me voy, fors de soupirs et plains.
> Plains sont mes jours d'ennuy et de tourmente;
> Mente qui veult, car mes cueurs est certains,[72]

Despite the *Deffence et Illustration*'s blanket criticisms, Marot's employment of gradation represents a clear progress over the earlier *rhétoriqueurs;* in one instance he adjusts the figure to his idea through

---

[70] Ronsard uses anadiplosis in a way not unlike Du Bellay, preceding it with a tight epizeuxis to intimate the hasty and excited flight from contemporary dissension and developing it into the expansiveness of anaphora to suggest the calm departure for the "îles fortunées":

> Toi, toi, Muret, apelent à leurs bors,
> Aus bors heureus des isles plantureuses,
> Aus bors divins des isles bienheureuses, (ed. Laumonier, V, 191)

And the vision of richness, preceded by the staccato of the *articulus* "Querelé, combatu, guerroyé," is evinced by the figure's inherent cumulativeness:

> Qui pert en se jouant un si bel heritage:
> Heritage opulent, que toy peuple qui bois . . . (XI, 22)

[71] *Ronsard, poète lyrique* (1923), p. 668.

[72] Eustache Deschamps (1882) *Oeuvres complètes* (1882), VII, 277.

the use of participles that keep the love theme in a continually progressing present:

> Dieu des Amants, de mort me garde!
> Me gardant, donne-moy bon heur,
> Et me le donnant prens ta Darde,
> En la prenant navre son cueur;
> En le navrant me tiendras seur , . . .[73]

It remained for the Pléiade to reduce radically the figure's monotonous expansiveness and to free the rhyme from an automatic mechanism:

> "De la simple parolle ilz sont venuz aux cris,
> Des cris à la fureur, furieux ilz ont pris
> Les armes en la main, comme un vent qui à peine . . ."
> "De vivre apres leur mort, un immortel honneur:
> Honneur, le seul loyer qui la vertu guerdonne,
> Loyer, qu'à la vertu la seule Muse donne."[74]

Quintilian related *gradatio* to polysyndeton because both figures accentuate the links among similar words (IX, iii, 50–55). D'Aubigné and Du Bartas in the generation following the Pléiade show a marked preference for asyndeton due to the fractured view it affords of a world in apocalyptic dissolution.[75] Even while describing scenes of apocalypse the Pléiade will hold to the essential relatedness and encompassing similitude of their vision by means of polysyndeton. In "Les Furies contre les infracteurs de foy" Du Bellay likens the three Farnese brothers to three Horsemen of the Apocalypse, "Par tout ou vous irez avecques vous chemine / Et la peste, & la guerre, & la palle famine: / Et ou vous ne serez, l'abondance & bon heur" (VI, 155), and extends the procedure into an elaborate description of death and Revelation XVI. He establishes prolonged connection between words by appealing to a wide variety of grammatical relationships: conjunctive, prepositional, adverbial and adjectival; but they are almost invariably stylized into a formulaic arrangement:

> *Comme* Heleogabale en ventre monstrueux,
> *Comme* un Sardanapale, ou *comme* un Epicure, (VI, 146)
> *Comme* la pieté, la justice & la foy,
> *Comme* il doit estre humain, *comme* en sa main royale (VI, 233)
> *Sur* Naples, & *sur* ceulx qu'on devoit secourir,
> *Sur* le danger de voir paisible l'Angleterre, (VI, 12)
> Mais tu ne feras rien ne *si digne* d'un Roy,

[73] "Chanson" III. Cf. Patterson, p. 169.
[74] Ronsard, ed. Laumonier, VIII, 322; Du Bellay, VI, 162. Cf. *Délie* 43, 281.
[75] See Imbrie Buffum, *Agrippa d'Aubignés "Les Tragiques,"* (1951), pp. 17–22.

> *Si digne* d'un Chrestien, ne *si digne* de toy, (VI, 153)
> Demeure en vos maisons, mais *toute* deffiance,
> *Toute* crainte & soupçon, *toute* meschanceté, (VI, 156)

Ronsard shares Du Bellay's preference for triplicity, especially when it is inherently required by his theme, and values altered formal arrangement when dictated by the need to vary rhythm:

> *Qui* croit en un seul Dieu, *qui* croit au sainct Esprit
> *Qui* croit de tout son coeur au sauveur Jesuschrist?[76]

When the connective configuration of words directs the eye vertically instead of horizontally, with the connective word beginning a succession of clauses, anaphora is formed, which the Pléiade used as frequently as any other figure. About half of the time Du Bellay resorts to an unrelieved series of clauses, each initiated by the relative pronoun *Qui*, where it is difficult to identify—either through Renaissance or modern poetic canons—any rationale for the figure's length, its location within the poem's structure, its function in context or its uniqueness with respect to other similar figures.[77] But when his anaphora is harmoniously paced with the poem's theme it becomes the very expression of an idea. In the third and final stanza of the anthology piece "D'un vanneur de blé aux vents" the double anaphoras coincide with the poem's simplicity and unite the sympathetic activities of gleaner and wind:

> De vostre doulce halaine
> Eventez ceste plaine,
> Eventez ce sejour:
> Ce pendant que j'ahanne
> A mon blé que je vanne
> A la chaleur du jour. (V, 16)

In the much longer "Ample discours au roy" his anaphora expands to embrace the complex activities of governing a kingdom. His grammatical protasis describing in unctuous detail the stealth to which the royal treasury is subject, "*S'il* vous plaist de reigler voz finances en sorte / Que les glueuses mains ne puissent retenir / Les deniers qui devroient

[76] Ed. Laumonier, XI, 45. Cf. Ronsard's

> *Loing* des combas, *loing* des guerres mutines,
> *Loing* de soucis, de soing & de remors, (V, 191)

But the measured cadence of his connectives often unfolds within the compass of a single line: "Tout Sceptre, & tout Empire, et toutes regions . . . S'il n'est vieil, s'il ne presche, & s'il n'est de sçavoir . . . Vos grandeurs, vos honneurs, vos gloires despouillés," XI, 84, 86.

[77] E.g., IV, 23; VI, 20, 198. Cf. VI, 145, 196 and Ronsard, ed. Laumonier VIII, 172; XI, 166.

en voz coffres venir," is placed in relief by a corresponding clause that describes the rapidity of punishment, "*Si* le juge luy fait la justice plus bréve." The concluding verse, "Mais sur tout, *s'il* vous plaist regler vostre despense / (Comme vous avez faict)" refers back to the initial verse, "*S'il* vous plaist de reigler voz finances en sorte," where repetition reinforces the impression that the recommended action has already been accomplished (VI, 201–202). Ronsard offers examples of anaphora that are remarkable for the ways in which the figure can direct poetic tone and thought or, through an alteration of form and function, can become another figure entirely. The body of "Les Isles fortunées" takes shape around verses beginning with *Ici* and *Là*. At times such lines come together to express the poet's excitement at the prospect of leaving a mutilated France for a prelapsarian paradise, "Là, nous vivrons sans travail, & sans peine. / Là, là toujours, toujours la terre est pleine," while at other times they are widely spaced so as to permit the poet an expanded description of his edenic dream.[78] If, however, the two repeated verses are precisely altered to give a piecemeal amplification of an idea that could be stated in one verse, the Renaissance rhetorician unfailingly identifies it as *merismus* or the Distributor:

> Donne (je te supply) que cette Royne mere
> Puisse de ces deux camps appaiser la colere.
> Donne moy de rechef que son sceptre puissant
> Soit maugré le discord en armes fleurissant.
> Donne que la fureur de ce Monstre barbare
> Aille bien loing de France au rivaige Tartare . . . .[79]

As we have stated, tropes can be incorporated into schemes and both can comprise figures of words, while figures of words can be employed in figures of thought. While this diagrammatic efficiency apparently possessed all of the self-contained rigor and visual progression of dialectical systems like Ramism—and, indeed the pictorial outlines of rhetoricians like Foclin and Talon resemble them in theory—astute analysts of rhetoric have always held that a clear separation between figures of diction and figures of thought, at the hands of a good poet, is often arbitrary and depends more on individual context than on rules of style (Quintilian, IX, iv, 117). For instance, Du Bellay often appeals in standard Renaissance fashion to the figure of thought commonly designated as prosopopoeia, and mixes it with tropical modes of rhetori-

[78] Ed Laumonier, V, 182. Cf. 184–185; I, 30.

[79] Ronsard, ed. Laumonier, XI, 31. Cf. Puttenham, p. 222, and Surrey's "Vow to love faithfully," *Tottel's miscellany,* ed. Hyder Rollins (Cambridge, Mass., 1965), I, 11.

cal address, as in the ironic dialogue of David and Goliath or the derisively mimicked conversations of the *Regrets*.[80] When he enters into the emotional and intellectual character of Charles V, however, the soliloquy expectedly moralizes and assumes allegorical proportions as it introduces the Wheel of Fortune and its lessons (V, 333–334, vv. 93–107); similarly, in Edoard's analysis of the "elegiaque Prosopopeïe," as he categorizes the "Vieille Courtisanne," most of his commentary bears on the poem's didactic and metaphoric depth.

Inevitably, then, all rhetorical figures form some kind of thought pattern; we have seen in successful poetic moments that numerous rhetorical constructs, depending on how large a segment of verse one wishes to cite, are juxtaposed and metamorphose, and that the effect of the passage relies largely on the disposition of those figures. But the Pléiade poets do resort to certain modes of expression that are traditionally classed as figures of thought, derived from dialectical places[81] and intended for amplification. These figures involve the formation of a single thought rather than the successive development of a line of thought (although several figures of thought can be arranged into an extended thought sequence) nor do they suppose a full intellectual grasp of the poetic subject. Maxims, proverbs, sententiae are examples of this kind of figure, and frequently lose the visual qualities inherent in Ramist disposition and in figures of words. Dialectic slightly disparges them, since they rely on traditional wisdom and thus amount to external, inartificial proofs. The Ramist desire, however, to make dialectic reflect the natural movement of thought finds its counterpart in rhetorical figures of thought in that they attempt to enforce the poet's point of view or mood through the imagined give and take, pauses and reflections of normal conversation. A random sampling from Ronsard and Du Bellay will suggest the variety of expression open to the poet and point to the ways in which some of the figures of words we have been discussing build figures of thought.

In the "Monomachie," following a brief anaphora in which is stated the moral of the encounter between David and Goliath, Du Bellay impassionately addresses the Old Testament God as his muse in an insistent optative that rhetoricians call deprecation, "O Dieu guerrier, Dieu que je veulx chanter, / Je te supply', tens les nerfz de ma lyre"

---

[80] Cf. Tuve, *Elizabethan and Metaphysical Imagery,* p. 73, and Ronsard, ed. Laumonier, VI, 40; XII, 299; XIV, 114.

[81] See William Crane, *Wit and Rhetoric in the Renaissance* (1964), p. 55, and Sister Joan Marie Lechner, *Renaissance Concepts of the Commonplaces* (1962), p. 128.

(IV, 120), after which he enters a *praeteritio* to say that he will not sing of Greek or Trojan heroes, but rather a simple shepherd. Anaphora is incorporated into Ronsard's feigned request addressed to Pontus; Foclin following verbatim Cicero (*De oratore,* III, liii, 204) and Quintilian (IX, i, 30), labels the figure as communication, or a deliberation and consultation with others, "Di moi, je te suppli, di moi que doi-je faire? / Di moi, si tu le sçais, comme doi-je complaire."[82] When he answers an assumed objection where fortune is blamed for his admitted wrongdoing despite his best intentions, his anaphora fulfills perfectly Quintilian's definition of the figure confession (VII, iv, 15): "Je sçai bien que je fais ce que je ne doy faire, / Je sçai bien que je sui de trop folles amours: / Mais quoy, puis que le ciel delibere au contraire?"[83] The means of interrupting the flow of thought (digression, apostrophe, reticence and correction) use figures of words for contrast or resemblance. The steadiness of Du Bellay's anaphora, used throughout "L'Antérotique," is broken by his contrasting use of *reticentia*

> Vieille, horrible plus que Meduse,
> Vieille, au ventre . . . hola ma Muse,
> Veux-tu toucher les membres ords,
> Qui point ne se montrent dehors? (I, 128)

whereas Ronsard's use of gradation reinforces the haltingly progressive use of correction:

> C'est ce bel oeil qui me paist de liesse,
> Liesse, non, mais d'un mal dont je vi,
> Mal, mais un bien qui m'a toujours suivy,[84]

The Pléiade's break with French rhetorical tradition was no more sudden than the coming of the Renaissance itself. We have seen similar uses of the same stylistic figures in the Marotic and Lyonnais groups as in Ronsard and Du Bellay. This is of course not surprising inasmuch as

---

[82] Ed. Laumonier, VII, 116.

[83] Ibid., VII, 170. Foclin discusses this figure with respect to Du Bellay and Ronsard in *La Rhetorique francoise* (1555), pp. 83–84.

[84] Ed. Laumonier, VII, 150. Cf. Marot's "Au Roy, pour le délivrer de prison," ". . . ainsi qu'une espousée, / Non pas ainsi, mais plus roide un petit" (vv. 30–31), Pernette du Guillet's "Qui dira que, d'ardeur commune / Qui les Jeunes gentz importune, / De toy je veulx . . . et puis holà! / Je ne sçay rien moins, que celà" (*Poètes du XVI^e siècle* [1953], p. 244), *Délie,* 382 and Du Bellay, V, 86. As with figures of words, figures of thought are carefully identified by poets and rhetoricians alike. In his commentary on Ronsard's "je me deulx. / Je me deulx? Non, mais dont je suis bien aise," Muret says "ceste figure est nommee par les Grecs ἐπανόρζωσις Les François la peuvent nommer, Correction," *Les oeuvres de P. de Ronsard,* p. 87 (cf. p. 9).

they all shared many of the same classical sources, such as the rhetorical system of Cicero and Quintilian, and it would have been indeed astonishing if the Brigade had been able to live up to its advance revolutionary notice. What we find, rather, is a more purified reintegration into the corpus of classical canons, a correspondingly tempered attitude toward certain precepts of rhetoric where the evolution is not away from figured language but instead from ornate to functional, and, on the whole, simply a shift in emphasis from poetic amusements to a serious and circumspect view of poetic composition, especially style.

# PART TWO

## CHAPTER III

# FROM POETIC THEORY TO PRACTICE

### ART AND NATURE

IT HAS OFTEN been observed that the contribution of the *Deffence et Illustration* can be measured as much by the enthusiastic attitude of its author as by the substance of its poetic doctrine. We have seen that this doctrine can be reduced largely to the main points of classical Latin rhetoric and poetic in both theory and practice. Under the guise of Corybantic madness that supposedly besets the poet and through the impulse of the desire for immortality, traditional precepts of rhetoric and poetic were accorded the status of a surpassing art. From the outset Du Bellay realized that, despite the handsome trappings of the theories of poetic inspiration, his *art* or *artifice* implied hard work and mastery of technique. In the *Illustration* he clearly outlined the required ascesis in an often quoted passage which he borrowed from Speroni and Horace: "Qui veut voler par les mains & bouches des hommes, doit longuement demeurer en sa chambre: & qui desire vivre en la memoire de la posterité, doit comme mort en soymesmes suer & trembler maintesfois, & autant que notz poëtes courtizans boyvent, mangent & dorment à leur oyse, endurer de faim, de soif & de longues vigiles. Ce sont les esles dont les ecriz des hommes volent au ciel" (pp. 105–106). To the "poete courtisan" he gives the ironic counsel of avoiding studious exercise when composing frivolous verse (VI, 131). But the Pléiade—and the Renaissance as a whole—held, at best, an ambivalent attitude toward art and technical skill in isolation. At times art appears to enjoy privileges unrelated to any referents in the natural world, as when Du Bellay blithely passes over the question of *L'Olive's* biographical validity, "Et mon Olive (soit ce nom / D'Olive veritable ou non) / Se peult vanter d'avoir premiere / Salué la doulce lumiere" (V, 63). Chamard and John Lapp have speculated on sources drawn from visual arts that may have contributed to the plastic images of his "Prosphonematique" and "Musagnoeomachie,"[1] thus elevating art to the status of a self-contained world. And certainly the Pléiade's numerous references to Rosy-Fingered Dawn are less an allusion to a natural phenomenon than to a stylized and prestigious epic prototype. At other times Du Bellay cautiously avoids "trop hault louer l'artifice ou j'ay employé une portion de mon industrie" (VI, 247).

[1] *Joachim du Bellay* (1900), p. 221; "Mythological Imagery in Du Bellay," *Studies in Philology,* LXI (1964), 122.

The crux of Renaissance discussions of art lies in its relationship to nature, not so much to the naturalism of the visible world as to the recognition of the intelligible in the physical and to the natural movement and functioning of the mind. This is as true of the self-conscious proclamations in Rabelais' prologues and Montaigne's legion statements as it is of the Pléiade's random and systematic reflections. Ramus' belief that art always presupposes nature, just as exercise assumes art, exemplifies the primacy of nature both in chronology and in value. Despite Du Bellay's allegations that human "artifice & industrie" determine linguistic improvement (p. 13) and the high esteem in which he held Vergil, at times he falls in step with the notion that the Golden Age of Homeric inspiration gave way to the iron age of Vergilian polish:

Montrant que la seule nature
Sans art, sans travail & sans cure
Fait naistre le poëte avant
Qu'il ayt songé d'estre sçavant . . .
Aussi les vers du temps d'Orphee,
D'Homere, Hesiode & Musee,
Ne venoient d'art, mais seulement
D'un franc naturel mouvement . . .
Depuis geinant tel exercice
Soubs un miserable artifice,
Ce qu'avoient de bon les premiers
Fut corrompu par les derniers.
De la vindrent ces *Eneïdes,* . . . (V, 117–120)

He repeats the same terminology and attitude in a poem to Saint-Gelais where he censures the laborious muse of "l'artifice miserable" (III, 96).

This paradoxical status of art, now venerated, now despised, arose from the related beliefs that, when characterized by an exclusive attention to technique or vapid rhetoric, art could deform nature. And when encumbered by an arcane doctrine it hides the primary substance of nature in an unintelligible obscurity. The most frequent image used to describe art's deformation of nature, *farde,* suggests at once the familiar Renaissance topos of the mask of appearance hiding reality and the Pléiade's criticism of appliquéd figures and colors. Thus the pernicious effects of artifice are viewed in both moral and aesthetic terms, in keeping with the poet's priestly role. The description of the Petrarchistic "style fardant" (IV, 211) coincides with the "artifice menteur" underlying mythological tales which "ne farde point mes paroles" (V, 388). Ronsard's blunt conclusion on the advantages of wandering contours over stylized craftsmanship, "D'artifice soigneux, toute peinte de fart; / Car toujours la Nature est meilleure que l'art,"[2] is essentially the same as that arrived at by the degenerate "courtisanne repentie":

> Adieu donc, fards, dont mon visage est peingt,
> Boetes, ou sont les couleurs de mon teinct . . .
> Et ne veulx plus, pour me faire plus belle,
> Changer par art ma forme naturelle. (V, 139)

The correlative objection advanced against art that excessive learning hinders "le style doux-coulant" found adherents in both Ronsard, "Je ne veux que ce vers d'ornement indigent / Entre dans une escole,"[3] and Du Bellay who disclaimed a lyric "plein de doctrine & antique erudition" in his introduction to the *Divers jeux rustiques.* But the contradiction surrounding the praise and blame of art is more apparent than real. We must heed the qualifications imposed on the terms *art* and *artifice,* since unalloyed art is criticized in various degrees for the corresponding imbalance it creates between carefully considered meaning and the spontaneous overflow of feeling. Du Bellay disdains a work "plein de doctrine," but not doctrine itself; he shuns a cultivated obscurity at the expense of the populace, since such showy pirouettes contravene the Horatian imperative to "mesler en sa doctrine / Le plaisir à l'utilité" (V, 359). The poet's rejection not of art but of constrained art, "qui produict naïvement en moy / Ce que par art contraint les autres y font naistre" (II, 195), finds its counterpart in the acerbic common sense of Aneau who objects to *L'Olive's* "huyle obscur" and "choses & parolles" on the rhetorical grounds of battology (pointless repetition) and indecorum (III, vi). In short, Du Bellay, like Cicero and Quintilian, conceives nature's superiority over art as proportional and not absolute, "le naturel faire plus sans la doctrine que

[2] Ed. Laumonier, XIII, 77. Cf. Robert J. Clements, *Critical Theory and Practice of the Pléiade* (1942), p. 213; Donald Stone, *Ronsard's Sonnet Cycles* (1966), p. 219; Jacques Peletier du Mans, *Art poétique* (1555), I, ii, 12; Montaigne, I, 20, p. 85; d'Aubigné *Les Tragiques,* II, 773–784; and Jamyn's "Les hommes, le plus souvent, adjoustent créance plus volontiers à la vérité quand elle est embellie de couleurs et de douceur de paroles: toutesfois, pourceque la vérité simple et nue se trouve parmy les vertueux plus luisante sans aucun artifice qu'autrement, à raison qu'elle est assez ornée de soy mesme et qu'estant fardée de paremens extérieurs, elle se corrompt. Le mensonge, au contraire, ne plaist sinon par l'apparence extérieure d'un embellissement emprunté s'evanouyssant et s'escoultant, si elle n'est polie de fards qui l'embellissent," quoted by Edouard Fremy, *L'Académie des derniers Valois* (1887), p. 361.

[3] Ed. Laumonier, VII, 325, variant.

la doctrine sans le naturel" (p. 103).[4] Art is both man's revenge on nature and his acceptance of its primacy.

In defining this dynamic relationship he employed the traditional complex of Latinate terminology surrounding the trichotomy of natural gifts of the mind (*ingenium*), art (*ars, disciplina, scientia, doctrina*) and exercise (*usus, experientia*). Taken together, they imply the learned mastery of methods inherent in successful examples which a gifted mind can judiciously use as guides in creating.[5] Since the terms are universal and go back at least as far as Plato (*Phaedrus,* 269d) it is no surprise that Renaissance writers make them the bases of discussions on dialectic, rhetoric and poetry without any necessary communication or reciprocal influence among those writers. In his coronation address, amid Horatian and Ciceronian adages and reminders to discipline the imagination, Petrarch elaborates the interrelations of *natura, ars, doctrina, ingenium* and their efficient cause.[6] The second chapter of Peletier's *Art poétique I,* in which he argues the interdependence of art and nature, is entitled "De la Nature et de l'Exercice." And the wording of Ramus' treatise on dialectic is strongly reminiscent of Du Bellay's treatise on poetry, "l'exercice monstroit le fruict de l'art, ainsi nous fault icy penser que non par l'art seullet mais beaucoup plus l'exercice d'icelluy et la practique faict l'artisant . . . ce n'est pas assez de scavoir que c'est de vertu, mais il fault mettre peine de l'acquérir et d'en user . . . Et vauldroit beaucoup mieux avoir l'usage sans art que l'art sans usage."

Indeed, Renaissance writers from various callings feel compelled to anchor their discussions of art, nature, experience and reason in unassailable logic. Writes Leonardo da Vinci: "La sperienza, interprete infra l'artifitiosa natura e la umana spetie, ne insegnia ciò che essa natura infra mortali adopera, da neciessità costretta non altrimenti operarsi possa · che la ragion, suo timone, operare le assegni . . . La sperienza non falla mai, ma solo fallano i vostri giuditi, promettendosi di quella efetti · tali che ne' uostri esperimenti causati non sono."[7] The

[4] This same phrase recurs in widely divergent Renaissance texts. Cf. "ad laudem atque virtutem naturam sine doctrina, quam doctrina sine natura valuisse," *Henrici Cornelii Agrippae ab Nettesheym . . . Opera in duos tomos concinne digesta, et nunc denuò, sublatis omnibus mendis, in φιλομούσων gratiam accurantissimè recusa* . . . (Leyden, n. d.), II, 4.

[5] Cf. Montaigne: "Feu mon pere, homme pour n'estre aydé que de l'experience et du naturel, d'un jugement bien net," I, 35, p. 220, and "L'art n'est autre chose que le contrerolle et le registre des productions," III, 3, p. 802. See also III, 10, p. 980. Discussions of this relationship inevitably entail related comment on principles that are basic to rhetoric; cf. *Conteurs français du XVI*e *siècle* (1965), p. 709.

[6] *Scritti inediti* (1874), pp. 312 and 316.

[7] Ramus, *La Dialectique,* pp. 153–155; *Scritti letterari* (1883), II, 288. Cf. Cicero's *Pro Archia,* VIII, 15, and Quintilian, II, xix, 2.

Quinte Essence addresses Pantagruel and Panurge in the same way: "Ce que fait les humains pansemens esgarer par les abismes d'admiration n'est la souveraineté des effects, lesquels apertement ils esprouvent naistre des causes naturelles, moyennenent l'industrie des sages artisans; c'est la nouveauté de l'experience entrant en leurs sens, non prevoyans la facilité de l'oeuvre, quand jugement serain associe estude diligent." Quintilian had used these categories interchangeably in postulating that "things" and "words" blend successfully by means of art, nature and exercise (II, x, 1; III, iv, 1), and that the similarity of logic, rhetoric and art lies in the ordered methods, practice and useful perceptions they share in common (II, xvii, 41–42). This perception is viewed either as certain judgment of evident facts or as purposeful wisdom (*consilium*) considering hidden facts where several arguments are compared (VI, v, 3); later he frames the opposition as *iudicium* against *ingenium* (X, i, 130). DuBellay appears to follow a similar line of thought in an octave from "Les Amours," if his grounding in Latin allows us to invest the French words with their original Latin meanings:

> Bien qu'imparfaict, j'ay toutefois des yeux,
> Non pour juger de vous parfaictement,
> Mais comme peult l'humain entendement
> Juger à l'oeil de la beauté des Cieux.
> Bien qu'ignorant, je n'aye receu des Dieux
> L'art & sçavoir d'escrire doctement,
> Si donnez vous suffisant argument
> De vous louër aux moins ingenieux. (II, 239)

The Renaissance implicitly made wisdom and virtue characteristics of reason, and thus saw the moral order of the universe as equally rational and virtuous. The Horatian requirement of mixing the useful with the sweet imposed a moral calling to which Du Bellay was always sensitive. For Quintilian the end of eloquence, knowledge and experience was goodness, and in an image with which the Pléiade as a whole was familiar he held that eloquence used for evil ends would make a stepmother of Nature (XII, i, 1; iv–v). Even Caesar in the *Gallic War* infused a moral tone in his formulaic *usus atque ratio* (II, xx; III, viii; IV, i). Although Du Bellay employs the same formula, it will be more instructive for our purposes to consider for a moment a transformation rather than a precise analogy. In his edition of Ronsard, Laumonier gives Horace's *Espistola,* I, ii, 19–22 as one of the sources for the "Ode au pais de vandomois" and contends that Du Bellay had Ronsard's poem before his mind's eye when he composed his famous "Heureux qui, comme Ulysse."[8] If that is so, then we witness the significant evolution of "virtus et sapientia" in Horace through "conseil" and "sçavoir" in Ronsard to "plein d'usage & raison" in Du Bellay, which not only points to a community of values but also places in a broader literary perspective the feelings of virtuous isolation and world weariness that underlie the intimate revelations of the *Regrets.*

Art, nature, exercise and their correlative values are therefore important to an understanding of Du Bellay's method and viewpoint in the *Regrets* and other collections. In the early sonnets where he proclaims his honesty, he presents the following sequence of poems as "estans de mon coeur les plus seurs secretaires"—the same expression he and Ronsard use in their communication with sympathetic nature: "Bois tristes & solitaires, / De ma peine secretaires" (V, 52), "Saincte Gastine, heureuse secretaire / De mes ennuis,"[9] but while he seems to say he will not work hard on his poetry, he really indicates that he will not work hard to become a poet. His sonnets are not going to be contrivances from a rattled brain and chewed fingers. Although the simplicity of his style will be like prose, he warns that this studied casualness is not easy. Near the end of the collection, in a group of sonnets replete with figures of sentence on art and virtue, Du Bellay follows the Longinian and Horatian tradition by claiming that perfect art imitates nature and nature is most effective when emended by art: "L'artifice caché, c'est le vray artifice" (II, 167). The significance of this and similar statements derives from the way in which art can mould nature to meet the shifting exactions of the poet's vision:

> Autant comme lon peult en un autre langage
> Une langue exprimer, autant que la nature
> Par l'art se peult monstrer, & que par la peinture
> On peult tirer au vif un naturel visage: (II, 171)

This affinity between poetry and painting was, of course, one of the basic assumptions of Renaissance aesthetic. Horace's famous "ut pictura poesis" became the catchword to express the conception, but its sententious simplicity and lack of elaboration in the *Ars poetica* led it to be so misconstrued that it often plays a doubtful and inconsistent role in the actual application of poetic theory. Aneau, himself the author of an emblem book entitled *Picta poesis* (1552), travesties Horace in his criticism of Du Bellay's recommended sad elegies, since the Quintil feels that painting should only delight (p. 117), and Du Bellay adds

[8] II, 95–96. Cf. Montaigne's "exercice de sagesse et de vertu," I, 11, p. 45, and Baïf's "C'est estre fol que d'estre sage / Selon raison contre l'usage," *Euvres en rime de Ian Antoine de Baïf* (1881–1890), V, 9.

[9] Ed. Laumonier, IV, 128. Cf. XVII, 163.

to the caricature by asserting that poetry and painting are alike in their mutual subjection to vulgar opinion (p. 182). The key words *au vif* cited in the verses above indicate rather a theory developed at length by the Pléiade's great manifesto, drawn from a non-Horatian source.

In the midst of numerous figures and ornaments that Du Bellay recommends to the would-be poet he includes the term *energies* (p. 35). Chamard and critics after him have charged Du Bellay with confusing Aristotle's *energia,* referring to the forcefulness derived from a vividly animated style, with Dionysius of Halicarnassus' *enargia* which refers to the high visual relief of character, idea or scene, caused by a figured style. Yet the poet's reference to Aristotle in "Le Poete courtisan" bespeaks a limited knowledge (VI, 129–130), and his "Prosphonematique" suggests only a casual acquaintance with Dionysius. Moreover, while a writer like Sebillet uses *enargie* to describe the uses of imposing vocabulary for drawing out a poet's conception (*Art poétique,* I, iv) and Peletier uses the related term *hypotypose* as "l'expression vive des choses par les moz" (*Art poétique,* I, ix), *energia* (or *energie*) has always tended to include all of these related meanings, as it does for Du Bellay. A close reading of Aristotle's *Rhetoric,* III, xi, finds *energia* linked to figured and ordered movement (*schema*), emotion and the reader's vicarious participation through visual immediacy; a medieval rhetorician like Isidore will use it in a similar way.[10] The conception became central to a later Renaissance poet like Sidney through readings of Aristotle, Quintilian and Scaliger.[11] But, if precise sources can be ascribed at all, it seems likely that Du Bellay's source was primarily Quintilian, since the figures and ornaments associated with *energies* are all found in the *Institutio* (VIII, vi) and Quintilian's discussion of *energia, enargia* and *hypotyposis* is the fullest Du Bellay could have known. In Book VIII and elsewhere a premium value is placed on vivid representation that would be true to nature, word pictures formed by the imagination for the mind's eye. The clear conceptions and powerful effects of these illustrations, engendered by a copiousness of thought and figurative language, are designed to persuade our minds and inspire emotions.[12]

[10] "Energia est rerum gestarum aut quasi gestarum sub oculos inductio," *Isidori Hispalensis episcopi Etymologiarum sive Originum libri XX* (1911), II, xxi, 33.

[11] Donald Lemen Clark, *Rhetoric and Poetry in the Renaissance* (1963), p. 85.

[12] This summary incorporates all of the basic terms (*illustratio, evidentia, oculis mentis, imago rerum,* etc.) of *Institutio,* IV, ii, 123; VI, ii, 32–34; VIII, iii, 61–63, 70, 88–89; IX, ii, 40–41. For a detailed account of the picture-making faculty of the imagination, see Grahame Castor, *Pléiade Poetics,* ch. 17. Cf. Montaigne, II, 37, p. 1613; III, 5, p. 826; and III, 11, p. 1012.

This type of imaging is fundamental to the close cooperation Du Bellay seeks between art and a superior nature: j'estimeroy' l'Art pouvoir exprimer la vive energie de la Nature" (p. 80). Since the painting nomenclature is partially metaphoric, the colors invoked refer more to varied verbal figures, the "couleurs de rhétorique," than to chromatic pigment. Ronsard, leafing through his books to sort out and choose "le plus beau," says "en cent couleurs je peints en un tableau, / Tantost en l'autre: & maistre en ma peinture, / Sans me forcer j'imite la Nature."[13] Du Bellay's dedicatory sonnet of the *Antiquitez* similarly purports to place before the king's and the public's eye "ce petit tableau / Peint, le mieux que j'ay peu, de couleurs poëtiques." His many allusions to painting and light effects are coupled with *energie* and the use of figures which body forth the poetic intention and express the general through particulars: "la nature / Au plus gay de sa peinture / Me figuroit les beautez" (V, 50), "magnificence de motz, gravité de sentences, audace & varieté de figures, & mil' autres lumieres de poësie: bref ceste energie . . . comme un peintre peut representer l'ame avecques le cors de celuy qu'il entreprent tyrer apres le naturel (pp. 40–41) . . . l'ornement & lumiere (p. 60) . . . l'ornement & illustration" (p. 74).

Nor should we take Ronsard's claim of facile imitation literally or as representative of a relaxed attitude toward the use of poetic diction. Like Quintilian, des Autelz closely associates copious figures, emotion and vivid representation with decorum,[14] implying a controlled use of abundant figures, and Du Bellay likens his word picture "richement ornée" more to sustained work than to loose fancy: "pour le vif la couleur, / N'employant nostre esprit qu'au labeur poëtique" (II, 215). Independently pleasurable sensuality and accurate naturalism are not sought through vivid and energetic representation as much as the accurate expression of the poem's argument or cause; teaching, moving and pleasing, then, work together. An examination of classical myth in the Renaissance shows that its vitality lies partly in the poet's cre-

[13] Ed. Laumonier, XV, 252.

[14] See my ch. II, note 41; Scaliger's chapter on "Efficacia" for the controlled use of figures of diction for persuasion to certain emotions, *Poetices libri septem* (1617), pp. 270–272; d'Aubigné, *Les Tragiques,* VII, 7–8; and W. F. Patterson, *Three Centuries of French Poetic Theory* (1966), p. 622. Jacques Tahureau expresses the same idea as Du Bellay in identical language: see *Odes, sonnets et autres poésies* (1869), pp. 66–67. Later Renaissance discussions of *chiarezza* are certainly close to Quintilian's requirement of clear illustration and conception and to the Pléiade's desired clarity of meaning. Cf. Clements, *Critical Theory,* ch. III; Antonio Minturno, *De poeta* (1559), p. 118 and *L'Arte poetica* (1725), p. 24; Tasso, "Discorsi del poema eroico," *Opere* (1824), III, 186. "Le jugement des yeux" unaccompanied by a judgment of the mind is unacceptable to Pontus in *Le Premier Curieux* (*The Universe of Pontus de Tyard, A Critical Edition of "L'Univers"* [1950], p. 122).

ative reaction to a story that crystallizes and universalizes his experience and vision, and partly in the extension of mythic tale to an ethical *exemplum* or explicit allegorization. Imagery, whether abundant or spare, florid or bleak, is responsible to the poem's intent and to the reader's reaction. The intention of lively portraiture in prose and poetry alike is a theme that is subject to countless variations. But however varied the rephrasing in theory, in expository writing, in lyric verse or in evaluative criticism, it is rarely disassociated from persuasion to a covert or overt moral point of view. Montaigne's statement in the "Au lecteur" of the *Essais* that ". . . je peins. Mes defauts s'y liront au vif," Du Bellay's self-proclaimed ability "au vif exprimer" Jean Du Bellay's "scavoir, vertu & conduyte" (p. 7), his advice to the poetic picture maker "Qui veult au vif imaginer la face / Du gentil Piéne, alors que sa vertu . . ." (II, 294) and Edoard's reference to the "Vieille Courtisanne"'s "vive representation de la devote creature introduicte en ses moeurs, actes, conditions, & evenemens respondans aux merites" (V, 181), despite different shades of emphasis, all stress the same relationship. *Energia,* then, is connected with the allegorizing nature of poetry; in the "Discours au Roy sur la trefve de l'an MDLV," following a series of *sententiae* on virtue, the causes and effects of Fortune and the triumph of La Paix over La Discorde, Du Bellay concludes:

> Si j'avois tant amis les cieulx & la nature,
> Qu'en mes tableaux je peusse au vif representer
> Quelque chose qui peust vostre esprit contenter. (VI, 15)[15]

Correspondingly, the failure of poetic figures to direct the reader's attention to a generally apprehensible truth, or of art to accord with nature led to the censure of "vaine peinture." Usually the tag was reserved for any body of poetry with pronounced and unrelieved substantive or structural pretentions. Ronsard charged the *rhétoriqueurs* with "forcing Apollo's light" for their too obvious versifying tech-

[15] Cf. *Deffence,* p. 43; II, 270; V, 26; VI, 195. It is perhaps not accidental that the verbs used by the Pléiade (*feindre*) and other Renaissance writers like Alberti (*fingiere*) in *Della pittura* to convey the meaning represented graphically by allegories and derived etymologically from *fingere,* find their semantic equivalent in the verb σχημᾰτιζω meaning figurative and imagined movement. Bruno lumps together philosophers, painters and poets, and concludes that "a man who does not know how to paint and feign is no philosopher," *Opera latine,* II, ii, 134. The Pléiade did, of course, legislate against any willful obscurantism implied by feigning. See Clements (*The Peregrine Muse* [1959], pp. 8–9): and Jean Seznec (*The Survival of the Pagan Gods* [1961], p. 112) for remarks on feigning, painting and allegory. In Aneau's *Picta poesis* poetry and emblems illuminate one another by holding eye and mind on such polarities as *ingenium* and *labor* (p. 17), *sapientia* and *eloquentia* (p. 20) and *natura* and *ars* (p. 54).

niques: "Sans plus il gastent l'encre, & broyant la couleur, / Barbouillent un portrait d'inutile valeur."[16] And Du Bellay's confusing *mea culpa* in the liminal sonnet of "L'Honneste Amour" seems to single out *L'Olive* for its "vaine peincture" and "feincte couverture" because it dwelled on "La non encor' bien comprise nature" instead of "imaginant le vif"; the attack is waged in "Contre les petrarquistes" with greater clarity and indignation:

> Mais cest Enfer de vaines passions,
> Ce Paradis de belles fictions,
> Deguizemens de nos affections,
> Ce sont peinctures vaines: (V, 71)

The maxim attributed by Plutarch to Simonides that painting is silent poetry while poetry is a speaking picture was common currency in Renaissance poetic discussions[17] and insists on the cooperation between senses and mind, imagery and meaning. Pontus de Tyard discusses the conception he wishes to communicate to others, "qu'avec quelque labeur i'ay depeint dans le tableau de mon esprit," and Pierre Motin bemoans the effort his thought requires, "Si tost que dans ma teste il a peint une image."[18] The close juncture of eye and mind and the near-identity of expression that involves them shows that poetry speaks with a meaning, a meaning that reflects the poet's point of view and to which he wishes to persuade his listener:

> Tout cela que l'oeil apperçoit,
> Tout cela que l'esprit conçoit,
> Est du poëte, & l'escritture
> N'est qu'une parlante peinture. (V, 68)

This persuasion to the poet's literal point of view appears in verses like "icy je vous supply mettre devant voz yeulx" (VI, 29), followed by a series of "Je voy," and in

> De quelle riche couleur
> Peindray-je ma poësie
> Pour descrire la valeur
> Que j'ay sur toutes choisie? (V, 41)

[16] Ed. Laumonier, XIV, 196.

[17] See Clements, *Picta poesis, Literary and Humanistic Theory in Renaissance Emblem Books* (1960), p. 174; Rosemond Tuve on Sidney in "Imagery and Logic: Ramus and the Metaphysical Poets," *Journal of the History of Ideas,* III (1942), 392; Le Caron's dialogue on poetry, "laquelle nous appellons la vive ou parlante peinture," quoted by Castor, p. 73; the accord between concept and internal visual design, Robert Klein, "The Figurative Thought of the Renaissance," *Diogenes,* XXXII (1960), 114; E. H. Gombrich, "Icones Symbolicae," *Journal of the Warburg and Courtaud Institutes,* XI (1948), 168–176.

[18] Pontus de Tyard, *Discours philosophiques* (1587), p. 2vo; Pierre Motin, *Oeuvres inédites* (1882), p. 66.

after which follow six consecutive "je voy" stanzas and then images based on tactile, aural and oral sensations.

Renaissance theorists of rhetoric and poetic ponderously label this scheme *pragmatographia* when "lively and ficticious" action is brought before the eyes, such as a battle scene, and ask that the figures and tropes be carefully controlled; in the process, the poet's general truth is praised over the historian's particular truth.[19] In the "Discours au Roy sur la poésie" Du Bellay opposes historian and poet, and lauds the broader truth derived from the artistic imitation of nature:

> Cestuy-là sans user d'aucune fiction
> Represente le vray de chascune action,
> Comme un, qui sans oser s'esgayer davantage,
> Rapporte apres le vif un naturel visage:
> Cestuy-cy plus hardy, d'un art non limité
> Sous mille fictions cache la verité,
> Comme un peinctre qui fait d'une brave entreprise
> La figure d'un camp, ou d'une ville prise,
> Un orage, une guerre, ou mesme il fait les Dieux
> En façon de mortelz se monstrer à noz yeux. (VI, 164)

In accordance with the desire to accompany *enargia* with auricular, "sensible," and sententious figures[20]—a kind of synesthesia leading to moral elevation—the vividly imaginative description of Ronsard's "Exhortation pour bien combattre" transcends the historian's role by deploying a multisensory scheme composed of tropes and figures that reinforce and complement one another: anaphora, compar, neologism and Sannazaro's antithetical traductio *vainqueurs-vaincus:*

> Je voy desja, ce semble, en ordre nos gendarmes,
> J'oy le bruit des chevaux, j'oy le choquer des armes,
> Je voy de toutes pars le fer etinceller
> Et jusques dans le ciel la poudre se mesler,
> Je voy comme foretz se herisser les piques,
> J'oy l'effroy des cannons, oeuvres diaboliques,
> J'oy faucer les harnoys, enfonser les escus,
> J'oy le bruit des vainqueurs, j'oy le cry des vaincus.[21]

### Variety and Imitation: Theory

On the surface Du Bellay's recommendation of *pragmatographia* runs counter to his sarcastic advice to the "poete courtisan":

> Arguments à propoz il te fault espier:
> Comme quelque victoire, ou quelque ville prise,

[19] Cf. George Puttenham, *The Arte of English Poesie* (1936), pp. 62, 238–239.
[20] Ibid., pp. 158–161.
[21] Ed. Laumonier, IX, 7–8.

> Quelque nopce ou festin, ou bien quelque entreprise
> De masque ou de tournoy: avoir force desseigns,
> Desquelz à ceste fin tes coffres seront pleins." (VI, 133)

But we must remember that a former Petrarchist is here addressing the excesses of Petrarchanism and that the poetic vices he decries are merely exaggerations of procedures he and many others continued to practice. The allusion to the thesaurus of themes refers to the abundance or *copie* prescribed by humanists, dialecticians, rhetoricians and poets. Through careful reading and study are acquired a wealth of material used in finding dialectical places, a stock of rhetorical commonplaces, turns of phrase, whole expressions, ideas and proverbial sententiae that could be mechanically applied as do the Petrarchists or skilfully reproduced through assimilation into one's cultural consciousness. Montaigne chides contemporary education where, instead of correcting judgment through applied sententiae, "chascun les couche en sa memoire" (I, 23, p. 114). Although the term embraced all forms of discourse, in a sonnet to Jodelle, Du Bellay lauds his *grave* tragedy, his *doulce* comedy and the *copieuse veine* of his lyric poetry (II, 285). Ronsard praises the artifice by which "meintes choses sont diversement portraittes," and Peletier's admiration of the "copieuse excellence . . . es auteurs anciens" is heard throughout the *Deffence et Illustration.*[22] The two ancient writers from whom Du Bellay's treatise draws the most, Cicero and especially Quintilian, provide an index for our understanding of his ideas, and show us again that varied imagery, expressed idea and intended effect are not separated. In *De oratore,* III, xxxiii, 136, Cicero assumes a necessary coexistence of effective style and copiousness of thought, while Quintilian, like Du Bellay in his respect for the ancients' store of knowledge and experience, recommends a copious flow and careful control of words, figures and sententiae.[23] So the requirement of *copie* applies equally to invention and style, *res* and *verba,* as the catchphrase "copia rerum atque verborum" would indicate.[24]

[22] Ibid., XIII, 85; Peletier quoted in Chamard's *Du Bellay,* p. 33; *Deffence et Illustration,* pp. 48, 84, 139. Du Bellay's equation of elegance and copiousness is anticipated by Pierre Saliat; see J. Chocheyras, "En marge de la *Défense et illustration,* Pierre Saliat: une préface critique de 1537," *BHRen,* XXVIII (1966), 677.

[23] V, x, 51; VIII, pr. 1; V, i, 15 and 108; XII, iv, 1: XII, v, 1. Following a description of a freshly picked bouquet of flowers, Ronsard concludes with the usual moral lesson, "cela vous soit un exemple certain" (ed. Laumonier, VII, 152) and commenting on Ronsard's *Amours I,* Muret holds that imagery must not contravene the poem's intention and must be meaningful in order to maintain logical relations: *Les Oeuvres,* p. 14.

[24] Cf. Erasmus' *De duplici copia verborum ac rerum.*

The two basic principles of the *Deffence,* imitation of the classics through the process that Faguet labeled "innutrition" and enrichment of the French lexicon, follow from this requirement. In successive chapters Du Bellay advises "copie et richesse d'invention" (p. 33) and "magnificence de motz, gravité de sentences, audace et varieté de figures" (p. 40). Ronsard's chapters on invention and style in the *Abrégé* are equally specific in their insistence that abundance of ideas and words be rationally guided toward a coherent meaning.[25] George Gascoigne, Du Bellay's English contemporary, asks "What figure might I find within my head?" in order to "expound the case" ("Gascoigne's Woodsmanship," vv. 131, 135). The poem's argument both orders and includes its accretive details. In addition to the "illumination" and greater intelligibility afforded by *copie,* it is sought so that art may imitate the "copieuse diversité" of nature, as Ronsard has it, and may create the impression of the unified diversity that inheres in nature, according to Pontus.[26] We have seen the requirement of copiousness implied in other related contexts as the desire for expanded invention and as the use of varied figures and lively portraiture in imitation of nature. The remainder of this section will address copiousness on a level of rhetorical and dialectical praxis to show how Du Bellay applied abundant themes and imitated nature through model authors.

### Variety and Imitation: Practice

After castigating the "poete courtisan" for his stockpile of poetic procedures, Du Bellay assails him further: "Il fault avoir tousjours le petit mot pour rire, / Il fault des lieux communs, qu'à tous propoz on tire, / Passer ce qu'on ne sçait, & se montrer sçavant / En ce que lon ha leu deux ou trois soirs devant" (VI, 135). Once again, he is not attacking a basic poetic premise as much as its misapplication. His remarks are foreshadowed in the *Illustration* where he opposes those who "sont contens n'avoir rien dict qui vaille aux ix. premiers vers, pourveu qu'au dixiesme il y ait le petit mot pour rire" (p. 110). Unlike Verlaine's categorical injunction, "Fuis de plus loin la Pointe assassine," he is not arguing against the pithiness of the tenth verse nor against its position,

[25] Ed. Laumonier, XIV, 13, 15. Cf. the Claude Deroziers translation of Dion Cassius' *Des faitz et gestes insignes des romains* (1542): "coppie de parolles, a icelle fin qu'elle (la loy) soit plus manifeste à tout homme," bk. XXXVIII, ch. 7, and Donald Stone, *Ronsard's Sonnet Cycles,* p. 180.

[26] Ed. Laumonier, I, 47; Pontus de Tyard, *The Universe,* ed. Lapp, p. 122. For a good illustration of the interrelation among *copia* of words, figures and commonplaces, *energia, enargia,* illumination, invention and style, see Montaigne, III, 5, p. 851.

but rather against the total subordination of the preceding nine verses. This is evinced by the imperative in the next clause, "mesle le profitable avecques le doulz," as Martial did, and by the subsequent stress on decorous verse that is formed of varied and sententious figures.

These recommended *sententiae,* along with *exempla,* proverbs, apophthegms and maxims, formed part of a corpus of commonplaces and folk wisdom that were traditional since antiquity. In the *Rhetoric* Aristotle distinguished the specific from the commonplace, since the latter could be applied to many situations, or in Du Bellay's words, "à tous propos on tire." Montaigne justified his culling of maxims on the broad basis of *experientia* and *usus:* "En l'experience et usage de cette sentence, qui est très-veritable, consiste tout le fruict que je tire des livres."[27] Commonplaces could be drawn from the plethora of commonplace books that circulated widely in the Renaissance, often in the form of Poetrias. Aristotle's *Topics* and *Rhetoric,* Cicero's *De oratore* and *Topica,* Quintilian's *Institutio oratoria* and the *Ad Herennium* were all adapted to this end, but the most popular were Erasmus' *De copia* for amplification and for themes his *Adagia* and the *Progymnasmata* of Aphthonius, whom Du Bellay read for the "Metamorphose d'une rose" (V, 182). Commonplaces were either stored for future use in the artificial memory, according to the recommendation of *Ad Herennium,* III, xvi, 28–29, and so violently opposed by Montaigne, as a treasury "de rare et antique erudition" according to Du Bellay; or else they were located in textbooks and instructional manuals, such as the manuals for the prince. Renaissance emblem books were used to teach rhetoric and educate princes by instilling in the memory a commonplace which was illustrated by a physical image of a virtuous subject.[28] In the "Ample discours au Roy" he tells François II that "les livres sont pleins, tant sacrez que gentils, / D'exemples infinis des Princes, qui jadis / Leurs sceptres ont perdus par paresse & par vice, / Et sur tout pour n'avoir honnoré la justice" (VI, 212–213).

Commonplaces invariably counseled traditional wisdom and rewarded virtue with praise and punished vice with dispraise. Since antiquity, praise of virtue and dispraise of vice presupposed a virtuous life on the part of the speaker or narrator. This reward and punishment were intimately bound up with the Renaissance world-view and brought to mind the theme of sublunary mutability embodied in the Wheel of Fortune. On the level of historical change, the Renaissance retained

[27] III, 3, p. 805. "A faute de memoire naturelle," he goes on to say, "j'en forge de papier," III, 13, p. 1071. Scaliger, for instance, associates *exempla* with inductive proof, III, 71.

[28] Cf. Robert Garnier's *Bradamante* (1949), vv. 237–238.

the medieval theme of the triumph of Vice over Virtue occasioned by the passing of the Golden Age. But in the Renaissance judgment and praise of virtue as an abstract quality open to allegorization became increasingly demonstrated in the concrete examples of human conduct and the vivid portrayals of moral types. In an elegy to the Cardinal de Chatillon, Ronsard describes Fortune dispensing and withdrawing Virtue according to her whimsy[29] and Du Bellay places even Diane de Poitier's immovable virtue above the realm of the moon and Fortune's province (V, 379). Occasionally he modifies the close connection between virtue and fortune, as in the "Ample discours au Roy" where he says that his own fortune, identified with nature, has forbidden him from being a soldier and so he will sing the king's virtue by conjoining *ingenium, ars* and *disciplina:* "J'emploieray mon esprit, ma plume & mon labeur" (VI, 234). But ordinarily he holds to the tradition of paraphrasing in an extended sequence the same basic commonplace, frequently drawn from Martial or the Greek Anthology, as an exercise in *copia;* praise for the man who can follow the difficult path of virtue when he is enjoying good fortune is immediately followed by a succession of *sententiae* bearing on the same theme:

> Fascheuse de nature est toute adversité,
> Mais trop plus dangereuse est la felicité.
> Le cheval furieux, aiant le mords pour guide,
> Tousjours en sa fureur ne desdaigne la bride:
> Le navire agité des vents impetueux
> Ne succumbe tousjours aux flots tempestueux:
> Et le cours du torrent tombant de la montaigne
> S'allente quelquefois au plain de la campaigne. (VI, 9)

The commonplace of fortune and virtue lent itself naturally to a multitude of variations during the Renaissance, since it subsumed the whole question of man's individual freedom. At times, Nature, Fortune, Destiny and Providence coalesce and subject man to their larger will.[30] But in as many cases submissive medieval moral virtue is supplanted by the Renaissance notion of personal accomplishment and ingeniousness where, as Alberti put it, ability directs fortune.[31] According to Mon-

---

[29] Ed. Laumonier, X, 333–334.

[30] Cf. ibid., I, 89; VIII, 105–114; X, 335; XIII, 212; and Du Bellay, V, 288.

[31] In the Proemio to "Della famiglia," *Opere volgari* (1844), II. Cf. Ronsard, ed. Laumonier, XVII, 195; Du Bellay, V, 393; Howard R. Patch, *The Goddess Fortuna in Mediaeval Literature* (1927), p. 25; and Descartes, *Discours de la méthode,* p. 64. The modern attitude probably dates from the conversation of Franciscus and Augustinus in the *Secretum.* See *Francesco Petrarca, prose* (1955), pp. 32–34, and for rhetoric and the individual as the cause of fortune, see pp. 70–76, *Epistolae familiares* (ed. Rossi and Bosco [1933–1942], XXII, 13, and *Epistolae seniles* (*Opera omnia* [1581]) VIII, 3.

taigne, "La fortune ne nous fait ny bien ny mal" because the mind is the "seule cause et maistresse de sa condition heureuse ou malheureuse" (I, 14, p. 67). Insofar as fortune is identified with nature, the notion can equally imply the triumph of art and human endeavor over the forces of nature. The most graphic example of this change is found in the "Hymne au Roy sur la prinse de Callais." After the temporary triumph of the allegorical persona Malheur over Fortune, Vertu decides to fight alongside Henri II. Soon, however, Du Bellay begins speaking of personal "vertu valeureuse" and of how the king's actions can overtake Fortune, "devancé par l'effect" (VI, 22).

The intent of the commonplace was to amplify a poetic discourse, to teach, please and move concurrently, since truth, beauty and goodness were ideally inseparable. In its dialectical function it could have the dual status of an intrinsic and an extrinsic argument. When considered as an inherent theme apart from the body of a poem the commonplace could be viewed as an intrinsic or artificial argument. Melanchthon's discussion on the nature of virtue and its adjuncts centers on their causes and effects, but when he attempts to persuade men to accept the beneficence of virtue, he resorts to rhetorical figures.[32] Similarly, Du Bellay's denial that Fortune has determined Henri II's virtue, following his analysis of

> Ceste dame Fortune, à qui pour sa puissance,
> Dont les divers effects nous donnent cognoissance,
> Sans en sçavoir la cause, on a d'antiquité
> Donné jusqu'aujourdhuy tiltre de deité. (VI, 10)

is a way of preparing an amplification of the king's personal qualities that follow in the poem. We have seen that in their function as rhetorical figures of thought, the grammatical structure of proverbs, aphorisms and other sententious matter is more amorphous than that of figures of diction. But with respect to their use within a whole poem, they are ordinarily reserved for the peroration of a poetic discourse, the sestet of a sonnet, the end of a stanza or any other meaning unit. And since they

[32] *Elementorum rhetorices libri duo* (n. p., 1572 [1st. ed.: 1519]), pp. 13–14. Cf. Richard Sherry's *Treatise on Schemes and Tropes* (1550), pp. 70–72. Ramus uses examples very similar to Du Bellay's to describe the effects of fortune and virtue (*La Dialectique,* pp. 69, 72). Montaigne dismisses the "imagination mesme de la vertu" as "jargon de colliege" (I, 37, p. 225), and further illustrates his condemnation by referring to "les deffinitions, les divisions et particions de la vertu" (II, 17, p. 644). His discussion of virtue and fortune in "De l'art de conferer" is a general denial of a stringent cause-effect syndrome (III, 8, pp 911–913), but elsewhere he speaks of "la cause generale," "l'effect d'une vertu" (III, 1, pp. 780–781) and "un effaict du sort plus que de la raison" (II, 21, p. 659).

are identical to inartificial arguments, Quintilian considers them in relation to the enthymeme as ways of relating the particular to the general (VIII, v, 3–8). The sententious "La hauteur (du sapin) n'est si ferme & asseurée / Que l'arbrisseau, qui croist par les campagnes" (IV, 120), derived from Horace's *Carmina,* II, x, not only sums up the particular action of the preceding verses, but also provides the moral focus for the whole "monomachie." The use of figures of thought to put the foregoing verses in broad perspective is certainly based on the poetic requirement of mixing the pleasant with the profitable and probably inspired Du Bellay's insistence that the epigrammatic tenth verse and the preceding nine be interdependent. This requirement has little if anything to do with the tone of the poem, for in an erotic "Chanson" of the *Jeux rustiques* he closes a stanza with the proverb "Qui ayme plus grand que soy, / Luy mesme se donne loy" and continues his argument with "Cela vous doit estre preuve" (V, 86), while in his "Lyre chrestienne" he ends a stanza with the ecclesiastical "Mais toutes choses ont leur temps" (IV, 137) and goes on to a discussion of mixing "le doulx à l'utile." Since in a dozen separate contexts Du Bellay stresses the mixture of components, the useful does not follow the pleasant in an inviolate order. For instance, a poem in the *Vers lyriques* that prefigures the *Antiquitez,* where "En ruines grosses / Le tens precipite . . . Maint palais de Romme . . . Regnes et empires . . . Maint peuple puissant" (III, 18–19), contains maxims on the ravages of time scattered at random, like the ruins themselves, from beginning to end; but this arrangement coincides with the poem's intent of persuading the reader to accept the eternal decline and regeneration of unstable life and of restating variations on a sententious theme.

Since belletrists often worked out of the same copy books, or at least with the same commonplaces, and used the same authors as models, the resulting similarity of expression is not surprising. The themes of the *Antiquitez* recur three more times in the *Vers lyriques* (pp. 38–39, 41, 51) and on numerous occasions in the *Poemata,* indicating the extent of the poet's preoccupation, and traditional topoi such as the Dying Rose, *ubi sunt* and *memento mori* appear in close juncture (IV, 28). A scholar of Chamard's scope can trace the commonplace that closes the first part of a long poem back through Rabelais and Erasmus (VI, 4) and even "O combien est heureuse," so severely censured in the *Illustration* (p. 114), is reworked in the *Vers lyriques* (III, 90). Du Bellay's astute editors have not failed to notice that too often his treatment of common themes and places is suggestive of "sententiae pueriles" and that his actual imitation of authors and refracting of themes are not always as naturally digested and reproduced as the *Deffence et Illustration* recommends.[33] Such serious charges deserve serious consideration. The next two sections, then, will examine the successes and failures of Du Bellay's imitations of literary models. Since translation is the most limited and most direct form of imitation, his translations of the *Aeneid* provide the most extensive demonstration of how he modified and applied his earlier ideas on imitation. *L'Olive* attests to the vast range of imitative possibilities open to the poet as he borrows and adopts imagery and thematic developments and as a result creates an impression of variety within a cohesive collection of sonnets. Both of these poetic endeavors show that in actual practice Du Bellay's translation, imitation and creation are cooperative activities differentiated by subtle gradations, and not mutually exclusive and clearly distinct categories.

### Du Bellay's Translations of the Aeneid

The random and polemic proscriptions in the *Deffence et Illustration* against translation are so colored by invective against the school of Marot and its defenders that we cannot take them as unqualified and absolute literary principles. Chamard clearly showed that Du Bellay's vituperation derived largely from the need to defend the hegemony of the French language against the *cicéroniens* and *virgiliens.* It was especially inspired by the publication of Sebillet's *Art poétique* which stole the Brigade's thunder and which defended adaptation and translation as the equals of poetic creativity.[34] After the battle had been joined and the enmity toward his adversaries somewhat relieved, Du Bellay could casually allow in the preface to his 1552 *Aeneid* translation that "Je n'ay pas oublié ce qu'autrefois j'ay dict des translations poëtiques: mais je ne suis si jalouzement amoureux de mes premieres apprehensions, que j'aye honte de les changer quelquefois à l'exemple de tant d'excellens aucteurs, dont l'auctorité nous doit oster ceste opiniastre opinion de vouloir tousjours persister en ses advis, principalement en matiere de lettres. Quand à moy, je ne suis pas Stoïque jusques là" (VI,

[33] Cf. the introduction of Eugénie Droz to *Les Antiquitez de Rome et les Regrets* (1945), p. xi; of Pierre Grimal to *Les Regrets suivis des Antiquitez* (1948), p. 32; of Verdun Saulnier to *Divers jeux rustiques,* pp. xxix and xxxiii; *Deffence,* p. 79; and Montaigne, I, 26, p. 171.

[34] Chamard, *Histoire de la Pléiade* (1961–1963), I, 183, 188. See also Joseph Vianey, *Les Regrets de Joachim du Bellay* (1946), p. 19, and Stephen G. Nichols, Jr., "Marot, Villon and the *Roman de la Rose,*" *Studies in Philology,* LXIII (1966), 135. The numerous publications of Saint-Gelais' *Aeneid* translation (1509, 1514, 1529, 1532, 1540) may also have goaded Du Bellay.

251). Neither his heated rejection of 1549 nor his mollified allowance of 1552 do justice to the subtle distinctions he raised in the *Deffence et Illustration* among imitation and the varieties of translation, or the problems these distinctions pose—problems and distinctions which he attempted in varying measure and with varying success to resolve and incorporate in his translations of Books IV and VI of the *Aeneid.*

In a spectrum ranging from blame to praise, Du Bellay's manifesto alluded to the activities of the *traducteur* who translates verbatim, the *translateur* who reproduces ideas closely, the *paraphraste* who reproduces ideas freely and the *imitateur* who so assimilates a literary model through innutrition that it becomes part of his instinctive cultural reference (pp. 32–39, 42, 46, 60). These varied activities correspond to the literary education proposed by Quintilian (X, XI) and coincide with part of the rhetorical-poetic rationale that underlies Du Bellay's treatise. We have seen how Chapter V of the *Deffence,* "Que les Traductions ne sont suffisantes pour donner perfection à la Langue Francoyse," introduces the system of Ciceronian rhetoric that will be Du Bellay's reference point for poetic terminology, and how the subsequent reduction of his remarks to invention and especially elocution aligns them with the dichotomy of *res* and *verba.* It is on the basis of this dichotomy that he criticizes translators and poor imitators who "s'amusant à la beauté des motz, perdent la force des choses" (pp. 34, 46). Imitation should benefit invention insofar as the transformation of a great author into one's intellectual background and literary memory provides a greater wealth of thematic and technical referents for the poet when he goes about "discovering" his subject. As such, imitation could not but enrich and copiously "illustrate" French letters in the new generation. But with the great stress placed on style by the ascending Pléiade—the creative formation of their uniquely personal expression—it was natural for one of their spokesmen to condemn word-for-word translation as a slavery that would vitiate their central purpose.

Du Bellay's conception of the worthy adapter alternates between the *translateur* and the *paraphraste,* and he came to see a successful rendition as a foreign author's natural inspiration revealed by a judiciously applied technique. To des Masures on his translation of Vergil's epic he wrote: "Autant comme lon peult en un autre langage / Une langue exprimer, autant que la nature / Par l'art se peult monstrer" (II, 171). He describes the necessary latitude he allowed himself in his version of the "Discours au Roy" of Michel de l'Hospital in order to remain close to the poem's theme and inspiration: "J'ay trahy ou traduit beaucoup plus de la moitié de nostre besogne, mays en vers alexandrins, car les aultres ne me satisfont en si grave matière, et m'eust fallu user d'une infinité de periphrases, dont je me feusse beaucoup eslongné de la nayfveté de mon autheur, que je m'esforce de représenter le plus au naturel qu'il m'est possible."[35] Even more liberally, in the preface to his translation of *Aeneid* IV he outlines at length his potentially dangerous theory of compensation which takes realistic account of transposing the metrical line of a synthetic language into the syllabic line of an analytic language: "il seroit mal aysé d'exprimer tant seulement l'ombre de son aucteur, principalement en ung oeuvre poëtique, qui vouldroit par tout rendre perïode pour perïode, epithete pour epithete, nom propre pour nom propre, & finablement dire ny plus ny moins, & non autrement, que celuy qui a escrit de son propre style, non forcé de demeurer entre les bornes de l'invention d'autruy. Il me semble, veu la contraincte de la ryme, & la difference de la proprieté & structure d'une langue à l'autre, que le translateur n'a point malfaict son devoir, qui sans corrompre le sens de son aucteur, ce qu'il n'a peu rendre d'assez bonne grace en ung endroict s'efforce de le recompenser en l'autre" (VI, 249–250).

Yet, his views on translation, although differently framed, are not basically original and do not represent the totality of the Pléiade's generation. In the tradition of the *Ars poetica* (v. 133), and perhaps following Vita, Etienne Dolet's *La Manière de bien traduire d'une langue en aultre* (1540) held that, through a requisite command of the foreign idiom, the translator should assimilate his author's tone and meaning and avoid word-for-word adaptation. Sebillet himself, whom Du Bellay praised in 1552 for his "docte artifice" in translation (IV, 181), stipulates the same command of idiom and avoidance of literal versions at the expense of meaning and harmonious style. On the other hand, the translations of the *Georgics* by Guillaume Michel in 1519 and by Richard Le Blanc in 1554 are completely verbatim, and Peletier, while acknowledging the superiority of original creation over translation, encouraged literal translation.

Divergent theories of translation and their execution were normal in an age when a considerable part of the standard collegial education consisted of translation exercises as well as poetic and rhetorical composition based on an assigned subject and argument. Although he had been away from Coqueret for several years when Loys Le Roy published *Plusieurs passages des meilleurs poëtes Grecs et Latins, citez aux Com-*

[35] *Lettres de Joachim du Bellay*, pp. 29–30.

*mentaires du Sympose de Platon* in 1558, the fragments translated by Du Bellay, heavily weighted with passages from Books IV and VI of the *Aeneid,* bear the characteristics of this type of compositional exercise.[36] Their various themes represent a compendium of Renaissance cosmography and poetic attitudes, such as the controlling force of the stars, the microcosm theme ("le monde est en nous," VI, 441), sublunary mutability, elemental composition, and the glory assured by poetry. Le Roy lauded Du Bellay's efforts for being "translaté," implying that he reproduced ideas closely, but in fact he frequently reproduces ideas freely and tailors them to the point of view of the Pléiade and its literary doctrines. For instance, in his translation of Pontano's *Meteora,* the line "Qui sont vulgairement nommez les douze Signes" is justified only within the Pléiade's reproachful attitude toward the "vulgaire odieux," not within the bland "duodena astra" of the text. And his advocacy of the trope antonomasia in the *Illustration* (p. 161), led him to expand the verse "Quum premit auratos Nephelaei velleris artus / Phoebus" into "C'est lors que le Soleil entre dans la maison / Du Mouton Phryxëan à la blonde toyson" (VI, 428).

Le Roy also admired the way in which Du Bellay preserved the rhetorical *sententiae* and "figures, couleurs & ornemens poëtiques" of the original texts. Although the compactness of the Latin "pervidimus omnem" in his translation of Manilius' *Astronomicon IV* (VI, 441) becomes the clumsy " Toute, en tout, & par tout nous l'avons recherchée," he was usually able to compensate for linguistic differences. By appealing to the tonic French rhyme, the complexities of Latin rhetorical figures and poetic rhythm are turned into tours de force of translation. The figure *traductio,* with its progressive variation developed from the same linguistic root, and the alliteration in Cornelius Gallus' "Pande, puella, collum candidum, / Productum bene candidis humeris" are deftly translated by Du Bellay's successive rhymes *undoiantes-blondoiantes-blanchissant* (VI, 422). Similarly, the internal alliteration in Juvenal's "Dii, majorum umbris tenuem & sine pondere terram" is accurately matched by Du Bellay's "Dieux, permettez qu'une legere terre / A tout jamais noz grandz peres enserre" (VI, 431).

Modern critics have not hesitated to admire his opuscules of Greek and Latin translation. Isidore Silver has shown in detail that Du Bellay's imitations of Pindar are independent of Ronsard's and that, despite his imperfect knowledge of Greek, his competent translation of

[36] Without pursuing the point any further, Marcel Raymond observed that Du Bellay's Latin translations resemble a "devoir d'école," *L'Influence de Ronsard sur la poésie française* (1927), I, 106.

Homer did not rely on extant versions.[37] His masterful command of Latin and his translation of Vergil's *Moretum* (V, 7), "moins traduit que transposé," according to Chamard's note, have elicited uniform praise from his commentators for having captured "le naif" of its author.[38] But his *Aeneid* translation, easily his most ambitious undertaking, has been censured by most of those same commentators for its conspicuous failure to approximate Vergil's genius, for the inevitably greater length of the French version, and yet it has received almost no detailed critical analysis.

His attraction to Vergil's genius reflected a major Renaissance predilection, for in that century the Augustan poet became progressively the exemplar of moral and patriotic conduct, a source book of themes, poeticized history and mythology, and the model of elevated style in poetry and rhetoric; for Du Bellay he was especially a source book and model.[39] A catchphrase used to describe Vergil's preeminence, derived from Quintilian (X, i, 86 and 106) and the *Ars poetica* (v. 323), compared his artistic mastery with Homer's natural inspiration as Demosthenes was compared with Cicero. Du Bellay frequently employs the formula in the *Deffence* (pp. 24, 28, 37) and elsewhere (II, 179, 274).[40] Vergil himself borrowed language, phrases, whole lines and entire episodes from Homer, but imitated creatively by reshaping and unifying so as to express the collective conscience of Augustan Rome. Du Bellay imitates Vergil in a similar way by using the mythological and historical past as seen in *Aeneid* VI to explain the present and add perspective to his vision in sonnets 6, 12 and 15 of the *Antiquitez.* He reproduces ideas freely in the "Hymne de Santé au seigneur Robert de la Haye" (V, 264–277) where in allegorical fashion he praises health and the eternal glory given by poetry; the transition between these disparate ideas is established by reference to the Vergilian underworld of *Aeneid*

[37] "Pindaric Parellelism in Du Bellay," *French Review,* XIV (1941), 461–472; "Du Bellay and Hellenic Poetry: A Cursory View," *PMLA,* LX (1945), 66–80.

[38] See Henri Weber, *La Création poétique au XVI*e *siècle* (1956), p. 415; Alice Hulubei's excellent "Virgile en France au XVIe siècle," *Revue du seizième siècle,* XVIII (1931), p. 57; Vianey, *Les Regrets,* p. 148; Chamard, *Histoire,* II, 213–214 and for l'abbé Goujet's judgment, p. 341.

[39] Vergil was also, but not primarily, the exemplar of patriotism for Du Bellay. For the debt of the *Illustration,* ch. xii, to *Georgics* II, see Alexander Haggerty Krappe, "Une Source virgilienne de la *Défense et Illustration de la langue française,*" *Revue du seizième siècle,* XV (1928), 342–343.

[40] Ramus, who used numerous excerpts of Du Bellay's translation of *Aeneid* IV to demonstrate dialectical method, says in the preface to *Scholae in liberales artes* (1569) that "cette méthode se trouve dans Virgile et dans Cicéron, dans Homère et dans Démosthène." Quoted in *La Dialectique,* p. 25.

VI, derived from the *Odyssey,* where one goes after death and where poor shades wander about. Free transposition of the underworld episode was not uncommon, witness François Habert's *Visions fantastiques* (1541) based on Book VI. But at times it is difficult to distinguish between imitation, close and free reproduction of ideas, as in the poem "Se perpetuo Faustinae memorem futurum" from the *Poemata.* The incipit, "Quod scelus admisi infoelix? quae numina laesi," and the fourth verse, "Iratos omnes huic decet esse Deos," recreate some of the language and basic ideas of the famous fourth and eighth verses of *Aeneid* I, "vi superum saevae memorem Iunonis ob iram . . . Musa, mihi causas memora, quo numine laeso," but Du Bellay applies their epic distance to his radically poignant love for Faustine. Vergil's broad human sympathy and melancholy appear to have held a highly personal appeal for Du Bellay.

Therefore, his willingness to forsake an earlier posture and translate two of the finest books of Vergil's epic bespeaks a commitment to a poet he imitated and freely adapted that transcends his earlier polemical mood. But the question remains: how can the translator conjoin *res* and *verba,* how can he capture the meanings of tonal change and shades of mood, "partie certes la plus difficile," in his author's idiom? The answer requires a close examination into the way Du Bellay addressed the problems of reconciling the Pléiade's poetic canons with his translations, of reproducing the sound, rhythm and syntax of Latin epic style, of his theory of compensation and of faithfulness to divergent cultural peculiarities. Since his translation of Book IV was the only one he saw through to publication, it must receive major consideration.

One of the basic tenets of the Pléiade, adumbrated in the *Deffence et Illustration,* is the alliance of poetry and music which implies close attention to rhythm and regularized rhyme. It is, then, surprising to find Du Bellay on one occasion egregiously abandon the considered rhyme recommendations of the *Illustration,* chs. VII–VIII; in the most poorly translated single passage of the two books he allows the narrative of Jupiter's agony to spill colorlessly into dialogue through the successive facile rhymes of similar roots and verb endings: entendit-estendit, vivoient-avoient, mande-commande, esselles-aïles, Dardanien-Sydonien (VI, 273). But usually the richness of the rhymes sustains careful distinctions and poetic value. In the passage of Book IV where the ghost of Anchises brings Aeneas back to the reality of his mission, the alternation between feminine and masculine endings reinforces the chiaroscuro of the description:

> Toutes les fois que la nuict froide & *sombre*
> Ce bas sejour couvre d'une obscure *ombre*

Toutes les fois que les astres *brulans*
Jettent sur nous leurs yeux *etincelans:* (VI, 281)

Du Bellay preserves the order and lambent cadence of Vergil's hexameter when the hero goes to meet his father in *Aeneid* VI, "spargens rore levi et ramo felicis olivae" (v. 230), and the author of *L'Olive* uses the rhyme to place in relief the Golden Bough which held a special meaning for him, "De la fertile & bienheureuse Olive" (VI, 355).[41]

The name that had the most special fascination for Du Bellay was, of course, Rome itself. Through the *Antiquitez* it resounds like the boom of a great drum, conjuring up cruel and noble visions of marching legions and victorious generals. Sonnet 6, developed from *Aeneid* VI, 781–787, articulates that imperial power, "Rome seule pouvoit Rome faire trembler." It appears that translation has here been the intermediary between imitation and creation, because Du Bellay anticipated the sonnet's martial rhythm in his translation, "Romme la grand', Romme, qui sa puissance" (VI, 388), which is barely implicit in Vergil's text, "auspiciis illa inculta Roma / imperium terris" (v. 781). Later, he again exceeds the Latin meter, "Nimium vobis Romana propago" (v. 870) to beat the same cadence, "Le sang Romain, le sang Romain, ô Dieux" (VI, 394). But in between these passages he successfully applies his theory of compensation when, after failing to meet Vergil's balance and concision, "vincet amor patriae laudumque immensa cupido" (v. 823) in his "Mais tout sera vaincu par la memoire / De la patrie, & l'ardeur de la gloire" (VI, 391), he more resoundingly adapts the unimposing "gener adversis instructus Eoïs" (v. 831) with the balanced "Contre Occident les peuples de l'Aurore" (VI, 391). Implied in Roman grandeur and the "memoire de la patrie" is the concept of *pietas,* easily the most difficult single word in Vergil to translate precisely since it connotes the maintenance of proper relations with the cosmos, Gods, Rome and family, and a sense of justice and responsibility toward all humanity. Du Bellay's compensation adapts well to this difficulty throughout his translation by rendering *pius Aeneas* now succinctly as "le bon Roy" (VI, 355), now resonantly as "Le pitoyable & magnanime Enee" (VI, 365), so that in the aggregate he hints at the word's collective meaning.

When Vergil's characterizations get in the way of Du Bellay's pe-

[41] Salmon Macrin's 1550 ode to Du Bellay refers to his "Felix Olivae" (I, 5). Although his antipathy toward the *rhétoriqueurs* forbade him from approaching the richness of Vergil's internal rhymes, as in "duras immittere curas" (*Aen.* IV, 488), he often compensated by fashioning the same rhythm: "deslïer les captives pensées" (VI, 291).

culiar preoccupations, he has trouble harmonizing rhythm and meaning. His strange desire to vindicate Dido's honor (VI, 249–252) led him to suppress the incriminating "Praebuerim sceleri brachia nostra tuo" in his translation of Ovid's *Heroides VII* (VI, 321) and to betray Vergil's evenness and epic repetition in "Speluncam Dido dux et Troianus eandem" (*Aen.* IV, 124, 165); at first he juxtaposes Dido and Aeneas as Vergil did, "Avec' Didon le Troien capitaine" (VI, 266), but then, while masterfully approximating the dactylic rhythm, he accentuates Dido at Aeneas' expense by substituting *la belle* for *dux* in "Didon la belle & le Troien ensemble" (VI, 268). In most cases, however, Du Bellay manages to reproduce closely the Augustan poet's characterization by matching his rhythm in dialogue and the point of view expressed by that rhythm. Many of Aeneas' actions are controlled by an awareness of his divine origin, "nate dea," and mission, but Dido throws his divine and noble lineage back in his face. Vergil suggests her anger through a striking enjambement and a grating succession of sounds, "generis nec Dardanus auctor, / perfide . . . cautibus horrens / Caucasus" (vv. 365–367), while Du Bellay achieves the same contrast through the rhymes *autheur-menteur* and similar sound values (VI, 282). Later, the insistence that calibrates Dido's lament, "Quin *morere,* ut *mer*ita es, f*erro*que av*er*te dol*orem*" (v. 547) becomes "*Meurs* plus tost, *meurs,* digne de ce *malheur*" (VI, 295). And when Vergil deploys an expansive movement to imply Anna's growing realization, "Hoc rogus iste mihi, hoc ignes araeque parabant" (v. 676), Du Bellay's verse is progressively expansive: "Ce feu, ce boys, ces beaux autelz secrez" (VI, 304). Dido's assonant prophecy of Hannibal, "Exor*i*are al*i*qu*i*s nostr*i*s ex oss*i*bus ultor" (v. 625), is only slightly altered by Du Bellay's "S*o*r de n*o*z *o*z, t*o*y, quiqu*o*nques d*o*is estre / N*o*stre vangeur" (VI, 301), but it is usually in alliterative effects that Du Bellay recreates the most faithfully. Even though he could not reproduce the metrical emphasis of Dido's fury in Ovid's "relinquas" (*Heroides VII,* 133) nor the enclitic structure in Vergil's "Mene fugis?" (*Aen.* IV, 314), the verbal precision of his "tu me fuys" (VI, 322) and "Me fuis-tu donq' " (VI, 279) equals the Latin models respectively when they are broken down into syllabic count. The Queen's suggestive description of the Massylian priestess' powers, "*vertere* sid*era retro;* / noc*tur*nosque *m*ovet *M*anis" (v. 488) returns as "*Tu* l*uy verr*as pa*r* ses *ver*s *murmur*ez / *Tir*er *de* nuict les esp*ris* conj*ur*ez" (VI, 291), while the meaning, sound, rhythm and syntax of "ni*gr*antem commixta *gr*andine nimbum" (v. 120) are preserved in "*Gr*osse de pluye & de *gr*esle menue" (VI, 266) and "*gr*avidam imperiis belloque frementem" (v. 229) in "*Gr*osse d' empire & superbe à la guerre" (VI, 273).[42]

The synclitic nature of Latin, as seen in the last example, authorizes some of the linguistic innovations the Pléiade sponsored for the enrichment of the language. The verbal substantives, neologisms and *provignement* recommended by the *Illustration,* ch. VI, recur in Du Bellay's translation as *songers* (VI, 258), *anuytoit* (VI, 289) and *gallées* (VI, 298, 335), but it is principally his *mots composés* that reveal the verbal texture of the *Aeneid.* This type of compression allows him not only to condense in his decasyllable, "Bache, Apollon, & Cere porte-lois" (VI, 261), all that is included in the more supple hexameter, "legiferae Cereri Phoeboque patrique Lyaeo" (*Aen.* IV, 58), but also to stress the role of Ceres the Lawgiver as Vergil did. Du Bellay's "Hecaté troy'-foy'-jumelle" (VI, 293) is no more and no less imposing than "tergeminamque Hecaten" (*Aen.* IV, 511), but the translation of Monaco (*Aen.* VI, 830) as *Port-hercule* (VI, 391) has almost no justification.

This procedure is nearly identical to the tropes antonomasia and periphrasis which imprint Du Bellay's personality on his translation. His *Dieu messager* (VI, 274) is an adaptation of Vergil's bland *Ille* (*Aen.* IV, 238), and his translation of *saltem placidis* (*Aen.* VI, 371) as *plus doux element* (VI, 363) evinces a Renaissance stylistic proclivity. Chamard's flat statement, however, that "Le latin ne dit rien de tel" about Du Bellay's version, "Source du Pau vers l'Aurore courant" (VI, 381), of "unde superne / plurimus Eridani par silvam volvitur amnis" (*Aen.* VI, 658–659) certainly maligns the translator's license to reproduce ideas closely, since the Eridanus and the Po are names for the same river and *l'Aurore* is suitable for "the world above." Du Bellay extends this license to rhetorical structure in *Aeneid* IV, 525–526, where he invents a chiasmus to suggest the interpenetration of nature implied in Vergil's text:

> Quand sur la terre, en *l'air* & sur *les eaux,*
> Bestes des champs & *poissons* & *oizeaux* (VI, 294)

Yet while this license betrays stylistic and structural preoccupations of the translator, it also coincides with Vergil's intent. The polysyndeton that Du Bellay employed in all types of poetry and that enjoyed popularity among the Pléiade,

[42] Cf. VI, 226, with *Aen.* IV, 131–132, where by preserving Vergil's initial consonants and zeugma Du Bellay recreates the military cadence and single purpose of the hunt; VI, 274, with *Aen.* IV, 247–248; VI, 302, with *Aen.* IV, 651; VI, 393, with *Aen.* VI, 857.

*Ores* le somme & *ores* le reveil,
*Ores* les clost d'ung eternel sommeil: (VI, 274)

accurately reproduces in several verses the rhythm of a single hexameter, "dat somnos adimitque, et lumina morte resignat" (*Aen.* IV, 244). To charge Du Bellay with redundance and systematic formulae is to charge the Roman poet with the same vices.[43] Vergil's avoidance of the fragmentizing effects of asyndeton corresponds to his pervading search for stylistic coherence and logical order. So when Du Bellay transcribes Dido's curse by means of polysyndeton, he is simply responding to a figure that Vergil employed several times in the same passage:

*Voicy* les sorts, *voicy* Phebus l'augure,
*Voicy* apres l'ambassadeur Mercure,
(VI, 283)

*Num* fletu ingemuit nostro? *Num* lumina flexit?
*Num* lacrimas victus dedit, aut misesratus amantem est?
. . . . . . . . . *Nunc* augur Apollo,
*nunc* Lyciae sortes, *nunc* et Iove missus ab ipso
(vv. 369–370, 376–377)[44]

Du Bellay's rejection of the alexandrine in favor of the decasyllable in his translations, thereby forcing many enjambements, and Saulnier's feeling that his poetry "ne se distingue pas dans l'art du rejet et de l'enjambement,"[45] require extended comment on this syntactical phenomenon. He rarely allows a pointless enjambement in his adaptations of the *Aeneid,* using it to establish emotional opposition, dramatic emphasis and descriptive action; the point of inquiry, then, should be to what extent this reflects Vergil's style and thought. The sense and syntax of the translation remain faithful to Vergil's skillful manipulation of enjambement for heightened emotional opposition, as in Dido's wavering indecision before her expected fall where Du Bellay maintains the Latin prolepsis, in the implied contrast between the invocation

[43] And indeed one of Vergil's major critics, Richard Heinze, makes this charge in Dido's plea to Aeneas. *Virgils epische Technik* (1915), pp. 425–426.

[44] The repetition of Du Bellay's "Desja desja" and of his anaphora "Je l'ay receu . . . Je l'ay logé . . . J'ay garanty" suggests Dido's frenzied "Iam iam" (v. 371) and "*Eiectum* litore, *egentem / excepi*" (vv. 373–374). Cf. VI, 303 with *Aen.* IV, 660. Elsewhere Du Bellay's fault lies in being actually less repetitive and rhetorical than his model (VI, 94–95).

[45] *Du Bellay,* p. 148. In another context Saulnier implicitly approves of the decasyllable, pointing out that the dactylic hexameter is longer than one alexandrine but shorter than two: "Joachim du Bellay et son *Regret* latin de la patrie," *Fin du moyen âge et renaissance* (1961), p. 272.

to Rome ("dum conderet urbem," *Aen.* I, 5) and the founding of Carthage, and in the description of Dido's actual decline and fall:

| | |
|---|---|
| Ce seul ici mon ame ballencée<br>A esbranlé:<br>(VI, 259) | . . . animumque labantem<br>impulit:<br>(vv. 22–23) |
| Qui de nouveau une vile a fondée<br>A petit prix:<br>(VI, 272) | . . . in finibus urbem<br>exiguam pretio posuit,<br>(vv. 211–212) |
| Pour toy je suis aux Libyques provinces<br>Faite haineuse, & aux Nomades princes:<br>Pour toy aussi le Tyrien m'honnore<br>Moins que devant:<br>(VI, 279) | Te propter Libycae gentes Nomadumque tyranni<br>odere, infesi Tyrii; te propter eundem<br>extinctus pudor,<br>(vv. 320–322) |

Even when Vergil's syntax does not authorize it, his meaning justifies the enjambement which Du Bellay uses in both books to establish the opposition of an affirmation to a negation: "Quand tu soumis ta royale grandeur / A ce meschant" (VI, 299; cf. *Aen.* IV, 597) and "Mais ilz voudroient quelquefois en ces terres / N'estre venuz" (VI, 346; cf. *Aen.* VI, 86). Concerning dramatic emphasis, Vergil's structure is often followed, as in the message sent to earth from Jove himself (*ab ipso*), "celeris mandata per auras / detulit" ("M'en a par l'air apporté la nouvelle / Jusques icy," *Aen.* IV, 357–358 and VI, 282). More often, however, Du Bellay either justifiably modifies the enjambement, "Exstinxti te meque, soror, populumque patresque / Sidonios urbemque tuam" ("Ta mort, ô soeur! en ruyne delaisse / Moy, ta cité, ton peuple & ta noblesse," *Aen.* IV, 682–683 and VI, 305), or else, retaining the sense, fabricates his own: "Osera-il aborder la Princesse / En sa fureur?" (VI, 277). But it is in the descriptions of action that Du Bellay's enjambement abandons the Latin structure in order to capture fully the meaning. His double adverbs emphasize Aeneas' prolonged stay in Carthage, "Es-tu icy au dormir arresté / Si longuement?" (VI, 296), while the Trojan captain's separation from Italy, "Finablement nous touchons l'Italie / Fuyant de nous" (VI, 345) and Palinurus' presumptuous wish to cross the Stygian marsh, "Entreprens-tu, sans congé, de passer / A l'autre bord?" (VI, 364) are similarly expressed.

Despite the adverse criticism heaped on his translations of Vergil's epic and the critical praise bestowed on his minor translations, the brief *Aeneid* passages he revised for Le Roy's anthology are in most cases inferior to the longer descriptive passages of Books IV and VI from which they are drawn. Two passages of cosmic proportion will show the importance of attention to detail in approximating Vergil's thought.

In *Aeneid* IV, 509–516, Dido invokes "ter centum deos," which Du Bellay translated as exactly "Trois cens Dieux" for the Le Roy collection (VI, 418). His 1552 version of "Bien troy'-cent Dieux" (VI, 293) is more accurate, however, since "ter centum" and "sex centum" were often used in Latin as vague exaggerations and here add to the mystery and magnitude of the scene. Among the deities invoked is Hecate in her role as three-faced goddess. His earlier translation is more faithful than his 1558 version, since "L'herbe nouvelle à la lune cuillir" is not only closer to Vergil's "ad lunam" than "L'herbe nouvelle on fauche au cler serain," but the implied reference to the goddess Luna is closer to Vergil's command of the language of Roman ritual. This ritual is repeated in the lower world when Anchises explains the nature of the soul. Du Bellay's translation of *Aeneid* VI, 724, mirrors Vergil's ordering of heaven, earth and sea, but in the Le Roy anthology he substitutes fire for heaven. The substitution is probably influenced by his translation of Manilius which immediately precedes in the collection and which orders the elements from fire through water. Du Bellay's new ordering creates a serious and confusing redundancy when Anchises proceeds to speak of the fiery life-spirit that issues from those elements. The confusion of the anthology translation is compounded six verses later when Du Bellay omits Vergil's verse "mens agitat molem et magno se corpore miscet." The ellipsis causes a mistranslation of Vergil's following verse and a misreference of the word *Inde* in "De cest esprit hommes, bestes, oyseaux," which is far more accurately reproduced in his translation of Book VI as "Par cest accord, hommes, bestes, oyseaux" (VI, 385).

His translation of Vergil's two books is, naturally, imperfect in more than a few places. It lacks the even faithfulness of des Masures' version, perhaps the best Renaissance translation of the *Aeneid.* But Du Bellay's work is far better than most of his critics have allowed, who may have paid too close attention to his earlier condemnation and not enough to the actual text of his translations. If he was a *traditore* to his energetic attack on translations, he was generally faithful in his own role as *traduttore.* In any case, it seems clear that most of his weaknesses stem from an excessive adherence to the poetic theories he outlined in 1549—yet the translator has an obligation to the idiom of his own generation—and not from a failure to appreciate the style or understand the inspiration of Vergil's great epic. Equally important, we see that after more mature reflection Du Bellay saw no absolute distinctions in theory or in practice between imitation, translation and poetic creativity.

### L'Olive

The cooperation among the varieties of imitation and translation in poetic creativity are seen as early as *L'Olive.* In the 1550 preface Du Bellay outlines the way in which art assists nature through imitation of "docte et ingenieuse" Latin and Italian poetry. His untempered answer to Sebillet, "je me vante d'avoir inventé ce que j'ay mot à mot traduit des aultres," is quickly qualified and explained by his contention that in his poetry there is "beaucoup plus de naturelle invention que d'artificielle ou supersticieuse immitation." What he means by "natural invention" is clearly, if blithely, articulated as a restatement of the natural memory—ingrained in the intellect and consubstantial with the normal flow of thought—described in *Ad Herennium* III, xvi, 28–29: "Si, par la lecture des bons livres, je me suis imprimé quelques traictz en la fantaisie, qui apres, venant à exposer mes petites conceptions selon les occasions qui m'en sont données, me coulent beaucoup plus facilement en la plume qu'ilz ne me reviennent en la memoire, doibt on pour ceste raison les appeller pieces rapportées?" Since in the *Deffence et Illustration* he advised the future poet to school himself in the precepts of antiquity, to study nature as it is faithfully imitated by classical writers and to assimilate these eternal literary archetypes on which he himself would develop variations, Du Bellay was not in the least disturbed by the results of natural invention: "Si deux peintres s'efforcent de representer au naturel quelque vyf protraict, il est impossible qu'ilz ne se rencontrent en mesmes traictz & lineamens, ayans mesme exemplaire devant eulx. Combien voit on entre les Latins immitateurs des Grecz, & entre les modernes Italiens immitateurs des Latins, de commencemens & de fins de vers, de couleurs & figures poëtiques quasi semblables?" Once again attacking the "rimasseurs" for having neglected the language's "nayfve proprieté si copieuse & belle," he especially stresses the need to "enrichir nostre vulgaire de figures & locutions estrangeres." But he makes the important qualification that he will strive to resemble only himself despite his borrowing of traditional figures. According to Du Bellay, then, the foremost question of *L'Olive* is how his borrowings, ranging from outright but limited translations to complete modifications of themes, images and structures, reflect his own natural inclinations; how assimilation and reproduction of archetypes, more than servile copying of appearances, allow him to remold tradition and establish a place for himself.

Du Bellay's commentators have generally applauded his innovations in the sonnet, have on a few occasions congratulated his choice of a poetic form that lends itself well to rhetorical configurations and discursive argument, yet most praise has been reserved for his later expansion of the sonnet sequence to include both elegy and satire.[46] Although *L'Olive* is the first of many French sonnet sequences in the Petrarchan tradition, the poet's early experiments with the form itself have often been relegated to the status of *juvenilia* and his critical comments on it are considered inadequate. Following Sainte-Beuve, Chamard pointed out that Du Bellay is more concerned in the *Deffence et Illustration* with abstracted forms of art than with its contents, and that his comments on the sonnet form are incomplete.[47] To be sure, his observation that the sonnet's adherence to certain rules and limits differs from the ode's considerable freedom (p. 121) and his later exaggerated opposition of the laborious Italian sonnet to the versatile ode (IV, 47) want further comment. But the search for freedom within accepted limitations essentially defines Du Bellay's attitude toward the sonnet, even in the early collections. Despite the unchallenged assumption that Ronsard regularized the French sonnet in the *Amours,* published in October, 1552,[48] we should credit Du Bellay's "XIII Sonnetz de l'honneste amour," published on February 1, 1552, with this accomplishment. There the four tercet rhyme schemes are created by alternating masculine and feminine rhymes in the CCDEED and CC DEDE dispositions. Since Ronsard refashioned several of these poems in his Cassandre sonnets and since Du Bellay's sequence is highly unified and Ronsard's is not, it would be absurd to suppose that Du Bellay imitated Ronsard's still unpublished manuscript. His initiative in the early sonnets is greater than is often conceded, and his awareness of the importance of rhyme and of the possibilities of innovation in the tercets is clearly seen in *L'Olive.*

Such a realization is, of course, essential when adapting Italian verse—where repeated tonic stress within a given verse diminishes the importance of rhyme—to French where rhyme is one of the primary determinants of meaning in a poem. On occasion, the poor quality of the rhymes *deffence-offence* (sonnet 63), in disregard of the *Illus-*

[46] See Grimal, p. 31; Max Jasinski, *Histoire du sonnet en France* (1903), pp. 56, 58; Alfred Satterthwaite, *Spenser, Ronsard and Du Bellay: A Renaissance Comparison* (1960), p. 64; Weber, p. 419; Chamard, *Du Bellay,* pp. 378, 522.

[47] C. A. Sainte-Beuve, *Tableau historique et critique de la poésie française au XVIe siècle* (1843), p. 344; Chamard, *Histoire,* I, 195–196.

[48] See Vianey, "Origines du sonnet régulier," *Revue de la Renaissance,* IV (1903), 88–90; Ronsard, ed. Laumonier, IV, xvi; Chamard, *Histoire,* IV, 97; cf. Saulnier, *Du Bellay,* p. 72.

*tration's* sound precepts for rhyming, may condemn a quatrain to a facile Petrarchan antithesis that prejudices the remainder of the sonnet. And while the end of the first tercet of sonnet 32 "Non la vertu, l'esprit & la raison" opposes not only the ephemeral pleasures of nature described in the preceding verses but also opposes the ten feminine rhymes that fade like those sensual attractions, it fails to correspond in meaning to the other line of masculine rhyme at the end of the sonnet, "Ny la rigueur de la froide saison." But Du Bellay's rhyming achievements lie in his more frequent awareness of the ability of semantically oppositional or complementary rhymes to forward the argument of a sonnet, and in this awareness we can appreciate how imitation can become creation.

As a possible source for Du Bellay's sonnet 13, Chamard proposes Giovanni Mozzarello's "O bella man che'l fren del carro tieni" which contains such uninspiring rhymes as *tieni-mantieni*. If this sonnet is indeed Du Bellay's source, then his major modification consists of lightening the grammatical punctuation so as to expand his poem into one fluid sentence where the B rhymes punctuate the flow of thought leading up to the main action in the first tercet, "a gravé le protraict":

> La belle main, dont la forte foiblesse
> D'un joug captif domte les plus puissans,
> La main, qui rend les plus sains languissans,
> Debendant l'arc meurtrier qui les coeurs blesse,
> La belle main, qui gouverne & radresse
> Les freinz dorez des oiseaux blanchissans,
> Quand sur les champs de pourpre rougissans
> Guydent en l'air le char de leur maistresse, . . .

The octave itself is composed of two balanced tableaux vivants in which the descent of *puissans* into *languissans* illustrates the debilitating force of "La belle main" and the background "pourpre rougissans" places the "oiseaux blanchissans" into broad relief. Again, the action in the sestet of sonnet 88 adheres to the CCDEED rhyme disposition:

> La forest prent sa verde robe neufve,
> La terre aussi, qui naguere etoit veufve,
> Promet de fruictz une accroissance pleine.
> Or cesse donq' l'hiver de mes douleurs,
> Et vous plaisirs, naissez avec' les fleurs
> Au beau Soleil, qui mon printemps rameine.

as *neufve-veufve* and *douleurs-fleurs* juxtapose affirmative and negative statement, while *pleine-rameine* abandon Petrarch's Christian *pietate-*

*onestate* in order to reinforce the idea of natural rebirth as the analogue of the poet's feeling.[49]

This careful attention to the rhyme as the normal terminus and focal point of each verse and his ability to establish the individual contribution of each of the sonnet's five basic rhymes to the collective statement augment the impact of enjambement as a means of amplifying various stages of the poetic argument. Sannazaro's pleasurable vision of *Arcadia,* "vedendo per li soli boschi gli affettuosi colombi con soave mormorio baciarsi," is filtered through Du Bellay's memory in sonnet 84 and condensed as the languid "Resvant au bien qui me faict doloreux, / Les longs baisers des collombs amoureux." As an index to the contrast between the scene he witnesses and the pain he feels, the second quatrain begins with "Heureux oiseaux, que vostre vie est pleine / De grand' doulceur!" where the overflow of plenitude into the following verse becomes the spatial coefficient of the poet's thought. Sonnet 103 formulizes its Petrarchan model by beginning the quatrains with "Mais quel hiver" and "Mais quele main." This rigidity gives way in the first tercet to "As-tu [Nature] donc faict une chose si belle / Pour la deffaire" which graphically reproduces the affirmation and denial of Petrarch's simple "far cose e disfar." That Du Bellay tries to distinguish his poem from his models by means of rhyme alterations is obvious in numerous sonnets. His sonnet 5, which changes Petrarch's Easter Morning to Christmas Eve, also modifies the character of the line endings. Whereas Petrarch's sonnet 3 alternates parataxis in the first quatrain with hypotaxis in the second, Du Bellay completely reverses the procedure in his quatrains; and while the last sestet of the French sonnet is hypotactic, his model for the last six verses, Ariosto's sonnet 2, is entirely paratactic. A convenient example of Du Bellay's transformation of one or perhaps two models simultaneously is the first quatrain of sonnet 3:

> Loyre fameux, qui ta petite source
> Enfles de maintz gros fleuves & ruysseaux,
> Et qui de loing coules tes cleres eaux
> En l'Ocean d'une assez vive course:

[49] References to Petrarch are from *Rime, Trionfi e poesie latine* (1951). The sonnet of Sansovino that Ernesta Caldarini suggests as a possible source affords thematic but not rhyme similarities to Du Bellay's tercet: "Nuove fonti italiane dell'*Olive,*" *BHRen,* XXVII (1965), 433. Sonnet 75's octave rhymes present the opposite arrangement, with the complementary *blanchissans-rougissans, verdissans-florissans* followed by the oppositional *decloses-encloses.* In sonnet 2 he transforms Sansovino's coloration and theme of Christian spirituality into a progression from physical to pagan spirituality, largely through the rhymes: "Son chef de l'or, ses deux levres des rozes"—"Mist en l'esprit ses semences encloses" (vv. 10, 13).

Caldarini proposes A. G. Corso's

> Fiume, che in Adria in più spacievol giri
> Ricco di mille fonti altier discendi,

in addition to Giovanni Guidiccioni's

> Arno, puoi ben portar tra gli altri fiumi
> Superbo il corno; & le tue Nimphe belle
> Riverenti venir a farle honore.

as sources from which the French sonnet is derived.[50] In both cases the description is primarily adjectival in order to stress the aura of the river's magnificence. Du Bellay's version stresses the river's movement for a different effect as, through verbal action and enjambement, the stream swells into the river and the river flows into the ocean.

If his enjambement focuses on rhyme precisely by disregarding the momentary stasis it assumes, his calculated use of assonance and especially internal rhyme accentuates the role of similar sounds and their thematic and semantic values, yet without ever contesting the importance of end rhyme through *rimes équivoquées*. The rhyming variations in lines like

> *Mere* d'Amour & fille de la *mer*
> Du cercle ti*ers* lumi*ere* souverene, (sonnet 52)

may seem contrived at first glance, and an examination of his source, "Figlia di Giove & madre alma d'Amore" shows that Du Bellay strove for the rhyme by inverting Lelio Capilupi's components. But the word arrangement integrates the personae into the mythological family that inhabits *L'Olive* and links it to sonnet 48 which begins "Pere Ocean, commencement des choses." Similarly, verses like "L'h*eur*eux malh*eur* de l'espoir qui m'attire, / Si le plai*sir*, suject de mon mart*ire*" (sonnet 46) with their similar sounds sustain the oxymoron that blends the theme of pleasure and pain. Du Bellay apparently delights in expanding a brief allusion to sound effects into the main attraction of his verse or in reducing disparate segments of his model into one commanding image. Sonnet 87 draws upon Girolamo Volpe's "dolce suono mormorate" and "Quest*o* vas*o* d'am*ono* & cr*oco* pien*o*" and, through a full range of linguistic resources including onomatopoeia, alliteration, assonance and internal rhyme, develops it into

> *Vent* doulx soufl*ant, vent* des *vens* souver*ain,*
> Qui *voletant* d'aeles b*ien em*panées
> Fais respir*er* de souëves halen*é*es
> Ta doulce Flore au *v*isage serain,
> Pren de mes *mains* ce *v*ase, qui est pl*ein* . . .

---

[50] P. 420.

Four sonnets later he welds Bernardino Tomitano's "rendete al Sole . . . l'oro" into "Rendez à l'*or* cete couleur, qui d*ore*." The internal rhymes, both perfect and imperfect, of the last two examples recur in *L'Olive,* frequently in a conventional 4 + 6 verse that avoids confusing one decasyllable with two five syllable verses and that repeats the same sounds in subtly altered sequences for an incantational effect. Brief examples drawn both from quatrains and tercets illustrate the pervasiveness of this internal rhyming through the full range of the sonnet.[51] The quatrains of sonnet 58 end with closely balanced lines that encompass similar but more randomly organized sounds:

> De tes yeulx s*ort* le feu qu*i* me dev*ore*.
> Donques le prix de celuy qui t'honnore,
> Est-ce la mort & le marbre endurcy?
> O pleurs ingratz! ingratz soupirs aussi,
> Mon feu, ma m*ort,* & ta r*i*gueur enc*ore*.

Sonnet 96 is patterned on Petrarch's *expeditio,* but while the Tuscan poet limits his negative enumeration to the octave, Du Bellay extends it throughout the sonnet in a procedure he will make famous in the *Regrets.* His first tercet introduces a series of internal rhymes which he doubles in order to vary the otherwise monotonous rhythm and amplify the richness of the subject he describes,

> Ny les pili*ers* des sainctz temples dor*ez,*
> Ny les pal*ais* de marbre elabour*ez,*
> Ny l'*or* enc*or',* ny la p*erle* tant *clere,*

although the second tercet contains the unfortunate alliteration, "Ny le *p*laisir *p*ouroit *p*laire à mes yeulx," initiated in the preceding verses.

Du Bellay's desire to expand his source, as with Bernardo Accolti's "Che l'cor mi tra' del corpo e'n cielo il porta," occasionally creates a halting rhythm unjustified by the sonnet's context and exceeding even Scève's most copious series of abstractions (cf. *Délie* 56): "Coeur, corps, esprit, sens, ame & vouloir emblent" (sonnet 4). But his progressively expansive invocations, such as "Sacrée, saincte & celeste figure" (sonnet 38) condensed from Francesco Maria Molza's cluttered "Santa, sacra, celeste & sola imago," and conclusions like "Saincte, pudique & chaste Cyprienne" (sonnet 104), rival those of the best sonneteers from Ronsard to Mallarmé. His powers of elaborative condensation are seen in sonnet 77 where his last tercet abandons his model, Petrarch's "Lieti fiori," to bring together all of the natural forces invoked and developed in the body of the poem: "je seroy' fleuve &

[51] Cf. "Ores qu'en l'*air* le grand Dieu du tonn*erre*" (sonnet 45) and "Chasse noz *jours* sans espoir de ret*our*" (sonnet 113).

rive, / Roc, source, fleur, & ruisselet encore". Ronsard, focusing partially on the same model and perhaps imitating Du Bellay, closes his sonnet in like manner, yet without ever indicating the particular value of each enumerated component "Tailliz, forestz, rivages & fontaines, / Antres, prez, fleurs, dictes le luy pour moy."[52]

Like the bee moving from one flower to another, to use the Pléiade's favorite description of their multiple inspiration, Du Bellay frequently condenses two or three sources into the development of a sonnet in a multitude of ways. His amalgamation may include imagery combined from Petrarch and Vergil followed by a revised passage (sonnet 31) from the *Orlando Furioso;* or it may comprise disparate segments from the same poet, as in sonnet 70 which brings together and alters a quatrain and tercet from the beginning of Petrarch's *Rime sparse* with those from another sonnet that is located near the middle of that collection; or, in sonnet 62, it can remold the theme of one sonnet from the *Rime* to the development of the following sonnet in Petrarch's sequence. But however ingeniously varied these borrowings may be, they rarely harmonize the individual charm and greatness of divergent poetic visions. Representative of that deficient coordination is sonnet 33 with its twin sources of Petrarch and Ariosto, and Du Bellay's extrapolation of those sources:

> O prison doulce, ou captif je demeure
> Non par dedaing, force ou inimitié,
> Mais par les yeulx de ma doulce moitié,
> Qui m'y tiendra jusq'à tant que je meure.
> O l'an heureux, le mois, le jour & l'heure,
> Que mon coeur fut avecq' elle allié!
> O l'heureux noeu, par qui j'y fu' lié,
> Bien que souvent je plain', souspire & pleure!
> Tous prisonniers, vous etes en soucy,
> Craignant la loy & le juge severe:
> Moy plus heureux, je ne suis pas ainsi.
> Mile doulx motz, doulcement exprimez,
> Mil' doulx baisers, doulcement imprimez,
> Sont les tormens ou ma foy persevere.

In the first half of the poem Du Bellay's awareness of rhyme value permits him to sustain tensions that correspond to the poem's argument: the coexistence of pleasure and pain. The paradoxically matched rhymes *demeure* and *meure,* the counterpoint of the two verses between them, and the grammatical similarities of verses 5 and 7, 6 and 8 that

[52] Ed. Laumonier, IV, 60.

offset the introverted rhymes ending those lines, all contribute to the mood of paradox and especially to a synthesis of sources, since verses 5 and 6 are basically Petrarchan while verses 7 and 8 come primarily from Ariosto. Petrarch's roughly sequential expansion and contraction of time, "Benedetto sia 'l giorno e 'l mese e l'anno / e la stagione e 'l tempo e l'ora," is reduced and unified by Du Bellay, and the Petrarchan beatitude is applied to Ariosto's knot that binds. But despite his plaintive assonance in that quatrain and his alliteratively descriptive use of *m*'s that seal the lips in the last tercet, the facile rhyming of *exprimez* with *imprimez* and the considerable distance between the D rhymes detract from that success. Even more serious, the apparent insertion of the Petrarchan passage separates "j'y fu' lié" (v. 7) from its supposed referent "prison doulce" and leaves that whole hemistich grammatically and logically vague. This vagueness is compounded by the substitution of "Bien que" for the blessing Petrarch gives his torment, since Du Bellay thus transforms the tension of paradox into a contradiction that he fails to develop. Moreover, the sudden and absolute address to the prisoners in Du Bellay's allegorization of Ariosto (v. 9) forces an uncomfortable contrast with the necessarily indecisive mood of the first quatrain. So it seems that Du Bellay was either unaware of the subtle distinction between the paradox he found in his two sources and simple contradiction, or else his imitation was unable to give rise to recreation in this sonnet.

Aneau was quick to realize these shortcomings and repeatedly brought them to the poet's attention. He corrected Du Bellay's grammatical referents in a sonnet overladen with logical connectives (20), and in his grammatical lesson on sonnet 10 he jocosely, although perhaps accidentally, stressed Ramus' important conceptual term *liens* in attacking the poetic logic: "Tout ce sonnet est de connexion mal jointe, & mal liez y sont les liens avec le feu & le trait. Car traitz liez ne font nul mal, & le feu pourroit bien brusler les liens." The significance of this criticism derives from the way in which the combined Trivium furnishes Aneau his aesthetic criteria, for he concludes his objection with the rhetorical terminology: "Appren donq à bien figurer." Du Bellay apparently learned his lesson well by sonnet 93 where we see him borrowing Petrarch's "effetto" and "cagion" as he moves from effect to the cause of his alternation between pleasure and pain. From there he proceeds to the logically introduced first tercet, "Madame donc," and incorporates Ariosto's Wheel of Fortune as the causal and pictorial analogue of the effect he undergoes.

The extent to which he learned his rhetoric properly remains a contentious point. Guido Saba occasionally admires it while Chamard invariably laments it.[53] But whether he was its master or its victim, normative rhetoric assumes a dominant position in *L'Olive* and therefore deserves more than the allusive treatment it has so far received. Du Bellay's condensation of Ariosto's "chiara eloquenzia che deriva da un fonte di saper" into "en esprit, en faconde" (sonnet 18) evinces a concern for the normal passage from invention to elocution in poetic composition. Salmon Macrin's 1550 dedication to *L'Olive* associates "Facunde Bellaï" with Horace and Quintilian (I, 4–5), and Du Bellay's own "l'ecolle de faconde" (sonnet 8) is a revealing paraphrase of Ariosto's "alti stili" and "scole insegnaro" that implies the persuasive power of a forceful style. Even when his eloquence succumbs to the ineffable beauty of his love, he is merely following a rhetorical topos that Curtius has traced from the beginning of poetry.[54]

The 1550 preface to *L'Olive* underlines the need to enrich French poetry with poetic figures, "elire pour decorer." But rather than compiling a list of the figures he uses, it is often more instructive to see how he modifies his borrowings to obtain those figures and to see how his borrowing accordingly alters the poetic vision. For instance, his modification of Navagero's loosely organized

> Quanto ringrazio il ciel et la mia stella,
> Ch'in sorte dato m'han si dolce ardore,
> Quanto amor, che t'aperse al cor la via.

to obtain the common polysyndeton we discussed in the last chapter,

> Combien le ciel favorable je clame,
> Combien Amour, combien ma destinée, (sonnet 22)

stresses the essential relatedness of the forces that pleasantly conspire against him. The modification may add only prolixity, witness the expansion of Petrarch's "destra" and "manco" into "main la plus forte" and "le flanc qui est le plus debile" (sonnet 69). Or it may restructure and refine the entire imitation, as the following example indicates. The octave of sonnet 24 flows more freely than Battista della Torre's sonnet which specifies Echo in the opening verse, paratactically arranges the

[53] Saba, *La Poesia di Joachim du Bellay* (1962), p. 80; Chamard, *Joachim du Bellay,* p. 186 and *Histoire,* I, 239–240.

[54] *European Literature and the Latin Middle Ages* (1963), pp. 159–162. In his commentary on "Ny de son chef le tresor crespelu" of *Amours I,* Muret surmises that Ronsard "n'a point esté asservi par les beautez corporelles de sa dame, ains seulement par le bon esprit, & par l'eloquence qui est en elle": *Oeuvres,* p. 25.

poet's address and presents the nymph's response by means of the balanced line called compar or isocolon

> Tu radoppi i miei tristi ultimi accenti:
> Tu col mio spesso il tuo dolor confondi:
> S'io grido Furnia, & tu Furnia rispondi; (vv. 5–7)

Du Bellay's reference to Echo is not made specific until his seventh verse where he eschews controlled balance in favor of the figure epizeuxis for heightened emotion: "Olive Olive: & Olive est ta voix." The progressively diminished voice created by this imbalance returns in "France, France, respons à ma triste querelle. / Mais nul, sinon Echo, ne respond à ma voix" (II, 59), where Echo enters as an indifferent witness to the poet's torment. In *L'Olive* Echo commiserates with him and Narcissus becomes the mythic analogue of the unfeeling Olive. Elsewhere Du Bellay makes similar verses physically intimate the idea of reflection between tercets and between physical and ideal beauty:

> Ceste beauté, seul miroir de mes yeux:
> Ceste beauté, dont la saincte merveille, (II, 249)

Similar configuration in sonnet 24

> Pareille amour nous avons eprouvée,
> Pareille peine aussi nous souffrons ores.
> Mais plus grande est la beaulté qui me tue.

intimates the reciprocity of pleasure and pain. Moreover, it frames the beauty of Narcissus which is the source of those feelings in Echo and ultimately the source of his own demise, and prepares the even greater beauty that plagues the narrator who finally individualizes his predicament in the last verse. The slight modification that Du Bellay effected in eschewing the third *egual* in

> Eguale arde ambidue fiamma amorosa:
> Eguale è'l nostro amor, pari le pene;
> Et ambidue già vinse egual bellezza.

preserves the desired duality of his second tercet. The restatement of the Echo-Narcissus myth to connect reflected beauty with death returns in sonnet 79:

> Le ciel courbé se mire dans ses yeulx:
> Echo respond à sa divine voix,
> Qui faict mourir les hommes & les Dieux.

The concern for the reflection in and through art of beauty and the emotion it causes responds to the 1550 preface's idea of "representer au naturel quelque vyf protraict." But although in that context Du Bellay is speaking of the inevitability of reproducing imagery similar to the poetry he imitates, his concern for vivid portraiture is greater than any of his models. Sonnet 74 attends to Olive's beauty, "Ce que le Ciel, les Dieux & la Nature / Ont peint en vous, plus vivante peinture," moving Platonically from her physical charms, "la vive et immortelle image," to her spiritual attraction, "au vif l'esprit te fera voir," and in the following sonnet he asks nature's help in painting his reaction to that beauty. These two sonnets are apparently Du Bellay's independent creations, and when in sonnet 29 he does borrow a passage from the *Orlando Furioso* he superimposes his own terminology and alleges this time that nature's forces "De ceste forme en moy si bien emprainte / N'effaceront la vive protraiture." His insistence on painting a convincing picture of her beauty and of his feelings relates to his rhetorical wish to convince the reader that she is worthy of his efforts and to persuade her that he deserves her consideration. He tells her in sonnet 50 that if he could express his true feelings "au vif," this "preuve certaine" would allow him to bend her will to his point of view and "mouvoir tout l'univers."

Aside from antithesis, which is so universal a thought pattern as to obviate any necessary association with rhetoric, the most recurrent figure in *L'Olive* is anaphora. Du Bellay works it into his self-inspired verse, superimposes it on his imitations and elaborates it when his models themselves use it. Leo Spitzer has shown how the four verses beginning with *La* in the famous "Idea Sonnet" (113) extensively direct the poet's and the reader's point of view.[55] The poem is written in a cyclic pattern from the fallen state of the speaker who begins with the universal occurrence of human transience, "sans espoir de retour." He then relates that occurrence to his personal experience which results from the universal condition. The *La* anaphora, borrowed from Bernardino Daniello and modified, gives the impression of rising through three modes of time, earthly, edenic and the poet's participation in both:

> La, est le bien que tout esprit desire,
> La, le repos ou tout le monde aspire,
> La, est l'amour, la, le plaisir encore.
> La, ô mon ame au plus hault ciel guidée!
> Tu y pouras recongnoistre l'Idée
> De la beauté, qu'en ce monde j'adore.

[55] "The Poetic Treatment of a Platonic-Christian Theme (Du Bellay's Sonnet of the Idea)," *Comparative Literature,* VI (1954), 193–217. Cf. the similar function of the *Ici-Là* anaphora of ch. II, p. 61.

Sonnet 81 is based on a similar but less successful deployment of the same anaphora which is absent from Du Bellay's apparent source, Ludovico Dolce. Beginning with the earthly "mon desir" in the first verse, the full *La* anaphora of the second quatrain directs the eye to the eternal values Olive incarnates, while in the second tercet it redirects the point of view back to earth and brings the poetic vision full circle:

> La n'est ma soif aux ondes perissante,
> La mon espoir & se fuit & se suit,
> La meurt sans fin ma peine renaissante.

Thematically, cyclic time and space can be seen as the correlatives of man's emotional experiences. They help to associate the poet's mental world with nature and the transformations of the sun, the moon and the elements, with the narrative lines of myth and the mutations of history. Since Fortune's Wheel bespeaks the instability of human existence, the cycle may suggest either desired rebirth or unwanted recurrence.

Cyclical development is one of the basic structural principles of many sonnets in *L'Olive* and of the sequence as a whole; it will become the major organizing principle of his later sequences. The linking of consecutive poems, through either the use of the same vocabulary and rhymes or similar thematic development, helps to make *L'Olive* a traditional sonnet sequence. Frequently the closing direction of a sonnet will be countered or complemented by the opening direction of the following sonnet (e.g., 13–14, 16–19, 86–87). The descent of sonnet 106, "Ainsi d'Amour le feu puisse descendre," is met by the rise of the following poem, taken from Saint Paul, "Sus, sus, mon ame," which introduces the group of religious sonnets at the end of *L'Olive* and the triumph of the Psalms' purgatorial flame over Eros' infernal fire: "D'un nouveau feu brusle moy jusq' à l'ame, / Tant que l'ardeur de ta celeste flamme. . . ." The end of the "Idea Sonnet" returns the speaker to earth whereas the following sonnet ends with elevation, "Courez par l'air d'une aele inusitée" and introduces the Icarus theme at the end of the collection. Even when they are not consecutive, many sonnets are placed in close proximity by the common source they share, as in the case of sonnets 29, 35 and 39 each of which reshapes two different stanzas from Bradamante's plea in *Orlando Furioso* XLIV, 61–66. Overall conjoining of sonnets is increased by the end of the first sonnet, "Egal un jour au Laurier immortel," and the end of the last sonnet, "Jusq' à l'egal des Lauriers tousjours verds," which announce the opening and the closing of the sequence, and by the liturgical rhythm that encompasses them between the Christmas Eve Sonnet (5), following the traditional explanatory invocations of sonnets 1–4, and the numerous rebirth sonnets at the end of the collection.

Du Bellay's peregrine muse led him to syncretize the Christian cycle with classical myth in an effort fully to join the activities of man with the workings of the cosmos. In *L'Olive* we encounter the standard conceits of her depersonalized attributes meeting the anthropomorphized forces of nature and of myth (sonnet 86) or the equation of her perfection with the harmonized elements. Yet this correspondence between the microcosm of man and the macrocosm of nature is usually associated with a rebirth motif or a cyclical movement: the setting sun of a quatrain that pacifies the elements rises again in the tercets where Olive "Semble renaitre avec la belle Aurore" (sonnet 27), the rising and falling wheel that controls the poet's fortune conjures up the movement of elements (sonnet 35), the progressively concrete descent from heaven which becomes "amoureux de la terre" and the resulting advent of spring contrasts with the poet's interior world of the last verse, "Un triste hiver sen' en moy renaissant" (sonnet 45) and the elements extend their sympathy as the poet's precious tear in the "jardin de son ame" brings forth "mile amoureuses fleurs" (sonnet 73).

This movement unfolds within both spatial and temporal dimensions. In sonnet 95 the reader's eye descends with the poet's tear as it blends with the water and rises as his mind is projected into the past:

> Dieu qui reçois en ton giron humide
> Les deux ruisseaux de mes yeulx larmoyans,
> Qui en tes eaux sans cesse tournoyans
> Enflent le cours de ta course liquide,
> Quand fut-ce, ô Dieu! qu'en la carriere vide
> De ton beau ciel, ces cheveux ondoyans,
> Comme tes flotz au vent s'ebanoyans,
> Deça dela voguoient à pleine bride?

In answer to his question, we are thrust further into an arcadian past when the Gods and time conspired to make "Renaistre l'or de l'antique saison." The reference to the passing of the Golden Age recurs in sonnet 101 where the descent of vices to earth in the first tercet is counterbalanced by the ascent of virtues to heaven in the second. Similarly, in sonnet 11 we descend through the imperfect and pluperfect tenses from a threatening sky to a tumultuous sea, and, as Du Bellay modifies Ariosto's temporal scheme, rise suddenly to a clearing sky in the present tense and in the presence of Olive rescued from the sea.[56] The same

[56] The imbalance created by the seven-syllable line and the perpetually altered time sequence in the "Complainte du désespéré" is a reflection of the poet's inner turmoil and his unmeasurable, dreamlike feelings that incorporate autobiography and myth.

poem of Ariosto is imitated and altered in sonnet 59 where Du Bellay's song charms the rocks and trees below him as Orpheus had done before the gates of Erebus; after snatching his prize from the "bord oblivieux" he returns in the last tercet to the upper world and the source of light.

A more extensive look at descent and return as expressed by myth will show some of the possibilities inherent in the procedure and Du Bellay's exploitation of them:

> Qui a peu voir celle que Déle adore
> Se devaler de son cercle congneu,
> Vers le pasteur d'un long sommeil tenu
> Dessus le mont qui la Carie honore:
> Et qui a veu sortir la belle Aurore
> Du jaulne lict de son espoux chenu,
> Lors que le ciel encor' tout pur & nu
> De mainte rose indique se colore:
> Celuy a veu encores (ce me semble)
> Non point les lyz & les roses ensemble,
> Non ce que peult le printemps concevoir:
> Mais il a veu la beauté nompareille
> De ma Déese, ou reluyre on peult voir
> La clere Lune & l'Aurore vermeille. (sonnet 16)

Following her mythological role, Diana descends from the moon in the first quatrain toward Endymion to whom Jupiter granted perpetual youth. The Endymion myth coincides well with the various themes of *L'Olive,* since it has usually suggested the vain search for lasting satisfaction, aspiring love and poetic dreams. The Moon Goddess is met by her sister Aurora as she rises in the second quatrain and who was traditionally accompanied by the Pleiads. Aurora—Olive's other surrogate—occasionally loved mortals, such as her "espoux chenu," the feeble-voiced Tithonus; she carried him away from the earth to assure his immortality, unlike Diana, but forgot to have Jupiter grant him perpetual youth. The tensive differences between the two myths is somewhat resolved in the sestet and the distanced point of view of the first verse is sharpened by Du Bellay's parenthetical "ce me semble" which interprets the significance of redness and whiteness and brings these colors together again in the last verse. The function of the two myths in the poem and the numerous equivalences between them and the poet's situation create concision and depth in Du Bellay's sonnet and suggest the Pléiade's theory of myth as a reflexion of supra-literal truth.

Depth is also created by the blend of scriptural and para-Christian themes, which he accomplishes in a single poem or by contrasting several poems. In sonnet 112, for instance, the Platonic "occultes Idées" that introduces the octave syncretizes rather obviously with the apocalyptic "Le Juste seul ses eleuz justifie" of the first tercet. More skillfully, the third verse of sonnet 76 (Isaiah XI, 6) and the remainder of the poem (Revelation VI, 12–14):

> Quand la fureur, qui bat les grandz coupeaux,
> Hors de mon coeur l'Olive arachera,
> Avec le chien le loup se couchera,
> Fidele garde aux timides troupeaux.
> Le ciel, qui void avec tant de flambeaux,
> Le violent de son cours cessera,
> Le feu sans chault & sans clerté sera,
> Obscur le ront des deux astres plus beaux.
> Tous animaulx changeront de sejour
> L'un avec' l'autre, & au plus cler du jour
> Ressemblera la nuit humide & sombre,
> Des prez seront semblables les couleurs,
> La mer sans eau, & les forestz sans ombre,
> Et sans odeur les roses & les fleurs.

give the poet's love a backdrop that ranges from the Old to the New Testament. The first Scriptural passage, dealing with the everlasting Branch of Jesse, prophesies an eventual reconciliation in the world of nature after innumerable afflictions, and the second passage prophesies the opening of the sixth Seal to unleash cosmic woes, announcing that martyrs will be avenged for their sufferings. Du Bellay thrusts us into a distant, mysterious future that adumbrates his deliverance from torment and blends the spirituality and vast dimensions of his sources with the olive branch, symbol of his enduring love.

Equally subtle is the way in which sententiae and exempla at the conclusion of numerous sonnets teach lessons that defy specific definition as either Platonic or Christian until the latter part of the collection: "Vivant par mort d'une eternelle vie" (sonnet 22), "Tu sers d'exemple, à qui ose aspirer / Trop hardiment à chose non mortelle" (sonnet 51), "Que l'homme en vain contre Dieu s'evertue" (sonnet 63), "Qui sans mourir, & sans voler aux cieulx, / Peult contempler le paradis en terre!" (sonnet 80), "Et morte soit tousjours pour moy la mort" (sonnet 110), and "Qui en mourant triomphe de la mort" (sonnet 111). Judging from the first tercet of sonnet 68

> Ainsi courant de sommez en sommez
> Avec' Amour, je ne pense jamais,
> Fol desir mien, à te haulser la bride.

which is recast in the Christian tercets of sonnet 6 of "L'Honneste amour,"

> Ainsi l'esprit dedaignant nostre jour
> Court, fuyt, & vole en son propre sejour
> Jusques à tant que sa divine dextre
> Haulse la bride au folastre dezir

it appears that Du Bellay continued to drape mythological deities in Christian robes and to practice this *contaminatio* of the Platonic dualism of Idea and matter with the Pauline war of Spirit and flesh, perhaps through the use of natural memory, over several years.

In *L'Olive* Du Bellay introduced the French sonnet sequence and leavened it with equal amounts of translation, imitation and original creation. Some of his sonnets, such as 83 and 113, are lasting anthology pieces, but many are merely technical successes and elicit our respect only on that level. The cyclical movement to which man and nature are subject returns in the *Antiquitez,* but the poet's point of view is considerably altered by the sights of Rome and their meaning. Sonnet 83 of *L'Olive,* for instance, presents a prelapsarian scene in which the universe is abstractly painted, steeped in perfection and lacks specificity of place. In the *Antiquitez* this Parnassian detachment and its final crescendo give way to a pilgrim's involvement with the world of fallen man and a concern for the causes that led to Rome's historical decline. The added dimension of Du Bellay's actual experience before the ruins of Rome, coupled with the scenes of his mind's eye, supplant the "double cyme" with its special and therefore limiting point of view that often dominates the sonnets of *L'Olive.*

# PART THREE

CHAPTER IV

# LES ANTIQUITEZ DE ROME

ROME: its very name, fated to rule the world according to Tibullus, invokes proud visions of legions marching triumphantly through a vast empire whose perimeter was coextensive with the frontiers of civilization, of marble temples whose blood-splashed altars offered sacrifice to benevolent gods, of Roma Aeterna whose seemingly superhuman accomplishments overshadowed its merely human mold. Its greatness was both created and reflected by Vergil, Horace and Ovid, while the poignancy of its dissolution summoned the attention of Renaissance humanists like Petrarch, Castiglione and Buchanan, all of whom Du Bellay knew and assimilated into his own testimony to the ruins of Rome. Even the impressions of a Poggio Bracciolini, which predate the *Antiquitez* by more than a century and which Du Bellay may not have known, demonstrate the same concern for the former greatness of the *magna parens,* mistress of the world, whose buildings were once believed to lie beyond fortune's reach but now lie prostrate like a giant corpse, concern for the lesson of fortune's inconstancy that Rome's fall teaches us, and yet also for the former dignity the ruins cannot fully hide.[1]

Of the numerous ideological and philosophical complications that defied full resolution in the Renaissance, the conflict of Classical and Christian visions of the world was preeminent. Christianity divided Renaissance humanists from the time of Rome, and "it certainly did not allow them in practice to mold their behavior in accordance with either the Greek or the Roman example. The ancient trust in the world's being more permanent than individual man and in political structures as a guarantee of earthly survival after death did not return, so that the ancient opposition of a mortal life to a more or less immortal world failed them. Now both life and world had become perishable, mortal and futile."[2] The basic disquietude of sixteenth-century man may be easily seen by contrasting Renaissance attitudes toward the secularized society. While men like Rabelais believed that despite their mortality they could become the authors of their own destiny and achieve an individual permanence, still, with Calvin, they were realizing that by

[1] See Poggio Bracciolini, "De varietate fortunae," in *Latin Writings of the Italian Humanists,* ed. F. A. Gragg (1927), pp. 112–116. Cf. Etienne Gilson, *La Philosophie au moyen âge* (1962), p. 341.

[2] Hannah Arendt, "The Concept of History: Ancient and Modern" in *Between Past and Future* (1961), p. 74.

its own fault and free will fallen nature had succeeded divine nature and in the process had divorced itself from its divine origin and from God, the source of its immortality.[3]

Du Bellay's vision of the ruins of Rome falls between these two polarities. He looked on the classical rubble and experienced conflicting responses that the medieval observer—if he looked at all—would not comprehend. Erwin Panofsky has explained that "the Roman ruins inspired the medieval mind with a mingled feeling of admiration for the lofty magnificence of the original buildings, demoniacal fear because these structures were the work of unbelievers, and pious triumph because their decay betokened the defeat of paganism."[4] Renaissance eyes came to see the ruins in a fresh way and sought to balance a calm archaeological interest in them with a nearly romantic sentiment. In literature as well as painting of the Renaissance, the theme of far-off Arcadian innocence and tombstone wreckage—both associated with Du Bellay's appreciation of the *Antiquitez*—appealed "not so much as a Utopia of bliss and beauty distant in space as a Utopia of bliss and beauty distant in time."[5] This generalization of an important fact correctly implies that such a spatial and temporal breach would not have held true during the Middle Ages. The full force of any latent nostalgia Du Bellay felt for the brilliance that was Rome revealed itself only when he got to Rome, where he was no longer removed in space from the ruins but only in time. Nostalgia, melancholy, sadness, regret—all these feelings obviously do mark his *Antiquitez,* but an awareness of the two separate reactions of the poet and their historical dimensions is a necessary part of our attempts to understand the poetry.

Chamard's *Histoire de la Pléiade* included a comprehensive study of the *Antiquitez;* but while his survey avoided a vague response to the poems, nevertheless it overlooked questions of thematic unity and relevant contexts. Of special interest to Chamard were the "plusieurs idées" treated in the sequence, but his discussion is basically a list of four themes: (1) "la grandeur colossale de la Rome d'autrefois," (2) Rome the "victime de la Némésis vengeresse," (3) Rome "tombée par les

[3] *Pantagruel,* ch. 8 and *Institution de la religion chrestienne,* I, iv, 1; see also Douglas Bush, "The Isolation of the Renaissance Hero" in *Prefaces to Renaissance Literature* (1965), pp. 91–106.

[4] "Et in Arcadia Ego: On the Conception of Transience in Poussin and Watteau" in *Philosophy and History: Essays Presented to Ernst Cassirer* (1963), p. 245. For comment on the Italian view of Roman ruins, see Jacob Burckhardt, *The Civilization of the Renaissance in Italy* (1961), pp. 149–155.

[5] Panofsky, "Et in Arcadia Ego . . ." in *Meaning in the Visual Arts* (1955), p. 303. This essay is a revised version of the one that appeared in the Cassirer collection originally published in 1936.

guerres civiles" and (4) Rome "le monceau de ruines"—a fact which induces men either to marvel at the sight or to meditate on various profound matters.[6] These four themes are, of course, present in the sonnets, but by sharpening Chamard's categories we will discover a slightly different grouping of topics, one which can provide us with a more revealing thematic map to the poems and at the same time help deepen our appreciation of the melancholy and nostalgia that pervade Du Bellay's collection.

With varying success, most of the sonnets seem to develop one of these four themes: (1) the fact of the present ruins (sonnets 3, 16, 20, 26, 29), (2) the symbolic value of the ruins (4, 7, 9–15, 17, 21–24), (3) the fact of the dead civilization (2, 18, 25) and (4) the living idea and spirit of Roman civilization (5, 8, 19, 27). The development in no one sonnet will encompass all four ideas, but one sonnet may treat one or two together. Moreover, unlike the sonnets of the *Songe* which insistently press only the first or second theme, the thirty-two sonnets of the *Antiquitez* (with the exception of sonnets 16–19) reveal no attempt to take up the four themes in consecutive order. But certain affinities of logic are evident among the four ideas: the meditative process may involve a movement from the inspiration of (1) and (3) to the broader reflections of (2) and (4) respectively. Similarly, a loose unity of association can relate sonnets (1) and (3) with (2) and (4). A brief examination of some representative sonnets can show how Du Bellay manipulates these four large themes.

1. The fact of the present ruins is for Du Bellay a strong visual reminder of the transitory quality of the world. As a man-made artifact, Rome becomes in its ruined state an *exemplum* of the inevitable decay that claims all things. Rome is "proye au temps, qui tout consomme," as the chiasmus in the poet's sententious paradox indicates:

   > Ce qui est ferme, est par le temps destruit,
   > Et ce qui fuit, au temps fait resistance. (sonnet 3)

   The same cosmic sadness, achieved through a masterful use of alliteration, imbues his awareness that

   > Ro*m*e vivant fut l'orne*m*ent du *m*onde,
   > Et *m*orte elle est du *m*onde le tu*m*beau. (sonnet 29)

2. Immediate implications of these ruins evolve, in other sonnets, into broader contemplations of the futility besetting any ambitious

[6] II, 41–44. For the vague response, see Sidney Lee, *The French Renaissance in England* (1910), pp. 200, 215, and Walter Pater, "Joachim Du Bellay" in *The Renaissance* (1902), p. 182.

worldly enterprise. In a sense, a collapsed process of meditation is at work: the physical rubble reminds man of his earthly mortality and this fact becomes symbolic of the mortality inherent in everything terrestrial. Sonnets of this second type reflect on the lessons of ambition, pride and decadent self-destruction. Rome's earthly aspirations were thwarted by Jove and Mars (4, 11, 12) when, like the Giants, the children of Chaos, the sons of Romulus threatened the hegemony and balance of the world. It is impossible ever to be like gods since they are always there, watching. But not only did the gods crush Rome, for human ambition itself, leading first to conquest, then to leisure and softness, finally brought on civil war (10, 21, 23, 31). A combined allusion to the macrocosm of pagan destiny and perhaps the microcosmic sin of Genesis suggests that both fatality and human frailty invested Roman ventures from their inception:

> Estoit-ce point (Romains) vostre cruel destin,
> Ou quelque vieil peché qui d'un discord mutin (sonnet 24)

As the civilization corrupted at home, the neighboring barbarians—long ago conquered by Rome—come back to erase their own defeat (sonnet 23). Barbarians, Romans, Giants—they all took part in the typical human cycle of aspiration and loss. And Rome is now an accumulation of stones. Du Bellay meditates on the ravages of time and discerns in the fall of empires his own expiration (sonnet 7). Suddenly glimpsing the omnipotence of time and realizing that all beneath the moon—man, his works, the powers of nature—will disappear one day, the poet boldly prophesies to the reader:

> Je ne dy plus la sentence commune,
> Que toute chose au dessous de la Lune
> Est corrompable & sugette à mourir:
> Mais bien je dy (& n'en veuille desplaire
> A qui s'esfforce enseigner le contraire)
> Que ce grand Tout doit quelquefois perir. (sonnet 9)

3. While these first two groups of sonnets are thematically connected in their melancholic contemplation of worldly decay, two other themes permeating the sequence explore a more optimistic idea. At times, Du Bellay drops the saddening perspective that envisions a futile end to human accomplishments and he exudes an altogether human delight for mortal creations. The other side of the fundamental dilemma that faced earlier poets like Villon and Chaucer—the flowers are fair though they pass; though passing, the flowers

are fair—asserts itself. Du Bellay can see that on an earthly scale there is a value and resilience in Roman achievement. In sonnet 18, by finding in Peter's successor the return to a pre-Roman pastoral world, Du Bellay intimates, albeit ironically, a rebirth of effort that characterizes human existence. The wish of sonnet 25 to be able to restore Caesar's genius and Vergil's art conveys an excited admiration for the matchless Roman splendor.

4. Recognizing that the visible ruins can recall human grandeur as well as earthly mortality, the poet dwells on the particulars of that Roman heritage. The spirit of Rome has survived along with the ruins, though "le temps destruit les republiques." The downfall of Rome "did not mean the annihilation, but the transfiguration of Roman grandeur," writes Alfred Adler, and "The sight of ruins did not always move to sadness, but to serene resignation."[7] Sonnet 8 affirms a belief in such endurance:

   Le temps ne mist si bas la Romaine hauteur,
   Que le chef deterré aux fondemens antiques,
   Qui prindrent nom de luy, fust découvert menteur.

   What the Empire means for the Renaissance observer is not eternally buried in the dross of sublunary earth (sonnets 5 and 9). Human endurance has refused to let the ruins halt the progress of Rome; conscious of its remote glory and of its recent new fame, the present city "fouillant son antique sejour, / Se rabatist de tant d'oeuvres divines" (sonnet 27).

In the *Antiquitez,* then, Du Bellay adopts no one rigid stance as he surveys the civilization's ruins. The sonnets in all four categories demonstrate the poet's many-sided mood. For different reasons, he had, in John C. Lapp's words, a "frequent poetic interest in the kinetic potential of objects,"[8] and he can perceive rebirth as well as decay. It is clear that Literary and Christian traditions, contemporary religious dissension and the Renaissance reverence for classical antiquity, exerted a combined influence on his view of the transitoriness and endurance of human achievement. On the one hand, Rome, like the world, was ephem-

[7] "Du Bellay's *Antiquitez* XXXI: Structure and Ideology," *BHRen,* XIII (1951), 194.

[8] "Mythological Imagery in Du Bellay," *Studies in Philology,* LXI (1964), p. 127. Because of this I cannot accept Alfred W. Satterthwaite's opinion that "Du Bellay's melancholy is unequivocally black" ["Moral Vision in Spenser, Du Bellay and Ronsard," *Comparative Literature,* IX (1957), 141] nor Frank M. Chamber's single-source theory that "the whole conception of the *Antiquitez* is due to Lucan" [Lucan and the *Antiquitez de Rome,*" *PMLA,* LX (1945), 946].

eral and the Christian should condemn the city of man, knowing that the City of God awaited him. On the other hand, Rome's history was a proud, admirable one and it elicited the new Renaissance culture's approbation.

The various points of view in the *Antiquitez* and the means of establishing them assume considerable importance, because the meaning of the experience before the ruins depends largely on the vantage point and attitudes of the person undergoing or witnessing the event, and on the person or object he addresses. This meaning is identified with and is conditioned by the poet's conception of his "cause." The initial sonnets of the *Regrets* relate to the reader the emotional "adventure" and psychological circumstances that occasion Du Bellay's point of view in the rest of that collection. As Ramus put it, "la vérité des choses comprises ès ars est ainsi naturellement proposée à l'esprit comme est la couleur à la veüe, et ce que nous appellons enseigner n'est pas bailler la sapience ains seulement tourner et diriger l'esprit à contempler ce que de soymesme il eut peu apercevoir s'il se fut là tourné et dirigé."[9] In turn, his cause determines what and how many details are selected and how they are seen. Saulnier has commented elegantly on the immense choice of material that must have faced Du Bellay in his attempt to conjure the image of Rome's greatness and Chamard slighted the poet's one-sided "peinture partielle" of modern Rome that fails in its presentation of "la vérité pure."[10] Du Bellay did not attempt a photographic account of Rome, but rather selected and arranged individual moments from the total spectacle that confronted him, excluding others, for the particular response they would elicit.

For any poetry that has at least one foot in rhetorical tradition, point of view is of utmost concern since rhetoric brings into being a specific or hypothetical audience and attempts covertly or overtly to gain its assent. Satterthwaite insists that Du Bellay "indulges in no personal statements of opinion at all, no reflections loaded with moral lessons. He is content to pass from description to description, from image to image, and to leave the reader to draw his own conclusions."[11] But this is true only in the sense that, as distinct from post-Romantic poetry, interest shifts from the private feelings of the poet to his expression as an artist, away from the personality of the arguer to the force of his

[9] *La Dialectique,* p. 61.

[10] Saulnier, *Du Bellay,* p. 76; Chamard, *Histoire,* II, 253.

[11] "Moral Vision . . .," p. 142. Cf. Northrop Frye, *Anatomy of Criticism* (1966), p. 319, and Henri Weber's astute observation that Du Bellay's impersonal address to the reader is a means of diverting attention from him to the argument he is expounding: *La Creation poétique au XVI*$^{e}$ *siècle* (1956), pp. 116, 418, 425.

argument. In a liminal sonnet of the *Regrets*—essentially, a poem about poetry—he claims that "la Muse demande / Le theatre du peuple & la faveur des Roys" (II, 58); and in the "Sonnets divers" he instructs the dramatized reader as to the proper attitude he should assume with respect to the poetic experience—not unlike the Ancient Mariner and the accosted wedding guest—before explaining the myth-laden octave and relating it in the last tercet to his Roman experience: "Cesse, passant, de t'en donner merveille" (II, 265). The same desire to teach and move through pleasure is central to the *Antiquitez*. The more openly allegorical *Songe* and the lesson of Ecclesiastes which opens and closes that sequence, "tout n'est rien que vanité," is brought forth in the *Antiquitez* through the use of naturalistic imagery or sketched historical development. After the simile of vapor condensation and rain, Du Bellay ends sonnet 20 with the ironic rhyme *soustenir-devenir* and the sententious proof "Monstrant que tout en rien doit un jour devenir." Even though the selection of events or analogies is inevitably limited, the conclusion creates at least the impression of moral omniscience. Instead of simply telling, the poet pleasurably but compellingly shows the involved reader what his reaction must be, and the imagined reader occasionally experiences the action through the eyes of the unobtrusive narrator:

> Ces grands monceaux pierreux, ces vieux murs que *tu* vois,
> Furent premierement le cloz d'un lieu champestre:
> Et ces braves palais, dont le temps s'est fait maistre,
> Cassines de pasteurs ont esté quelquefois.
> Lors prindrent les bergers les ornemens des Roys,
> Et le dur laboureur de fer arma sa dextre:
> Puis l'annuel pouvoir le plus grand se vid estre,
> Et fut encor plus grand le pouvoir de six mois:
> Qui, fait perpetuel, creut en telle puissance,
> Que l'aigle Imperial de luy print sa naissance:
> Mais le Ciel s'opposant à tel accroissement,
> Mist ce pouvoir es mains du successeur de Pierre,
> Qui sous nom de pasteur, fatal à ceste terre,
> Monstre que tout retourne à son commencement. (sonnet 18)

We witness the calm, pastoral origin of Rome in the first quatrain, accelerate through history in the second to the zenith and transformation of Imperial power in the tercets and, along with the poet, didactically complete the cycle. The last four verses can be read as a quatrain built on introverted rhymes and thus heighten the shock of Rome's collapse by countering the sonnet's traditional divisions.

Familiar second person address is varied by altering the speed of verses and thus making the reader experience Rome's life from a shifting perspective, but the didactic function of that address is the same. In the expansive verses that begin sonnet 27 Du Bellay establishes complicity with the implied reader (or viewer) by giving him his cue, "emerveillé," and justifies that wonder in the second half of the quatrain by radically accelerating the rhythm as he passes in review the glories of Rome:

> Toy qui de Rome emerveillé contemples
> L'antique orgueil, qui menassoit les cieux,
> Ces vieux palais, ces monts audacieux,
> Ces murs, ces arcz, ces thermes & ces temples,

The beginning of the next two stanzas controls the reader's vision by the imperatives "Juge" and "Regarde apres," while the last tercet controls his conclusion as well, "Tu jugeras," that the spirit of Rome attempts to revive its lost grandeur.

Perspective (but not the conclusion it leads to) is modified not only by changing grammatical person, but also by shifting pronouns within the same person for an altered viewpoint. The reader may perceive the action from a distance through the limiting "Qui a veu quelquefois" (sonnet 28) or he may be more involved through the more general "Non autrement qu'on void" (sonnet 20). Quintilian had discussed person change, classifying it somewhere between trope and figure of thought, in terms of the effect it intends (IX, iii, 22–23), and Renaissance critics treated narrative style where the poet speaks in his own person, dramatic or imitative style where he assumes the reaction of another person, as in prosopopoeia, and combinations of the two.[12] Du Bellay evinces a similar concern in all types of poetry; his desire in the "Prosphonematique" to paint the king's glory "au vif" leads to a continually displaced point of view and altered address (III, 61), in an amorous piece the narrator apostrophizes mythological deities and reports their dialogue (III, 138), and his satire especially relies on multiple perspective, such as his derisive collation of sequential portraits and implied conversations of Pierre de Paschal that obliquely suggest the narrator's opinion (VI, 113). Not only is form of address inflected in the *Antiquitez,* but also referents are transferred within the same pronoun. Such transfer creates a desirable vagueness at the beginning of sonnet 31 where Du Bellay enumerates forces that had nothing to do with Rome's fall:

> De ce qu'on ne void plus qu'une vague campaigne,
> Ou tout l'orgueil du monde on a veu quelquefois,

[12] See Bernard Weinberg, *A History of Literary Criticism in the Italian Renaissance* (1961), I, 61.

> Tu n'en es pas coulpable, ô quiconques tu sois
> Que le Tygre & le Nil, Gange & Euphrate baigne:

The pronoun *on* refers to different points of view in the past and present, while Lucan's concrete "Non tu, Pyrrhe ferox" becomes the purposefully indecisive "quiconques tu sois." The referent of *tu* is altered and specified in the first tercet as the poet apostrophizes Rome, "Tu en es seule cause, ô civile fureur," and in the last verse he returns to subordinate clauses and the third person, "La Romaine grandeur, trop longuement prospere, / Se vist ruer à bas d'un plus horrible sault," which is vague enough in meaning to include both Rome and the barbarians as witnesses to the turn of Fortune's Wheel. The crucial witness, of course, is the alternately objective or subjective narrator. A near translation of a sonnet by Castiglione ("Superbi colli, e voi sacre ruine") allows him to bring the ruins which he apostrophizes into close focus and describe their significance in the second person as a means of relating his own reaction to a more general occurrence in the last tercet:

> Tristes desirs, vivez donques contents:
> Car si le temps finist chose si dure,
> Il finira la peine que j'endure. (sonnet 7)

The image of Rome that inspires his feelings becomes his own creation to the extent that he modifies and yet preserves the driving alliteration of his model: "Qui le seul nom de Rome retenez" ("Che 'l nome sol di Roma anchor tenete"); "Las, peu à peu cendre vous devenez, / Fable du peuple & publiques rapines!" ("E fatte al vulgo vil favola al fine").

The *Regrets* tell of the literary fortune Du Bellay had hoped to make in the Eternal City, of the Golden Fleece he would like to have brought back to France,[13] and from the beginning of the *Antiquitez* to the end he presents himself as the intercessor who can recreate, or at least adumbrate for us, the glory that once was Rome. In his dedication to Henri II he claims to have painted "en ce petit tableau . . . de couleurs poëtiques" so that it "Se pourra bien vanter d'avoir hors du tumbeau /

[13] "Heureux qui, comme Ulysse, a fait un beau voyage, / Ou comme cestuy là qui conquit la toison" (*Regrets,* 31). The apparent dissemblance between the stories of Ulysses and Jason, and the ill-fitting allusion to Jason in this sonnet may be justified on the grounds that the Jason myth estabilshes continuity between the two collections, since it is also found in *Antiquitez* 10, and that it may be an allusion to the Order of the Golden Fleece which was awarded to Catholics of noble lineage for distinguished accomplishment. The allusion, and many similar ones in volume II, could have been inspired by the momentous abdication of Charles V, the first act of which was his resignation as Grand Master of the Order on October 22, 1555, during Du Bellay's stay in Rome. The captured Fleece symbolizes virtue rewarded (II, 184), and the poet refers to Charles as the Master of the Fleece (II, 271).

Tiré des vieux Romains les poudreuses reliques." The antithetical beginning of sonnet 1, "Divins Esprits, dont la poudreuse cendre," introduces the theme of the surviving animus of lifeless stones, the weighty archaisms "Gist," "loz" and "abas," and the triple invocation that surrounds Du Bellay's stance as the earthly priest who can recall the spirits from the Elysian Fields. If he lacks the skill of Orpheus, Amphion or Vergil (sonnet 25), he at least can claim to be the first French poet to have sung Rome's name (sonnet 32). The significance of his conscious use of art, whether demonic or poetic, to summon Roman achievement before our eyes derives from his conception that surpassing art has made Rome endure beyond the grasp of nature and fortune:

> Qui voudra voir tout ce qu'ont peu nature,
> L'Art & le ciel (Rome) te vienne voir:
> J'entens s'il peult ta grandeur concevoir
> Par ce qui n'est que ta morte peinture.
> Rome n'est plus: & si l'architecture
> Quelque umbre encor de Rome fait revoir,
> C'est comme un corps par magique sçavoir
> Tiré de nuict hors de sa sepulture.
> Le corps de Rome en cendre est devallé,
> Et son esprit rejoindre s'est allé
> Au grand esprit de ceste masse ronde.
> Mais ses escripts, qui son loz le plus beau
> Malgré le temps arrachent du tumbeau,
> Font son idole errer parmy le monde. (sonnet 5)

The insistent conjoining of art with nature and the powers of heaven, which Du Bellay added to his models in *L'Olive* 23, 74 and *Songe* 12, is seen again here in his modification of Petrarch's "Chi vuol veder quantunque po natura / E'l ciel tra noi, venga a mirar costei." The ruins, the "morte peinture," do not permit the viewer to understand their full and hidden meaning; only art, as the alliterative final verse tells us, assures the survival of its *idole* (from εἴδωλον) with its appropriate meanings of vision, phantom, portrait, image or idea.

Alliteration, rhythm and rhyme themselves are effective means of recreating the various faces of Rome and of directing the narrative "point of view" as well. Before Ronsard's recommendation of "lettres heroïques," *m* and doubled *r* on Vergil's example, and probably before Peletier's stress on "l'expression vive des choses par les moz: savoer ét, les soudeines e hatives, par moz briéz e legers: et les pesantes ou de travalh, par moz lons e tardiz,"[14] Du Bellay separates alliterative and

[14] Ronsard, XVI, 347; Peletier, *Art pöetique,* I, 9.

rhythmic statement from flat didacticism and impels it toward a significant formality and even ritualism:

> Nouveau venu, qui cherches Rome en Rome
> Et rien de Rome en Rome n'apperçois,
> Ces vieux palais, ces vieux arcz que tu vois,
> Et ces vieux murs, c'est ce que Rome on nomme.
> Voy quel orgueil, quelle ruine: et comme
> Celle qui mist le monde sous ses loix,
> Pour donter tout, se donta quelquefois,
> Et devint proye au temps, qui tout consomme.
> Rome de Rome est le seul monument,
> Et Rome Rome a vaincu seulement.
> Le Tybre seul, qui vers la mer s'enfuit,
> Reste de Rome. O mondaine inconstance!
> Ce qui est ferme, est par le temps destruit,
> Et ce qui fuit, au temps fait resistance. (sonnet 3)

The narrative sequence of sounds caught by the unnamed reader's ear reinforces emotional effects, but he is unceasingly reminded that he is not experiencing the real object of mimesis as much as the object transmuted into symbolic form and meaning. The theme "Rome n'est plus Rome" (*Regrets,* 131)[15] with its martial cadence is insistently hammered throughout the sonnet by the two close repetitions of the city's name in the first quatrain (vv. 1, 2) and by the similar repetitions in the first tercet (vv. 9, 10) which condense respectively the meanings of the two quatrains. In order to insure the swift recurrence of the name in three of the four instances, Du Bellay resorts to the rhetorical device of hyperbaton, the inversion of customary word order for special emphasis. This emphasis ironically undercuts the implied Imperial might because it opposes Rome's glorious past to its faded present, an affirmation to a negation. The "nouveau venu" 's field of vision narrows in its triple descent from the large "palais" to the "arcz" to the anonymous "murs" as he progressively discovers that the only vestige of Rome's past is the hollow echo of its name: the imperative "Voy" of the second quatrain is really an invitation to hear the descriptive alliteration. Equally descriptive are Du Bellay's rhetorical figures: the zeugma, following the antithesis involving the abstract *orgueil* and the concrete *ruine,* fractures verbal and logical continuity in a rhythmically unbalanced line; and the traductio *seul monument-seulement* creates a short-

[15] Cf. Scève's *Délie* 20, "A Romme alla, a Romme desolée," and Andre Six, "Explication française: Du Bellay, *Antiquités de Rome*-Sonnet III," *Romance Notes,* VIII (1967), 281–284.

ened refrain that underlines Rome's diminished stature.[16] The only new thought added to the synoptic first tercet is verse 11 which visually escapes its stanza and comes to rest in the last tercet—the logical accommodation of statement to form. Du Bellay repeated precisely the pattern involving enjambement of these two verses in *L'Olive* 103 for the same effect, and will do so again to conjoin the tercets in *Antiquitez* 29, *Songe* 11 and "Amours" 15. While successful sonnets do not always inhabit a world of logic, their forms do. And just as the world of dialectic is composed of unchanging propositions, the stichic or strophic components of poetry which belong to that world assume the permanence of art, despite the lesson of inconstancy they teach.

Much of Du Bellay's craftsmanship in the *Antiquitez* lies in his knowing when the sonnet's stringent conditions should be overlooked and when they can be turned to advantage by adhering to them. Often he intentionally disregards the theoretical divisions of strophic forms and just as often exploits the force of rhymed words as means of directing poetic statement. In the first quatrain of sonnet 8, for instance,

> Par armes & vaisseaux Rome donta le monde,
> Et pouvoit on juger qu'une seule cité
> Avoit de sa grandeur le terme limité
> Par la mesme rondeur de la terre & de l'onde.

the A rhymes connote a global dominion and enclose rhyme words whose suggested limits only reinforce Roman hegemony. This assertion is made more specific in the second quatrain by a veiled allusion to Octavian Augustus, grandnephew of Julius Caesar, and by a reference to the papacy's eventual power, "Mesura le hault ciel à la terre profonde"; the power of empire is thus simply transformed into spiritual strength. Sonnet 11 brings together the similarly rhymed verses "Ce peuple adonc, nouveau fils de la Terre," and "Puis se perdit dans le sein de sa mere"; Rome rose from and disappeared into Cybele the Great Earth Mother who, along with her mate Saturn, was among the oldest and most important Roman deities and whom Du Bellay glossed in the famous sonnet 6. The antagonism between divine will "juste jugement," and human actions, "ferme fondement," is again amplified through alliteration and rhyme in the final tercet of sonnet 24.

[16] Zeugma bespeaks an inarticulate dialectic based either on cause and effect or on proper and opposite cause, as in Ronsard's "Regrettant mon amour, & vostre fier desdain," ed. Laumonier, XVII, 266. Saulnier points out the Latin meaning of *monument* as "a reminder of a past event" in "Commentaires des *Antiquitez de Rome*," *BHRen*, XII (1950), 139. Traductio is found in Du Bellay's anonymous model, *Romam-Roma-Romae*, in addition to extensive alliteration: "viden' velut ipsa cadavera," "Vicit ut haec mundum, visa est se vincere: vicit."

The poet's concern—we could say obsession—over these human actions is not limited to the classical line of Roman literature which guarantees its survival, but extends as well to the former majesty of the crumbled ruins he sees before him. Whether it be a triumphal arch or the Temple of Vesta with its eternal flame, Rome's buildings reflect its culture and aspirations. Its massive construction and even its serene remains show that Rome built for eternity. Roma Aeterna surely became a literal and unalterable reality for whoever looked upon the formal splendor of Augustan architecture. Roman geography and architecture assume an important role in most of the *Antiquitez* as Du Bellay seeks the reasons for Rome's physical demise and attempts to recreate the compass of its strength in the construction of his sonnets. Some of his attempts suffer from the excessive rigidity that characterizes some Roman architecture. Sonnet 19 builds an extensive anaphora of six verses beginning with *Tout,* and relieves it only by the imposing synonym *Rome* which begins the seventh verse. In sonnet 4, on the other hand, it is the rhyme words and octave-sestet opposition that make the implicit but rather obvious commentary.

Celle qui de son chef les estoilles passoit,
Et d'un pied sur Thetis, l'autre dessous l'Aurore,
D'une main sur le Scythe, & l'autre sur le More,
De la terre & du ciel la roundeur compassoit:
Juppiter ayant peur, si plus elle croissoit,
Que l'orgueil des Geans se relevast encore,
L'accabla sous ces monts, ces sept monts qui sont ore
Tumbeaux de la grandeur qui le ciel menassoit.
Il luy mist sur le chef la croppe Saturnale,
Puis dessus l'estomac assist la Quirinale,
Sur le ventre il planta l'antique Palatin,
Mist sur la dextre main la hauteur Celienne,
Sur la senestre assist l'eschine Exquilienne,
Viminal sur un pied, sur l'autre l'Aventin.

The imperfect tense of all A rhymes and the B rhymes composed of nouns in the first quatrain and adverbs in the second, all preserve the relative animation of the octave which describes Rome's assault on heaven and its defeat; the unrelieved rhyme words in the sestet, however, are the names of six of Rome's seven hills which pin down the captured victim like dead weights and also display the poet's disregard for precise Roman geography. Sonnets 2 and 26 are more accomplished in their attempt to represent physically the dominion of Rome through the disposition of the sonnet and the figures it contains. In the first instance the self-conscious narrator details the seven wonders of the ancient world in a colorless list marked by unevenness of verse and stanza. This unevenness is sustained until the end of the poem when he states his proposed undertaking:

> ... quant à moy, pour tous je veulx chanter
> Les sept costaux Romains, sept miracles du monde.

Repetition of the mystical *sept* and juxtaposition of the physical fact of Rome with the spiritual in the balanced hemistichs—figures of words a rhetorician would identify respectively as reduplicatio and compar—amplify Rome's catholicity and calm assurance.

The clearest example of Du Bellay's verbal imitation of Rome's physical and temporal dominion is sonnet 26:

> Qui voudroit figurer la Romaine grandeur
> En ses dimensions, il ne luy faudroit querre
> A la ligne & au plomb, au compas, à l'equerre,
> Sa longueur & largeur, hautesse & profondeur:
> Il luy faudroit cerner d'une egale rondeur
> Tout ce que l'Ocean de ses longs bras enserre,
> Soit ou l'Astre annuel eschauffe plus ta terre,
> Soit ou soufle Aquilon sa plus grande froideur.
> Rome fut tout le monde, & tout le monde est Rome.
> Et si par mesmes noms mesmes choses on nomme,
> Comme du nom de Rome on se pourroit passer,
> La nommant par le nom de la terre & de l'onde:
> Ainsi le monde on peult sur Rome compasser,
> Puis que le plan de Rome est la carte du monde.

His invitation to *figurer* Rome's greatness is an invitation to create its physical image for the mind's contemplation,[17] and that is precisely

[17] As is also evident from the similar imagery in IV, 220:

> On peult feindre par le cizeau
> Ou par l'ouvraige du pinceau
> Toute visible chose,
> Mais d'Amour le seul poingnant traict
> Vous peult figurer le protraict
> De ma tristesse enclose.
> On peult diffinir au compas
> De tout ce qu'on void ici bas
> La forme en rond unie,
> Mais on ne scauroit mesurer
> Le mal que me fait endurer
> Mon amour infinie.

The nexus of seeing and understanding is at the heart of Muret's comment on Ronsard's first Cassandre sonnet, "Qui voudra voir": "Le poëte tasche à rendre les lecteurs attentifs: disant, que qui voudra bien entendre la nature d'Amour, vienne voir les effects qu'Amour produit en luy," *Les Oeuvres*, p. 1. For Johannes Scotus Erigena, every attempt at definition outlines the shape of a universal, and the dialectical category of *topos* implies the area in which ideas are traced.

what he does in the first tercet by using three rhetorical figures that function together. The epanalepsis *Rome-Rome* in the first tercet illustrates the "egale rondeur" which introduces the serialized four elements in the second quatrain, literally encompasses the ancient and modern world and graphically outlines the idea of the last tercet that Rome can be measured only in global terms. The combination in the same line of enallage or the change of verb tense for dramatic effect (*fut-est*) with compar follows Quintilian's recommendation[18] and supports Du Bellay's argument that Roman civilization is simply transformed. Rome once defined the frontiers of the Western World and now that world is shaped by the Roman patrimony. Chamard's note indicates only Horace and Ovid as the sources for Du Bellay's idea in the tercets and we find Rome's world dominion similarly framed in his "Patriae desiderium" as "Roma orbis patria est, quique altae moenia Romae" (v. 11). But this theme and the inseparable theme of cultural transformation take on greater significance because the classical sources of the sestet are complemented by Biblical sources (Zechariah II; Revelation XVI, XXI) that can be seen in the octave.

The rise and decline of Imperial might and the transformation of the temporal strength of the Palatine into the spiritual strength of the Vatican find their natural expression in the cyclical rhythm of these sonnets. This rhythm generally operates on the related levels of the microcosm and the macrocosm which conspire against Rome's permanence, and for their realization Du Bellay dramatizes traditional motifs. Sonnet 31 associates the impersonal wheel of fortune with the civil war between Caesar and Pompey, while the mirrored action of the Giants and Romans in the octave and sestet of sonnet 12 and the forceful opposition of these poetic divisions in *Songe* 7 repeat the tragic rhythm of areté-hubris-nemesis. The microcosm relates the internal human

[18] IX, iii, 80 and VIII, iii, 66–70. The figures of words here create the figure of thought called *commutatio* by rhetoricians; see Quintilian, IX, iii, 85; [Cicero], *Rhetorica ad Herennium,* IV, xxviii, 39; Horace's *Epistles,* II, i, 257. Although poetry that is oriented toward rhetoric tends to repeat similar combinations of figures and formulaic phrases, the function and tone of such repetitions often differ considerably, witness the styling of

> C'est ores, mon Vineus, mon cher Vineus, c'est ore,
> Que de tous les chetifs le plus chetif je suis (*Regrets,* 42)

which closely resembles the configuration of verses 9–10 of the sonnet under discussion, but not at all the mood and intent. Quintilian's additional recommendation in IX, iii, 80, of compar combined with traductio appears in Du Bellay's adaptation of Sannazaro, "Et osent les vaincuz les vainqueurs desdaigner" (sonnet 14), which intimates Rome's steady confidence even in defeat, while Ronsard uses it to imprint France's victory in the heat of battle: "J'oy le bruit des vainqueurs, j'oy le cry des vaincus" (ed. Laumonier, IX, 8). Cf. Laumonier IX, 103: "Meintenant le veinqueur, meintenant le veincu."

causes of Rome's decline, such as the civil war which is seen "Comme l'humeur en un corps vicieux" (sonnet 23), and adheres to the Renaissance theory that good health relied on the correct proportion and distribution of the four bodily humors. Since the composition of human anatomy corresponded with the four elements that compose the natural universe, sonnet 22 presents Rome's physical disappearance in terms of a discordant relationship of the natural elements. Again, sonnet 13 invokes Fortune's Wheel, descends in cosmic value through the elements from "la fureur de la flamme enragee" which corresponded to hot and dry choler to the moist and cold phlegmatic element "Qui tant de fois t'a couvert de son onde," and ends with the fitting antithesis, "la grandeur du rien." Correspondence of the natural, human and supra-human that pervades these sonnets along with Renaissance cosmology as a whole, warrant a more extensive look at four different cyclical poems and the ways in which Du Bellay's rhetoric serves his poetic cause.

Sonnet 16, which lacks the self-intrusion of the poet with its impersonal *on,* claims an ambivalent and ironic understanding.

Comme lon void de loing sur la mer courroucee
Une montaigne d'eau d'un grand branle ondoyant,
Puis trainant mille flotz, d'un gros choc abboyant
Se crever contre un roc, ou le vent l'a poussee:
Comme on void la fureur par l'Aquilon chassee
D'un sifflement aigu l'orage tournoyant,
Puis d'une aile plus large en l'air s'esbanoyant
Arrester tout à coup sa carriere lassee:
Et comme on void la flamme ondoyant en cent lieux
Se rassemblant en un, s'aguiser vers les cieux,
Puis tumbler languissante: ainsi parmy le monde
Erra la Monarchie: & croissant tout ainsi
Qu'un flot, qu'un vent, qu'un feu, sa course vagabonde
Par un arrest fatal s'est venuë perdre icy.

Since it shares certain prosodic and thematic similarities with other sonnets in the collection it seems, through its multiple and perhaps paradoxical logic, to argue the usual *contemptus mundi* lesson; but in fact it urges us to mourn ephemeral glory. This ironic outcome depends chiefly on the poem's structure and its metaphorical development. Just as Du Bellay discarded conventional topics of the Petrarchan sonnet in composing the *Antiquitez,* he here disregarded the standard sonnet separation of quatrains and tercets. In comparing the rise and fall of Rome to similar processes in nature, he chose to divide the poem at verse 11, and in the middle of that verse. The one long sentence that comprises the sonnet moves resolutely through the analogies of waves, wind and fire to the central fact of Rome. The uniform punctuation and grammatical dependency of all three *comme* clauses serve to blend the similes together. In addition, words in one unit occasionally recur in another: *ondoyant* (vv. 2 and 9), *flotz* (vv. 3 and 13), *aigu* and *s'aguiser* (vv. 6 and 10), *arrester* (vv. 8 and 14) and of course the formulaic *comme* and *ainsi.* Moreover, Du Bellay so fashioned his three similes that features of one element overlap another; the waters, for instance, are a *montaigne d'eau, le vent* causes the wave's *gros choc,* and *la flamme* shines in the sky, the dominion of *l'aquilon.*

By juxtaposing words and running the clauses together, Du Bellay merges the three illustrations of growth and decline drawn from the world of nature. In like manner, although he seems to present a sequence of immediately significant rhymes—for example, the first eight rhymes are all appropriately verbals, suggestive of the energies of nature—he actually, in various ways, undermines the apparent meaning. First of all, the firm rhyme of *ondoyant* and *abboyant* has a basis in sense, but a comma halts *ondoyant,* and *abboyant* must grammatically proceed to the next verse where its meaning is subverted by *se crever.* In the same way a trick of syntax upsets the pairing of *tournoyant* and *s'esbanoyant.* Secondly, Du Bellay toys with his rhymes to produce unexpected oppositions: although *lieux* rhymes with *cieux* and both plural forms connote expansiveness, *lieux* goes syntactically into the singular *un* (v. 10) and *cieux* descends into *tumber.* And while *monde* and *vagabonde* make for a perfect coupling in meaning, *vagabonde* is incomplete without the contradictory *arrest* (v. 14).

Such typographical and grammatical techniques not only tightly integrate the three similes with one another and with the last three verses but they underscore as well a pattern of incongruities—unexpected alterations of our initial impressions. Exactly why this pattern exists becomes clear when we analyze the implications of the three elements: water, air and fire. The relentless logic of the poetic argument (Come . . . Comme . . . Comme . . . Ainsi) suggests that just as huge waves split, furious winds dissipate and shimmering fires wane, so the Roman Empire, a creation of human civilization, must also decline and decay. This triple metaphor from nature that subsumes the destiny of a man-made thing is derived from the hierarchy that separated the four elements, placing earth (the lowest and heaviest) at the dregs of the cosmos and fire (the highest and lightest) at the edge of the lunary realm. Clearly the imaginative function of the elements was to associate human actions with the workings of the universe.

Du Bellay employs this metaphoric frame of reference in a complicated manner. There are actually five planes of matter in the poem: (1) the inferior earth—dry land, the *de loing* of the speaker's vantage point; (2) the higher stratum, water; (3) even higher, the winds and air; (4) the highest plane, fire; (5) and, once again, the lowly region of *la Monarchie, le monde.* Significantly, the only spatial movement begins and ends with earth, the dull sublunary zone of eternally futile human efforts; the poem journeys out and back, but the important borders are fixed by the key words that open and close the sonnet: *de loing* and *icy.*

The course of Rome, as it expanded and contracted, is like the swelling and collapsing of natural forces, and inasmuch as it was a thoroughly earthly (and indeed un-Christian) venture it was doomed to fall. The three similes function to place Rome under the rule of "physical" laws and not to imply "moral" or Christian judgments. Like Roman ambition, each element achieves a form only to return to formlessness. Waves aspire—to crash, winds blow—to die, flames sharpen—to wither; and it is their terminations that receive the greater emphasis, at the beginning of verses 4, 8 and 11. Entrophy constantly threatens the natural world: mountainous waves with *mille flotz,* the expanding winds *d'une aile plus large,* the solitary flame once *en cent lieux,* now *en un*—they all run down, their noise and fury ending in silence. Despite their great or manifold powers, they each encounter the inescapable *arrest fatal;* the place may be *un roc,* the time *tout à coup,* the personified attitude *languissante.* Cosmologically, diminishment follows expansion. It is important, then, that nature's eternal flux be described in present participles, verb forms which dramatize the tension of active forces. These forces do have a temporary cessation, expressed by infinitives (*se crever, arrester, tumber*), but Rome, once *croissant,* met an irrevocable fate, one underlined by the finality of the present perfect *s'est venuë.*

Therefore, in this sonnet the structure, syntax and metaphoric comparisons work in unison to integrate and sharpen the conclusion drawn in the last tercet. The poem starts and finishes at the earthly locus of the poet, amid evidence of vanity and immortality, after ranging beyond human confines. *Ainsi parmy le monde* cannot be noticeably divorced from the previous examples because the inevitability of history closely parallels the inevitability of nature; the enjambement of verses 11–12 stresses the point and prevents the example of Rome from receiving too much separate attention. Versification, along with the unvaried punctuation and repetitive clausal structure, support the logic of the argument. But is the poem simply a subtle but didactic pronouncement, a traditional contempt of the world lesson? It would seem not. For one thing, the described activity of the three elements occurs in a continuous or eternal present (*-ant*), and the observations we make with Du Bellay (*on void*) are impersonal and timeless. Opposed to these seemingly illustrative images is the fate of imperial Rome which, while compared with the elements, is fatally different. Nature is eternally cyclic, the wind and fire are phoenix-like. Although Rome—like the elements, like the water breaking on the rocks—is historically transformed in a circular pattern (sonnet 18), the magnificence of its Golden Age died once as it lived but once.[19]

That the three similes chosen to exemplify the principle of rise and fall are not truly similar enough produces, at the end, a note at once sad and ironic. Anonymous waters, winds and fires cannot die the particular and lasting death of Caesar's Rome; there is, it turns out, an abyss between the lessons of nature and the human condition. In his attempt to see the Roman ruins from a detached perspective, the poet fails. Nostalgia and sadness—arising from an ambivalent sense of being proudly human yet uniquely mortal—become, finally, the sentiments that overshadow Du Bellay's apparent interest in *contemptus mundi* or *ubi sunt* themes. So it is that in the last line Du Bellay masks his sense of loss by using an explicit spatial metaphor, as the empire *erra parmy le monde* until *sa course vagabonde* reached an end, when the decayed monuments before him tell a story whose dimensions are temporal. *Les Antiquitez de Rome* is a poetic unit, and this sonnet must be read in logical relation to the poems that precede and follow it. Like some of the others, its subjects is the scattered ruins, the futility of human endeavor; unlike the others, it does not make a pointed moral preachment. It is an eternal note of sadness, a mood and not a moral, that closes the poem.

The basic simile of sonnet 30 again suggests an imprecise resemblance between the natural cycle and the evolution of Rome:

> Comme le champ semé en verdure foisonne,
> De verdure se haulse en tuyau verdissant,
> Du tuyau se herisse en epic florissant,
> D'epic jaunit en grain, que le chaud assaisonne:
> Et comme en la saison le rustique moissonne
> Les ondoyans cheveux du sillon blondissant,
> Les met d'ordre en javelle, & du blé jaunissant
> Sur le champ despouillé mille gerbes façonne:
> Ainsi de peu à peu creut l'empire Romain,

[19] Cf. Ronsard's "La matiere demeure, et la forme se perd," quoted by Laumonier in *Ronsard et sa province* (1924), p. 213, and "Mourir, quand la forme en une autre s'en va," ed. Laumonier, VIII, 178.

> Tant qu'il fut despouillé par la Barbare main,
> Qui ne laissa de luy que ces marques antiques,
> Que chacun va pillant: comme on void le gleneur
> Cheminant pas à pas recueillir les reliques
> De ce qui va tumbant apres le moissonneur.

Despite the assertions of Chamard that the sonnet was inspired by the *Georgics* I, 314–317 and of Vianey that it came from an epigram of Martial,[20] a close examination of the theme and its development shows the more likely and more fitting source to be Mark IV, 26–29, since Christianity represented the present state of Rome's evolution from Du Bellay's historical vantage point. To emphasize the perpetually changing present, Du Bellay skilfully resorts to the figure *gradatio*. Far from mechanically establishing the chain sequence between the end of one verse and the beginning of the next verse as the *rhétoriqueurs* did, he sets the connecting words (*verdure-tuyau-epic-saison*) inside the verse and instead uses the verbal A rhymes to describe the continuity of action and the adjectival B rhymes to indicate the effect of that action. The importance of continuity established by the figure between the quatrains is that man is involved in a legitimate relationship with nature and partakes of its plenitude. But in the sestet where we are suddenly thrust into the past (vv. 9–12) and where the excess of relative pronouns impedes the flow of thought, cooperative harvest turns into plunder. The smooth transition of the quatrains (*assaisonne-saison*) becomes antithetical enjambement in the tercets, "ces marques antiques, / Que chacun va pillant," which comments unfavorably on the anonymous and undistinguished situation of the humanist in sixteenth-century Rome. And when we return to the present and to the original comparison at the end of the poem, the resemblance of the humble gleaner slowly moving "pas à pas" to the increase of Rome's power "peu à peu" creates a subtle but devastating irony. Due to the poet's careful insertion of Rome's example within the larger simile drawn from nature, the sonnet moves from present to past and back to present. But the cycle is incomplete since the ironic awareness at the end precludes a return to the optimism of the outset.

Yet Rome survives because of its artistic and intellectual contribution to its humble survivors. Sonnet 6, perhaps the best known of the collection, substantiates this survival by using *Aeneid* VI, 781–787 as its basis and point of departure:

> Telle que dans son char la Berecynthienne
> Couronnee de tours, & joyeuse d'avoir

---

[20] Chamard, II, 27; Vianey, *Le Pétrarquisme en France au XVI*e *siècle* (1909), p. 325.

> Enfanté tant de Dieux, telle se faisoit voir
> En ses jours plus heureux ceste ville ancienne:
> Ceste ville, qui fut plus que la Phrygienne
> Foisonnante en enfans, & de qui le pouvoir
> Fut le pouvoir du monde, & ne se peult revoir
> Pareille à sa grandeur, grandeur sinon la sienne.
> Rome seule pouvoit à Rome ressembler,
> Rome seule pouvoit Rome faire trembler:
> Aussi n'avoit permis l'ordonnance fatale
> Qu'autre pouvoir humain, tant fust audacieux,
> Se vantast d'égaler celle qui fit égale
> Sa puissance à la terre & son courage aux cieux.

We are here at the important moment where Anchises takes his son Aeneas by the arm and prophesies Rome's future greatness through the myth of the Berecynthian goddess Cybele, and the *Aeneid* itself roughly marks the transformation of Roman folklore into mythology. Looking back into an imaginary past just as Vergil did, Du Bellay insists on the gradual transformation of mythos in the first quatrain into the logos of historical reality. His sonnet preserves the Vergilian concern for establishing parentage between Troy and Rome, and to this end the two quatrains are drawn together by repetitions (*plus-plus, ceste ville-Ceste ville*) and by parallel structure (vv. 1–2 and 5–6). Radical distinctions are blurred and antitheses are mitigated by a mute *e* at the caesura (vv. 7, 14). But the one long sentence that comprises the octave is formed of balanced repetitions of sounds and words, *Telle que dans son char-telle se faisoit voir,* which in fact oppose legendary Troy to superior Rome and Rome's glorious past to the inglorious present, *jours plus heureux, plus que la Phrygienne. Foisonnante en enfans,* despite its mortal reference, is grammatically less limiting than *Enfanté tant de Dieux* of the first quatrain. The return of sonnet 5's insistent quatrain rhymes *voir-revoir* appears reinforced by the iterative prefix *re-* which bore the full idea of repetition in the sixteenth century; but these rhymes and the compar of verse 8 with the confrontation of "grandeur, grandeur" at the caesura actually deny the possibility of repeating Rome's greatness.[21] Completed actions (*fut-Fut*) and passivity (*se faisoit voir-se peult revoir*) characterize most of the slow, elegiac octave. But toward the end *le pouvoir* (v. 6), the only B rhyme that is not an infinitive, is placed in relief and introduces a series of explosive alliterations.

[21] The facile rhymes *voir-revoir,* in disregard for the precepts of the *Illustration,* ch. 7, and the unequal syllabic count of verses 12 and 14 are perhaps justified by the ironic distance they create between form and meaning. Cf. Ferdinand Brunot, *Histoire de la langue française* (1927), II, 267.

In the couplet formed by verses 9 and 10 Du Bellay exchanges the paraphrase and hypotaxis of the octave for parataxis and martial resonance in which he alters narrative perspective by naming *ceste ville* and dramatically asserting its power. Rhetorically, the use of *Rome* forms a polyptoton, a figure of diction that repeats various forms of one word in a single thought, while the juxtaposition of the two verses is of course anaphoric. Quintilian recommends the figure for either contrast or reaffirmation (IX, iii, 36–37); here, and elsewhere (I, 78; VI, 13), Du Bellay uses its rhythm and structure to enforce and reinforce the idea—the two verses affirm one another and the ideas of resemblance and military strength.[22]

The last four lines form a quatrain and resume the elegiac tone and hypotactic structure. This third stage in the sonnet's development relegates Rome's momentary power to the past and completes the movement from Rome's mythic origin to its realization to its ultimate destiny. Finally, the analogies of "Oeuvres et noms finablement atterre" in sonnet 7 and the cyclic return of Rome to Cybele the Earth Mother in sonnet 11 argue an ambivalent reading of the last verse which implies at once Rome's dominion and its demise, "fit égale / Sa puissance à la terre."

Du Bellay's integration of Vergil and other Latin poets into his sonnets is a way of bearing witness to the various meanings of Rome and of revealing the reality of its greatness. In the opening sonnets of the collection Du Bellay presents himself as the mystic poet who can invoke and restore the "poudreuses reliques." Again, sonnet 15 pieces together fragments from Aeneas' descent to the nether world and his own witness to the torment of the condemned shades (*Aeneid* VI, 325–439):

Palles Esprits, & vous Umbres poudreuses,
Qui jouissant de la clarté du jour
Fistes sortir cest orgueilleux sejour
Dont nous voyons les reliques cendreuses:
Dictes, Esprits (ainsi les tenebreuses
Rives de Styx non passable au retour,
Vous enlaçant d'un trois fois triple tour,
N'enferment point voz images umbreuses)
Dictes moy donc (car quelqu'une de vous
Possible encor se cache icy dessous)
Ne sentez vous augmenter vostre peine,

[22] His use of polyptoton is similar to *Aeneid* IV, 83, and VI, 247, which he translated around the time he was composing the *Antiquitez*. *Regrets* 136 uses a similar structure (vv. 12–13), latinism ("liberté contrainte") and paraphrases *Aeneid* VI, 425, as well. Cf. *Aeneid* V, 447–448; XII, 640; Cicero, *Pro Deiotaro,* IV, 12.

> Quand quelquefois de ces costaux Romains
> Vous contemplez l'ouvrage de voz mains
> N'estre plus rien qu'une poudreuse plaine?

The Latinate hortatory subjunctive following a hopeless wish (*ainsi,* v. 5: *sic*) and the infinitive construction (v. 14) are both found in Vergil's passage. An imbalance between the brief clarity of creation and the dominance of shadowy destruction is supported by the melancholy A rhymes that deal only with ashes, dust and shadows. *Umbres* refers to the ancient belief that unless a person received proper burial, his soul would be forced to wander as a shade and never attain peace in death. The disheveled ruins of Rome evidently do not constitute proper burial. While the first quatrain presses the rapidity of Roman creation, the long parentheses of the following verses accentuate the difficulty of the spirits' return. The spirits which pass over the encircling Styx are not capable of answering an invocation. Only the cyclic return of *poudreuse,* of dust to dust, is assured. But the scattered ruins of Rome and the spiritual presence they belie survive in Vergilian accounts of their greatness and as well in Du Bellay's testimony to their full history.

This sequence tells the story of Rome's—and, one step beyond, of man's—transience and endurance. As the intermediary which translates the complex lessons of Roman history for the reader, *Les Antiquitez de Rome* brings nature and art into coincidence by resolving even the dead ruins into the sounds and sights of a palpable reality. Du Bellay's shifting moods control our awareness of and reaction to the way's Fortune's cycle transforms civilization, and this cycle structures his vision and conditions its expression. Seen through a veil of reminiscent nostalgia, his intermittently impersonal longing for the peace and glory of an ideal past gave way to a bitter and more personal accusation against Rome's too real present in the *Regrets.*

## Chapter V

# LES REGRETS

### Fortune's Wheel

The line of the circle, then, infers and encompasses the larger meanings of human experience—heaven and hell, life and death, death and rebirth. In *L'Olive* cyclic movement structures poetic myth and Scriptural allusion, while in the *Antiquitez* it equates with the humanistic poet's view of history. Both poetic myth and the humanist's vision enter the context of the *Regrets* in which Du Bellay claims to relate his own personal story of aspiring to the Golden Fleece and literary fortune, disappointment with prosaic reality and renewed hope on his return to France.

As the emblem for the ebb and flow of his life he chooses the Goddess Fortuna, "ceste aveugle Deesse," along with the values and assets she traditionally possesses. Fortune's wheel is often seen in the medieval sense as the great equalizer (sonnets 70, 96, 97, 105 and 107). But she lacks the clear delineations of the literary stereotype we find in the later *Discours* because in the *Regrets* Fortune serves as a generalization for the oppressive forces that surround the poet, and coalesces with such conceptions as fatality, destiny and necessity.[1] As the persona that shadows him throughout the collection, she becomes the analogue of his initiation into the full range of experience, and the correlative of the lessons he learned in Rome. In sonnet 107 the glance cast over Rome which fully scans the horizon becomes, as in the *Antiquitez,* a reflection on the cycle of temporal destruction and recreation. At the outset Du Bellay looks back on his formerly blissful innocence, "N'estant, comme je suis, encor' exercité / Par tant & tant de maux au jeu de la Fortune" sonnet 3), while the conclusion of the sequence is described as "Depuis ayant le cours de fortune suivy" (sonnet 185).

Ovid's *Tristia,* the literary model after which the dedication of the *Regrets* is patterned, develops the concept of *ambigua Fortuna* (V, viii, 15–18) in a passage to which Du Bellay seems to allude in sonnet 123. An awareness of Fortune's duality, "Estant son naturel de n'estre jamais une" (sonnet 51), alters the poet's attitude toward reality and consequently toward poetry as his life's reflection. Opposed to the two-dimensional Petrarchan ideal, he insists on the complexities of his ex-

[1] The confusion of Fortune with fate, at least, was common to numerous poets used by Du Bellay as models: cf. Pontano, *Carmina,* I, 38; Sannazaro, *Arcadia,* sonnet 44; Burchiello, *Sonetti* (1757), p. 26.

perience of sixteenth-century Rome. His complaints and amusements are gordian and inextricably woven into the sequence. Critics have emphasized the tonal complexities of Du Bellay's other collections of this period,[2] and he himself acknowledges the mixture of honey, salt and gall in the "Ad lectorem." He goes on in the dedication to defend his combination of dulcit melancholy and saline comedy, for "les moyens de plaindre sont divers." But if laughter and tears are mixed in the *Regrets* the proportion is not always the same.

Melancholy, the product of spleen according to Renaissance physiology and the equivalent of earth, the basest cosmological element, pervades the first third of the collection. This mood of sadness is an index to the poet's increasing feeling of Fortune's indifference to his merit. Whereas four years in Rome completely dispelled any youthful visions of innocence he may have entertained about the modern-day city, he insistently proclaimed his actions innocent of reproach and unworthy of Fortune's castigation. In "France, mere des arts" he plaintively understates his position, "Si ne suis-je pourtant le pire du troppeau," but with the increase of satire his alliteration and internal rhyme strengthen his invective against fortune: "Le malheur me poursuit & tousjours m'importune . . . C'est qu'on dit que je n'ay ce malheur merité, / Et que digne je suis de meilleure fortune" (sonnet 43), ". . . je veulx desormais Fortune despiter" (sonnet 56). Yet Fortune, as every Renaissance person knew, is not evil; she is fickle and her blessings are often mixed. In Chapter III we saw that the variable relationship between Fortune and virtue was grounded in cause and effect, although the cause may be unknown to man and the effect uncertain. Despite Du Bellay's assertion at one time that Fortune threatens him with self-alienation, "N'estant de mes ennuis la fortune assouvie, / Afin que je devinsse à moymesme odieux" (sonnet 41) and despite his tacit acceptance of the adage that "fault faire vertu de la necessité" (sonnet 56), he more frequently holds that she disregards virtue and at the same time makes it more evident to the individual through self-knowledge:

> Par la bonne fortune on se trouve abusé,
> Par la fortune adverse on devient plus rusé:
> L'une esteint la vertu, l'autre la fait paroistre:

[2] Verdun Saulnier, *Du Bellay* (1963), p. 100 and Joseph Vianey, *Les Regrets de Du Bellay* (1946), pp. 92 and 169. The kind of tonal complexity we find in the *Regrets* was proverbial in Renaissance poetry; Gascoigne speaks of "The costly taste, of honey mixed with gall" (Dan Bartholmew's Dolorous Discourses," v. 30). Cf. Juvenal's *Satires,* VI, 180–181: "Quotiens animo corrupta superbo plus aloes quam mellis habet."

L'une trompe noz yeux d'un visage menteur,
L'autre nous fait l'amy cognoistre du flateur,
Et si nous fait encor' à nous mesmes cognoistre." (sonnet 51)

As the poet perceives and philosophizes on the sources of his misfortune, the elegiac tone and betrayed expectations prepare and give way to the ironic-satiric point of view; elegy and satire could scarcely be reversed. Ironic fate creates ironic man, the man of innocent conduct yet whose experienced eye allows him to see with an oblique glance and understand the discrepancy between pretentions and deeds, appearance and reality, fortune and virtue.[8]

Du Bellay's passage from melancholy to satirical irony is characterized by a disjunction between himself and other men, between what he seems to say and what he really means. Earlier in the "Chant du désespéré" he had brought together the isolation occasioned by his deafness with his cry of outraged innocence:

D'ou me viennent, sans ma faulte,
Tant de remors furieux?
O malheureuse innocence, (IV, 109)

But from the initial four sonnets, which are basically poetry about poetry, to the end of the *Regrets,* Du Bellay specifically relates this innocent isolation to the low style, "une fureur basse," as the only fitting expression of Fortune's lessons: "Une adresse j'ay pris beaucoup plus opportune / A qui se sent forcé de la necessité."

When the wheel turns and we fall, then we know how unstable, how different from lofty Parnassus and unchanging Eden this world is. Fortune is a symbol for a condition of this world, and knowledge of this condition is irrevocable and parallel to eating of the forbidden fruit. A still naïve Du Bellay had followed Apollo on the uncommon path. As we are all subsumed under the edict passed on our first parents, Adam and Eve, this should be an uncommon path indeed. The path to Parnassus' heights seems to require a state of innocence which enables one to paint an abstract and idyllic vision of the universe. In his innocence Du Bellay felt a "saincte fureur," possibly like the poet who "Dedans l'onde au cheval tout nud s'ira plonger"; one is allowed to be naked in Eden or on Parnassus' slopes. This verse from sonnet 2 carries an insistence not found in its source, the prologue to Persius' *Satires,* although it retains the perspective of the "outsider" (*semipaganus*). As an outsider he continually contrasts his verse with the

[8] Cf. Scaliger, *Poetices libri septem* (1617), p. 322: "Ironia contrarium indicat: constituta est in disunctione." Quintilian discusses the ironic coloring of a man's life and style in IX, ii, 46.

poetic abstractions he sees around him, and wishes to tell his sonnets of the complexities of his experience:

> Mais suivant de ce lieu les accidents divers . . .
> Je me plains à mes vers, si j'ay quelque regret:
> Je me ris avec eulx, je leur dy mon secret,
> Comme estans de mon coeur les plus seurs secretaires. (sonnet 1)

The point is that he is "picqué du souci qui fascheux m'importune." Despite his avowed willingness both to laugh and lament, the etymology of *accidents* points to the downswing of Fortune's Wheel. The source of his inspiration is his agitation at the ways of men and the "maux au jeux de la Fortune." He is not in Paradise, so it is better for him to write of the world. This world is not Parnassus or Eden where holiness guides one's path, but rather a place of contrary forces and a variety of needs.

### The Satiric Reaction

The introductory sonnets claim to add a dimension of personal involvement by relating in non-literary language those actual events which cause emotion. Du Bellay gently intimates that he has fallen from the higher path to a lower, more common one, in keeping with the fallen state of Roman society. Deprecation of one's work is a common Renaissance posture, but upon consideration the reader realizes that his fall is really a voluntary choice to be true to his experience: "Je ne veulx point fouiller au sein de la nature" (sonnet 1), "Je ne veulx fueilleter les exemplaires Grecs" (sonnet 4). Whereas he often damns the object of his satire with faint praise by overstating its worth, whether it be a Petrarchan *blason* (sonnet 91) or Venetian mannerisms (sonnet 133), he praises himself with faint damning by understating his poetic effort. It would be dishonest to disregard the evils which trouble him. Thus, his plain style indicates an honest refusal to paint a picture more beautiful than the world presents, and he will follow the "chemin plus batu" unacceptable to conventional poetry. This more beaten path would paradoxically seem to create an original poetry because so many poets try to climb Parnassus that there are few poets of the earth.

Of course, Du Bellay's disclaimer of conventionality makes his theme all the more conventional. The question does not center on originality as opposed to convention, but rather on which convention—the high road or the low—he will choose and how he chooses to interpret that convention. While the majority of theorists like Sebillet, Peletier, La Fresnaye and the young Du Bellay held that great poets should avoid the beaten path, others like Piccolomini shunned the "altri dotti" in favor of the low, satiric muse, and still others combined the clichés in their praise and dispraise.[4] Du Bellay's derision of rich Petrarchan fiction, "Je ne peins mes tableaux de si riche peinture, / Et si hauts argumens ne recherche à mes vers" (sonnet 1), in favor of simple, ungarnished truth and the "vivante peinture" (sonnets 91 and 159) coincides with the anti-Petrarchan movement of the mid-1550's. Throughout the collection he frames his deunuciation of two-dimensional *res* and *verba* in traditional rhetorical terms.[5] Subject and theme have become separate with the result that poetic substance yields to rhetoric which celebrates its own self. Architectural structure has succumbed to mere verbal and grammatical structure. His distrust of false conceptions is stated through Quintilian's *electio,* "Ores je ne veulx plus telz argumens eslire" (sonnet 186). The concern for expression that is the spatial coefficient of thought, "Qui se peult beaucoup mieulx representer que dire . . . Il vous peindra la forme" is apparent from from his desire to satirize ecclesiastical ceremony in a sestet refashined from Horace (sonnet 119), and is heightened by the surrounding sonnets which press the invitation to see a varied spectacle.

The most significant implication of the choice of the low road and the plain style is that it announces the self-conscious narrator's presentation of the satirist in the Horatian tradition, and satisfies the requirement of rhetorical decorum in general that satire adopt the low style. In the initial sonnet this style derives from a studied indifference that intimates both the forces that work on him and his reaction to them, "Soit de bien, soit de mal, j'escris à l'adventure" (sonnet 1). *Adventure* refers at once to the poet's casualness and to the working of Aventure, Fortune's surrogate.[6] He continues simul-

---

[4] Cf. Vianey, "La Part de l'imitatiton dans les *Regrets,*" *Bulletin Italien,* IV (1904), pp. 31–32; Henri Weber, *La création poétique au XVI*e *siècle* (1956), p. 417; Guido Saba, *La Poesia di Joachim du Bellay* (1962), p. 170; E. R. Curtius, *European Literature and the Latin Middle Ages* (1963), p. 158. Ronsard's "Hymme de la Mort" (1555) which Du Bellay may have had before him, seems to bridge both conventions in its rejection of the "chemin frayé qui conduit sur Parnasse"; elsewhere, Du Bellay praises Ronsard's verses which "Du double mont sont en France venus, / Courent (hardis) par sentiers inconnus" (II, 213). Pierre Grimal astutely observed in passing that even Du Bellay's melancholy theme and development are rhetorical in nature *Les Regrets suivis des Antiquitez* (Paris, 1948), pp. 22, 32).

[5] See Robert J. Clements, "Anti-Petrarchanism of the Pléiade," *Modern Philology,* XXXIX (1941), p. 20.

[6] Cf. Howard Patch, *The Goddess Fortuna in Mediaeval Literature* (1927), pp. 39–40. Horace admires the humble sage (*sapiens*) who can withstand the assaults of Fortune in *Satires* II, vii, 83–87, whereas in *La Parfaicte Amye* Antoine Héroet allows that "amour est dessoubz la nature, / Dessus fortune, et ne craint adventure / N'aultre accident," *Oeuvres poétiques,* ed. Ferdinand Gohin (1909), III, 1577–1579, p. 73.

taneously to describe and demonstrate his casual method in the sestet:

> Aussi ne veulx-je tant les pigner & friser,
> Et de plus braves noms ne les veulx deguiser
> Que de papiers journaux ou bien de commentaires.

The object of his satire for the moment is those poets, namely Ronsard, who do not write as he does. Chamard's note to this sonnet indicates Du Bellay's rejection at the outset of Ronsard's high-flown muse of the *Hymnes;* the last quoted lines, along with sonnet 92 ("En mille crespillons les cheveux se frizer"), also deride Ronsard's fascination of the 1552 Cassandre sonnets: "Qui or peignant les siens jaunement longz, / Or les frizant en mille crespillons."[7] Du Bellay's outlined method is elaborated in the following sonnet where his debt to the tradition of satiric style is even more evident:

> Quant à moy, je ne veulx, pour un vers allonger,
> M'accoursir le cerveau: ny pour polir ma ryme,
> Me consumer l'esprit d'une songneuse lime
> Frapper dessus ma table ou mes ongles ronger
> Aussi veulx-je (Paschal) que ce que je compose
> Soit une prose en ryme ou une ryme en prose,
> Et ne veulx pour cela le laurier meriter.
> Et peult estre que tel se pense bien habile,
> Qui trouvant de mes vers la ryme si facile,
> En vain travaillera, me voulant imiter.

In one breath he refuses to strive for Parnassian perfection, and his subsequent denial, "Je ne veulx retracer les beaux traicts d'un Horace" (sonnet 4), rebuts the numerous passages in which the Augustan poet invites the would-be poet to chew his nails in his concern for the untrodden path to immortality and counsels the *limae labor* that will polish and refine his verse.[8] Yet he subscribes to the Horatian belief that satire, like comedy, should be a "cotidianae vitae speculum" characterized by a common approach to life in an everyday, conversational language capable of addressing unified themes in a variety of ways:

> La Satyre (Dilliers) est un publiq exemple,
> Ou, comme en un miroir, l'homme sage contemple
> Tout ce qui est en luy ou de laid ou de beau. (sonnet 62)[9]

---

[7] Ed. Laumonier, IV, 42, variant 7.

[8] Cf. *Satires,* I, x, 64; I, iv, 11; *Ars poetica,* 285–295; and Cicero's *De oratore* III, 31. See especially M.A. Screech's excellent introduction to *Les Regrets et autres oeuvres poëtiques* (1966), pp. 17–23. The Jolliffe-Screech edition contains the passage from Jean Britannus that will be referred to presently.

[9] *Satires* II, iv, 9; *Epistles* II, i, 168; *Ars poetica,* 89.

Horace goes on to warn, as do all those in the Ciceronian tradition, that the plain style of satire with its pleasant negligence is difficult to imitate and relies on the techniques of rhetorical composition.[10] The Golden Mean of the first Satire and the Murena Ode must be observed in thought, style and action,

> Lime le jugement & le rend plus subtil:
> Mais qui trop y demeure, il envoye en fumee
> De l'esprit trop purgé la force consumee,
> Et pour l'esmoudre trop, luy fait perdre le fil. (sonnet 72)

and Horace's distrust of poetic fury is neatly summed up:

> Bref, loue qui vouldra son art & son mestier,
> Mai cestui-là (Morel) n'est pas mauvais ouvrier,
> Lequel, sans estre fol, peult estre bon poëte. (sonnet 146)

Moreover, the Horatian satirist, who hesitates even to list himself as a poet, cares little for the immortal laurels assured by the *genus grande.*

A Renaissance gloss of Horace, like Jean Britannus' 1536 commentaries, will commonly refer the reader to Quintilian for the techniques, tropes and figures that are desirable in expediting satire. Du Bellay apparently heeds this advice in his use of Quintilian as a source book for the types of figures he will cull from Italian and principally classical Latin poets, but his conception of satire and the genres adjunct to it is still basically Horatian. While Quintilian suggests the use of sarcasm, urbane wit, contradiction and proverbs (VIII, vi, 57), he wishes to exclude invective from satire's province (VI, ii, 16). Horace expands the domain of satire to include the fringe areas of mime and even invective, and argues that it should extend beyond prosaic casualness to parody and elevated emotion.[11]

The *ad hominem* invective we occasionally find in the *Regrets,* the blunt and didactic expression of feeling, runs counter to Horace's theory of satire but remains consistent with his practice. Du Bellay variously directs stinging sarcasm at the territorial designs of the papal court of Paul IV (sonnet 119), Ronsard at play in the fields of Grace (sonnet 3) or the treacheries of Le Breton (sonnet 58). As early as 1550 in the "Musagnoeomachie" we see him plying "la corde puissante / De ma Lire menaçante." Despite a momentary lapse of strength but not intention in the *Regrets* he adapts the theme of Ulysses' vengeful

[10] *Satires* II, i, 3; *Ars poetica,* 240–243; cf. *Orator,* 75–90.

[11] *Satires* I, x, 5–17; I, v, 9; II, i, 13; *Ars poetica,* 93. The "bien dire en mesdisant" of sonnet 143 suggests the classical understanding of *bene dicendi* as both technical mastery and moral stance, or means and ends. Cf. Quintilian, II, xv, 34 and II, xvii, 37.

bow and fits a barb to his lyre string "pour faire ma vengeance" (sonnet 130). But in further obedience to Horatian dicta he tempers invective with variety, good timing, taste and humor. Associating himself with "Ce ruzé Calabrois" in sonnet 62, Du Bellay claims that "sans espargner personne . . . je morde en riant." His bite is demonstrated in the following series of sonnets when again he adapts Horace and threatens a "chien envieux" with "Un traict . . . de rage envenimé . . . un fouet, une Megere, / Un serpent, un cordeau, pour me venger de toy" (sonnet 69). Since Horatian, like Aristotelian, invective is reserved for serious wrongs, Du Bellay sets up a mock-serious gradation of offenses. Sonnet 65 is constructed around a series of dependent clauses that sustain the reader's suspense until "le petit mot pour rire" at the end, and relies on an acceleration of tone and rhythm that continues through the last tercet:

> Tu ne crains la fureur de ma plume animee,
> Pensant que je n'ay rien à dire contre toy,
> Sinon ce que ta rage a vomy contre moy,
> Grinssant comme un mastin la dent envenimee.
> Tu crois que je n'en sçay que par la renommee,
> Et que quand j'auray dict que tu n'as point de foy,
> Que tu es affronteur, que tu est traistre au Roy,
> Que j'auray contre toy ma force consommee.
> Tu penses que je n'ay rien dequoy me venger,
> Sinon que tu n'es fait que pour boire & manger:
> Mais j'ay bien quelque chose encores plus mordante.
> Et quoy? l'amour d'Orphee? & que tu ne sceus oncq
> Que c'est de croire en Dieu? non. Quel vice est-ce doncq?
> C'est, pour le faire court, que tu es un pedante.

*Mordante* is purposely made feminine to rhyme with the Italianate *pedante:* the Roman pedant, as in the following sonnet, is a caustic, chewing creature which abusively devours an excess of knowledge. Similarity of intent, structure and disgusting animal imagery hold the poem together. The satirist normally treats the minor foibles of man, like pedantry, and leaves major failures to philosophers and police officers. Here alkaline humor mixes with the acid of invective, both entailing a recognition of incongruities, which any satirist must accomplish if he wishes to assure the sympathy of his audience. In fact, the intent and technique of Du Bellay's invective are never far from those of satirical irony. Horror and laughter are bluntly juxtaposed in the tercets of sonnet 97, "Ceste frayeur se passe, & suis contraint de rire," and identical alliterations are distinguished only by their contexts of irony, "Ceulx qui sont vaillans, vanteront leur valeur" (sonnet 5) and of vituperation, "Sur les vers je vomis le venim de mon coeur" (sonnet 14).

Both early and late Renaissance poets employ "poetry as a living picture" for the purpose of satire, often through an accumulation of infinitives to parody a series of actions. Whereas a precursor like Berni groups infinitives to suggest random background action, Du Bellay's arrangement outlines gesture and conversation with more precision, after which he casts a retrospective glance at the action with a *voila* to intimate its meaning (sonnets 84, 85 and 113). The English critic Henry Peacham assigns this latter function to the derisive figure mimesis and poets like Magny, Ronsard and d'Aubigné follow the pattern with precision.[12] Despite any variations he may have instituted, Du Bellay's overall conception of satirical mime is well within classical tradition for it incorporates the three types in the New Comedy which Horace helped establish. We find the buffoon whose actions are laughed at by others, "Et rien, que le Breton, ne nous peult faire rire" (sonnets 57 and 120), the imposter, "Ces vieux Singes de Court, qui ne sçavent rien faire, / Sinon en leur marcher les Princes contrefaire" (sonnet 150), and the ever-present ironic narrator who makes himself laugh, in accordance with Aristotle's famous definition of *Rhetoric* III, xviii, 1419b: "Si je ry, c'est ainsi qu'on se rid à la table, / Car je ry, comme on dit, d'un riz Sardonien" (sonnet 77). As with invective, Du Bellay's burlesque is inseparable from the varieties of irony which complicate the poem's structure and increase the reader's mental participation. The mechanical burlesque of sonnet 86, akin to Bergson's "mécanique plaqué sur le vivant," moves into ironic damning with faint praise in the final tercet as the poet comments on the social ballet he has witnessed and ends with verbal irony as his *s'en* aurally completes the tercet's two triple negations in contrast with the three *grave* of the opening:

Marcher d'un grave pas & d'un grave sourci,
Et d'un grave soubriz à chascun faire feste,
Balancer tous ses mots, respondre de la teste,
Avec un *Messer non,* ou bien un *Messer si:*

---

[12] *The Garden of Eloquence* (1954), pp. 138–139; Cf. Ronsard's

Discourir de Jacob & des predestinés,
Avoir S. Paul en bouche, & le prendre à la lettre, . . .
Voylà tout le sçavoir de vostre belle loy. (XI, 74–75)

and d'Aubigné's

. . . marcher mignonnement,
Trainer les pieds, mener les bras, hocher la teste, . . .
Voila pour devenir garce du Cabinet, (II, 1282, 1283, 1298)

See Weber, p. 453, n. 1, for Magny and p. 623.

Entremesler souvent un petit *Et cosi,*
Et d'un *son Servitor'* contrefaire l'honneste,
Et, comme si lon eust sa part en la conqueste,
Discourir sur Florence, & sur Naples aussi:
Seigneuriser chascun d'un baisement de main,
Et suivant la façon du courtisan Romain,
Cacher sa pauvreté d'une brave apparence:
Voila de ceste Court la plus grande vertu,
Dont souvent mal monté, mal sain, & mal vestu,
Sans barbe & sans argent on s'en retourne en France.

The tableau transcends the pointless laughter of pure mime parody to attain the corrective laughter of satire, as Horace wished it to, because the purposely distorted reflection derives from the actions and conditions of the dehumanized society that besets the poet. Elsewhere, his elevated emotion ironically blends with burlesqued ecclesiastical jargon, "Les regrets, les ennuys, le travail & la peine, / Le tardif repentir d'une esperance vaine" (sonnet 24.)[13]

By the very nature of its indirection and meaning more than it says, irony mitigates direct attack and controls emotion. The ironist prefers the indirect approach because his social position may be precarious, "Les vers chantent pour moy ce que dire je n'ose" (sonnets 14 and 42), but mainly because direct rebuke militates against good satire which seeks to move the reader to anger or laughter. The ironic satirist gains the sympathy of his audience by instilling in it his own ideas and feelings. He must appear honest and not subject to whimsy, even though satire by any definition is unfair; it seldom presents its subject straightforwardly and never presents both sides, however much this might be desired.[14] The poet's apparent casualness, then, belies his predetermined purpose. Fortune's caprice notwithstanding, he must present a consistent outlook, "Et n'ay changé d'estat ny de condition . . . Aussi ma qualité ne baisse ny ne monte" (sonnet 74), and yet he must employ a varied technique to retain his audience. For this variety the Renaissance satirist relied heavily on rhetorical persuasion. The greater variety of rhetorical devices, coupled with the similar use of individual figures, and more skillful control of poetic logic in the *Regrets* allow a more detailed analysis of these procedures than in any other sonnet sequence of Du Bellay.

[13] Cf. Rabelais, I, 19 and II, 7, for "le tardif repentir." For the ironic mixture see *Ad Herennium* IV, xxxiv, 46.

[14] Cf. "I am very well up in the opposite calling, too: I mean the one with love for a base; for I am a truth-lover, a beauty-lover, a simplicity-lover, and a lover of all else that is kindred to love. But there are very few who deserve to have this calling practiced upon them." *Lucian,* tr. A. M. Harmon (1947), III, 33.

## RHETORIC AND SATIRE

Reminiscent of Quintilian's advice to affect a listener and convey a larger meaning by ironically repeating words (IX, iii, 29) is sonnet 38 where Du Bellay expresses his wish to free himself from sycophancy and dependence on others. The dispossession of the octave expressed by an extended series of *sans* that introduces negative qualities, and the aurally similar possessive adjectives *son-sa* of the sestet that marshals favorable actions, establish a tensive contrast between Du Bellay's actual condition and his ideal. The jolting contrast of aspiration and failure and the "espoir malheureux / Ce que possede moins celuy qui plus y pense" (sonnet 19) also appear through the juxtaposition of concrete and abstract words in the introduction to the *Regrets,* "j'ay sur mon doz chargé la pauvreté" (v. 42), and in sonnet 32, "m'enrichir d'ennuy, de vieillesse & de soing" where he, unlike Jason, reflects on the emptiness of his quest. Occasionally, the verbal redoubling that creates the impression of balanced presentation, whether in praise of arcane subjects, "D'une saincte fureur sainctement agité," "Je n'entre si avant en si profonds secretz" (sonnets 3 and 4) or in the "Ainsi donc" (sonnet 17) that logically sets off quatrains and tercets, is the same repetition that destroys equilibrium in the poetic argument and shifts it from direct statement into ironic overstatement.

Whether they are achieved through hyperbole or litotes, verbal and other shades of irony are rarely more than one verse or one word away from melancholy. Although "les moyens de plaindre sont divers," similar techniques are mixed and interchanged. The first thirteen verses of sonnet 5 ironically arrange the spectacle of modern Rome, while the balanced redoubling of the fourteenth, "Moy, qui suis malheureux, je plaindray mon malheur," places the contrasting mood in relief. On the other hand, the similarly enumerated melancholy of sonnet 79 gives way in the last verse to an ironic thrust at clerical ignorance.[15] On the level of persuasion the poet thus gains both the reader's sympathy and amused attention. And on the related level of personal experience we again discover that behind the most minute shade of irony of word or manner in his poetic transformation of society is the dramatic irony of Fate that contrasts anticipation with disappointment and thus transforms the poet. The soliloquy that flashes back on his earlier intentions is

[15] Cf. C. E. Nelson, "Enumeration and Irony in *Les Regrets* of Du Bellay," *French Review,* XXXVI (1963), 271. In an authorial commentary on the structure and meaning of a comparably enumerated sonnet, La Ceppède observes that the two parts of each verse correspond "comme des effects à leur cause" (*Les Théorèmes spirituels* [1613], I, iii, sonnet 20).

rudely interrupted by the imperfect tense and the subsequent reflections on life's vanity:

> Je me feray sçavant en la philosophie,
> En la mathematique & medecine aussi:
> Je me feray legiste, & d'un plus hault souci
> Apprendray les secrets de la theologie:
> Du lut & du pinceau j'esbateray ma vie,
> De l'escrime & du bal. Je discourois ainsi,
> Et me vantois en moy d'apprendre tout cecy,
> Quand je changeay la France au sejour d'Italie.
> O beaux discours humains! je suis venu si loing,
> Pour m'enrichir d'ennuy, de vieillesse & de soing, . . .

The grammatical detachment of the poet in the last verse, "Ayant fait, comme moy, un malheureux voyage," contrasts with the impersonal beginning of the previous sonnet, "Heureux qui, comme Ulysse, a fait un beau voyage." Thus the field of observation is enlarged from words and personalities to the central fact of life and the play of Fortune.

We have seen that the cultivation of the low style corresponds to the satirical task, and that careful control of language in this style helps establish the ironic point of view. This is simply another way of restating and resolving the traditional dichotomy between art and nature. Du Bellay believes "que la nature / Par l'art se peult monstrer" (sonnet 148), but in a Horatian maxim he stipulates, as any Renaissance writer would, that technique should be unobtrusive: "L'artifice caché, c'est le vray artifice" (sonnet 142). So when he says "J'escry naïvement tout ce qu'au coeur me touche" (sonnet 21) he does not claim purely spontaneous composition, as *naïvement* might imply; rather, he shows a conscious concern for a style that betokens a casual attitude. Sonnet 36 offers such an example where, after alluding to the three colorless years spent in Rome by means of monotonous assonance, periphrasis and repetition, he continues

> Tant me tarde (Morel) que Paris je revoye,
> Et tant le ciel pour moy fait lentement son tour.
> Il fait son tour si lent, & me semble si morne,
> Si morne & si pesant, que le froid Capricorne
> Ne m'accoursit les jours, ny le Cancre les nuicts.

The various figures that structure the passage—traductio and anadiplosis among others—would be apparent to the scrutiny of any poet like Du Bellay who was schooled in rhetoric as figures that stress the gradual transformation of the subject and expand a single poetic argument. His return to more direct statement in the conclusion summarizes the heaviness of time on his hands and specifies that "la nature / Fait toute chose longue." While this prolonged recourse to disguised technique may violate modern aesthetic or post-Romantic notions of "honesty," it is nevertheless at the very heart of Renaissance poetic and the principles of the *Deffence*. Use of "ornemens poëtiques," enjoined by the *Deffence* and operative in the previous sonnet sequences we have examined, is everywhere apparent in the *Regrets*. Spontaneous overflow of feeling is tempered or even precluded by the occasionally rigid styling, whether in widely separated or sequentially related sonnets. The similarly framed figure epizeuxis is utilized to represent haste and emotion in sonnet 8, "Cela (Ronsard) cela, cela merite bien" and in sonnet 53, "Vivons (Gordes), vivons, vivons, & pour le bruit." The figure compar which solidifies the center of *Antiquitez* 6, "Pareille à sa grandeur, grandeur sinon la sienne," again designates virtue and solidarity in *Regrets* 135, "La police immuable, immuable les lois," and 137, "Je vey ce beau Lyon, Lyon que tant je prise."

From the point of view of Renaissance poetic canons, it would be insufficient and partially incorrect summarily to pronounce Du Bellay's poetry rhetorical without asking why and how his tropes and figures are elaborated. While some verses appear to come from the same mold and similar schemes are often deployed with similar intent, identical configurations can create different effects. The epanalepsis (*Rome-Rome*) and the balance of *compar* in *Antiquitez* 26 argue Rome's former global dominion and the persistence of its influence:

> Rome fut tout le monde, & tout le monde est Rome.
> Et si par mesmes noms mesmes choses on nomme,

This verbal arrangement is reduced to casual conversation in *Regrets* 42 where *ores-ore* stresses the opposition between the vivid present and an implied past:

> C'est ores, mon Vineus, mon cher Vineus, c'est ore,
> Que de tous les chetifs le plus chetif je suis,
> Et que ce que j'estois, plus estre je ne puis,

The hyperbaton (*je suis*) of the second verse, suggestive of similarity in the previous instance, insists on the poet's virtuous but unblest isolation from Roman vice. Whereas the *Antiquitez* sonnet speaks at once of finality and continuation, the altered verb tenses in the *Regrets* sonnet (v. 3) speak of complete divorce from a former condition.

It is no surprise, then, to see like figures repeated in force and in varying or comparable situations. The formulary pattern of numerous sonnets in the *Regrets* has often been cited as evidence of a reaction to contemporary Italian satire,[16] and in Chapter II we explained the Pléiade's shared preference for polysyndeton as a means of expressing a unified vision. With only slight structural variations, in the *Regrets* this figure always describes perfection, celebrates the departure for a promised land where virtue reigns, or disparages the vice and dissension the poet sees around him. It thus unites widely separated sonnets and supports the thematic integrity of the collection:

> Sortons (Dilliers) sortons, faisons place à l'envie,
> Et fuyons desormais ce tumulte civil, (sonnet 50)
> Fuyons (Dilliers) fuyons ceste cruelle terre,
> Fuyons ce bord avare & ce peuple inhumain, (sonnet 116)
> Je voy (Dilliers) je voy serener la tempeste,
> Je voy le vieil Proté son troppeau renfermer, (sonnet 129)[17]

By judiciously culling from an open book or by exercising the literary memory through innutrition, poets often conjured up time-honored images and themes that functioned as figures of thought and upon which they worked variations. These allusions were drawn both from the elevated style of classical poets the Pléiade always admired, such as Vergil's thematic image of the poet as lamenting swan around which sonnet 16 centers,[18] and from the low style of contemporary poets which the *Deffence* originally spurned (p. 114), as in sonnet 48. Even when their character and sources are dissimilar they underline the sequence's basic concerns. The Ulysses theme and the "livre du monde" theme (sonnet 59) which Montaigne and Descartes revive in their pages on education, both correlate the idea of undergone experience. Such thematic images were a kind of *locus proprius*. They corresponded to the "special topic" of classical rhetoric with its particular subject refer-

[16] See Vianey, *Le Pétrarquisme en France au XVI*[e] *siècle* (1909), pp. 336–360; Chamard, *Histoire de la Pléiade* (1961–1963), II, 242; Raymond T. Hill, "The Influence of the *Noie* on the Poetry of Joachim du Bellay" in *Essays in Honor of Albert Feuillerat* (1943), pp. 85–92; Saulnier, *Du Bellay*, p. 83; and Weber, p. 425. We could of course go back as far as Quintilian who cites the ironic use of praeteritio in IX, ii, 47, or Cicero's *Pro Sexto Roscio Amerino*, I, 1–2, for a prototype of the figure aetiologia used throughout *Regrets* 79.

[17] Cf. sonnets 90, 148 and Olivier de Magny's *Les Souspirs* (1874) 67, p. 49: "Vivons, Belle, vivons & suivons nostre amour."

[18] Chamard cites *Aeneid XI*, 456–458 as the source of Du Bellay's sonnet; it is just as likely, however, that he had in mind the famous canto XXXV of *Orlando Furioso* which also elaborates the theme of the Golden Fleece. Cf. Ronsard, IV, 6, variant and VI, 26 of the 1914–1919 Laumonier edition. Eugénie Droz speaks of Du Bellay, "le cerveau farci de textes latins, de souvenirs classiques, de centons qui pendant des années, a rêvé d'un voyage en Italie," *Les Antiquitez de Rome et les Regrets* (1945), p. xi. See also Grimal's edition, pp. 23, 29, 31. These centos must be considered along with other rhetorical figures, for they are often similar in source and function.

ence, as opposed to the universal reference of the commonplace. In this effort the poet was guided by his rhetorical training for the principles of decorum and suggested procedure. Du Bellay's sonnet 9, "France, mere des arts, des armes & des loix," may well have been inspired by Petrarch's "Armarum legumque," as it is occasionally pointed out, but any encomium of a country required an initial or final tribute to "its race, founders, government, its advancement in learning and literature."[19] It is within this larger tradition that he works variations on the same theme with his "la France fut enceincte / Des lettres & des arts" (sonnet 190) and "Mere des ars, ta haulteur je salue" (III, 69).

Vergil was a favorite source for these themes and centos, and Du Bellay heaps praise on his inspiration, "Virgile eut ce Daemon, & l'eut Horace encor" (sonnet 147). Pastiche verses in the *Regrets,* "O trois & quatre fois malheureuse la terre" (sonnet 114) and elsewhere, "O trois-fois malheureux & quatre fois, celuy" (VI, 210) incorporate the Vergilian formula "terque quaterque" that Du Bellay would have found in his readings and translations of Vergil (*Geor.* II, 399; *Aen.* I, 94; IV, 589; XII, 155). Certain verse fragments from Vergil are integrated into the *Regrets* and recur, just like specific rhetorical tropes, to establish unity and thematic progression. Sonnet 17, which follows the theme of lamenting swans in the previous sonnet, condenses and moves resolutely through *Aeneid* VI, 305, 313, 326, 639 and 713:

> Tu as attaint le bord ou tout le monde court . . .
> Qui nous chasse bien loing : car, pour le faire court,
> Nous n'avons un quatrin pour payer le naulage . . .
> Bien avant dans un bois te perds avec ta dame :
> Tu bois le long oubly de tes travaux passez, (vv. 3, 7–8, 11–12)

*Aeneid* VI, 713, which Du Bellay incorporates into the description of his infernal existence at the beginning of the *Regrets,* returns in the last tercet of sonnet 174 where he leaves the hell of Rome and returns to Marguerite at the court of France.[20]

Such passages are found not only in single collections, but also in his combined poetic efforts ranging through translation, imitation and recreation. Anchises' cosmological speech (*Aen.* VI, 724–727), which appeared in Du Bellay's *Aeneid* translation (VI, 385), was considerably reworked in his translation for the Le Roy anthology (VI, 443), is included in the octave of *L'Olive* 64 for the sake of praising his love, indi-

[19] Charles S. Baldwin, *Medieval Rhetoric and Poetic* (1928), p. 21. Cf. Screech, p. 66.

[20] The Vergilian underworld, on which the cyclic return of *Antiquitez* 15 centers, creates the unity of *Regrets* 134, 136 and 137.

cates the permanence of Rome's influence in the first tercet of *Antiquitez* 5, survives intact in the octave of *Regrets* 125 and intimates his perilous existence in the first tercet of *Regrets* 128. This continued and apparently limitless adaptability of Vergil to the divergent needs of the sonnet is not good by definition, since it can prolong faults of understanding or linguistic difficulties. When he has trouble in skillfully adapting the continuation of Anchises' speech (*Aeneid* VI, 730) from his translation to the Le Roy anthology he naturally has difficulty when he incorporates it in his sonnet; the result is the clumsy syntax of sonnet 117, "De substance de feu dit estre noz esprits." But even when Vergil's vague *machina* of *Aeneid* IV, vv. 88–89, "pendent opera interrupta, minaeque murorum ingentes aequataque machina," is loosely translated to the point of mistranslation in Du Bellay's "L'oeuvre imparfait des superbes murailles, / Et des palais le front audacieux" (VI, 263), the poetic refraction of Vergil's lines in the *Regrets* evinces consummate talent. Although the description is of Carthage's unfinished buildings, Du Bellay combines it with the legendary "altae moenia Romae" of *Aeneid* I, 7 in his melancholy praise of Rome's lost grandeur, "Le brave front de ces palais Romains" (*Antiquitez* 9) and in "des palais Romains le front audacieux" (*Regrets* 31). In the later ironic sonnets where melancholy turns to irony, the *Aeneid* is used as background for depicting curial degeneracy (*Regrets* 103). Sonnet 109 focuses on the "pendent opera interrupta" and on the reform-minded Pope Marcellus II who died "au milieu de son oeuvre entrepris."

Adaptations of both themes and model rhetorical figures imply a stylized attitude toward poetry, and are both forms of innutrition whether by artificial or natural memory. Both, then, are fundamental to poetry that claims to work with preexisting material. Vergil, for instance, furnishes not only figures of thought but also figures of style which Du Bellay employs in precisely the same way. In his reading and translations of Vergil his eye would have crossed the figure anadiplosis that prolongs and defines an idea, as in "n'ay prouvé que la peine, / La peine & le malheur d'une esperance vaine" (sonnet 35).[21] The figure always illustrates the poem's theme and is never gratuitous. It is usually found in sonnets that emphasize the duration or monotony of action, and coincides with the need to expand the emotional or physical dimensions of a thought. Sonnet 82 sets out to increase the reader's awareness and convince him that Rome is a microcosm of the world, replete with

[21] E.g., "videt et lacerum crudeliter ora, / ora manusque," *Aeneid* VI, 495–496. Cf. *Aeneid* II, 405–406; *Eclogues* VI, 20–21 and X, 72–73; *Regrets* 25, 30, 83, 126 and 145; Ronsard, ed. Laumonier, XI, 83.

buffoons and impostors: "Veulx-tu sçavoir (Duthier) quelle chose c'est Rome? / Rome est de tout le monde un publique eschafault."

From the frequent recurrence and apparent uniformity of such rhetorical devices, both in their sources and adaptations, one should not of course conclude that Du Bellay applies them with no regard for the subtle variations in actual experience or for contours of the imagination. Among these figures, antithesis receives most present-day censure as being "mere rhetoric."[22] But rhetoricians of any pre-Romantic period are quick to criticize antithesis which derives from the simple desire for balance or "fausses fenêtres." Close analysis shows that numerous antitheses in the *Regrets* are carefully imbalanced and this imbalance directs the narrative point of view. Balance may be strongly inferred through internal rhyme and assonance, as in the polarity of the old and young man in sonnet 73: "Si sale qu'un vieux bouq . . . Comme est un jeune loup" and "Comme un fangeux pourceau . . . Comme d'un fin regnard." The declarations that introduce them, however, are unevenly paired, "j'ay en horreur" and "je ne crains rien tant," as are the stanzas of sonnet 67 which alternate unevenly between "je ne puis voir," "je me fasche," "me deçoit" and "me degouste." Appreciation for the difference in tone is crucial for the reader's understanding of the poet's intent. The intent, or at least the result, of sonnet 29 is to damn his fate but implicitly to praise himself with a faint damning:

> Je hay plus que la mort un jeune casanier,
> Qui ne sort jamais hors, sinon aux jours de feste,
> Et craignant plus le jour qu'une sauvage beste,
> Se fait en sa maison luy mesmes prisonnier.
> Mais je ne puis aymer un vieillard voyager,
> Qui court deça dela, & jamais ne s'arreste,
> Ains des pieds moins leger que leger de la teste,
> Ne sejourne jamais non plus qu'un messager.
> L'un sans se travailler en seureté demeure,
> L'autre, qui n'a repos jusques à tant qu'il meure,
> Traverse nuict & jour mille lieux dangereux:
> L'un passe riche & sot heureusement sa vie,
> L'autre, plus souffreteux qu'un pauvre qui mendie,
> S'acquiert en voyageant un sçavoir malheureux.

The quatrains rely on a semantic imbalance between the similarly aligned "jeune casanier" and the "vieillard voyager." Intensified by

[22] Alfred W. Satterthwaite ["Moral Vision in Spenser, Du Bellay and Ronsard," *Comparative Literature,* IX (1957), p. 149] and Frédéric Boyer [*Joachim du Bellay* (1958), p. 91] reduce antithesis in the *Regrets* to absolute opposition. I find Weber [pp. 422, 425] and Saba [p. 75] more convincing in their insistence that antithesis responds to poetic vision and varies accordingly.

pressing internal rhymes, "Je hays plus que la mort" exceeds in strength the modest "je ne puys aymer" to receive the poet's full disapprobation. In the tercets, attention is diverted from the young fool to the more extensively treated weary traveler who is overwhelmed by his many unsatisfactory experiences. Both alternatives in the poet's dilemma appear undesirable. But the old voyager, who like Du Bellay experiences life at first hand and reflects upon it, has better reasons for seclusion than the young recluse. The passage from the self-directed irony of "leger de la teste" to the "sçavoir malheureux" creates a mood that dominates not only sections of this collection but the "Patriae desiderium" and the "sage malheureux" (IV, 141) of his lyric poetry as well.

So rhetorical tropes and figures in the *Regrets,* far from being a static appliqué, dynamically express and direct the line of the poet's thought. By repeating similar words or abruptly juxtaposing opposites, by both traditional and unconventional use of figures, Du Bellay's art expresses *au vif* the variety inherent in nature and the subtleties of his emotions and opinions. Rhetorical schemes thus delineate the gradations and reversals of his fortune and of his corresponding reaction. In the anthology piece "France, mere des arts" the transformation of the simile "comme un aigneau" into metaphor by means of allegorical development deepens at once the identification with the wandering lamb, the sense of tragic irony in the poet's isolation and the feeling that his fortune is causally out of line with his character. Nor are figures expressive of gradation and reversal mutually exclusive. The aural and semantic alteration inherent in the figure traductio can embroider the theme of lyric's curative powers in a rectilinear progression from "tormente" to "en pleurant je les chante, / Si bien qu'en les chantant, souvent je les enchante" (sonnet 12). Or it can combine with chiasmus, which abruptly modifies the point of view:[23]

> Si l'importunité d'un crediteur me fasche,
> Les vers m'ostent l'ennuy du fascheux crediteur:
> Et si je suis fasché d'un fascheux serviteur,
> Dessus les vers (Boucher) soudain je me desfasche. (sonnet 14)

These two patterns of ideas are further conveyed through figures of thought which can adjoin or incorporate tropes and figures of words in order to mirror the informal dialectic of normal conversation. Heedless of the division between octave and sestet, sonnet 63 combines gradatio

[23] Cf. sonnets 41, 110 and 140; Magny's *Souspirs* 148.

and chiasmus to form the figure of thought communicatio, a request for advice in making a decision (Quintilian IX, i, 30):

> . . . quel homme est-ce, Lestrange?
> Lestrange, entre nous deux, je te pry, dy le moy.
> Dy moy, quel est celuy qui si bien se deguise,
> Qu'il semble homme de guerre entre les gens d'eglise,
> Et entre gens de guerre aux prestres est pareil?

Sonnet 33 makes a similar request and shows the same indecision:

> Que feray-je, Morel? dy moy, si tu l'entends,
> Feray-je encor icy plus longue demeurance,
> Ou si j'iray revoir les campaignes de France,
> Quand les neiges fondront au soleil du primtemps?
> Si je demeure icy, helas, je perds mon temps
> A me repaistre en vain d'une longue esperance:
> Et si je veulx ailleurs fonder mon asseurance,
> Je fraude mon labeur du loyer que j'attens.
> Mais fault il vivre ainsi d'une esperance vaine?
> Mais fault il perdre ainsi bien trois ans de ma peine?
> Je ne bougeray donc. Non, non, je m'en iray.

The review of diverse causes and their effects demonstrates how unobtrusive can be the logic of the poem's basic argument; the accelerated momentum of the plea coincides with the poem's only plastic image, the melting snow on the French landscape.

This impression of casual honesty in a conversational tone is enhanced by a variety of discourse. *Licentia* or *oratio libera* (Quintilian IX, ii, 27)—a speaker's risky but honest reproach of his audience—appears in sonnet 85, "Ne suivre en son parler la liberté de France . . . Ne dire à tous venans tout cela que lon pense," as a means of contrasting Roman duplicity with the unguarded speech of the French. Innumerable variations on this theme occur throughout the collection: Du Bellay reasons with himself in sonnet 48 about the virtue of speaking his mind and the need to restrain "la liberté de sa plume," and initiates imaginary conversation with others (subiectio: Quintilian IX, ii, 15) in sonnets 18, 28 and 75 where the point of view fluctuates continually throughout the dialogue. Similar thought patterns reveal subtly altered points of view; his monologue addressed to animate objects or actual persons is couched either in an exclamation which receives no answer (sonnet 9) or in an interrogation which expects no answer (sonnet 15).

Figures of thought thus reflect and recreate the flow of relaxed speech and constitute both the visual and aural disposition of thought. Du Bellay's continued interest in *dispositio* (*despense*) is articulated in his admiration for architecture's "vivante peinture" with its "artifice & despense admirable" (sonnet 159) and for its "mil argumens / Variant le desseing" which closely parallels his poetic style, "je bastis, d'un nouvel artifice" (sonnet 157).

Driving concern in this group of sonnets for the meaning of architectural order and the relative position of components has its literary counterpart in the sonnet's structure. Arrangement of single verses and stanzas can frequently be taken as an index to the source of Du Bellay's melancholy or satiric intent. The point-by-point correspondence in sonnet 6 between octave and sestet from the initial verses ("Las, ou est maintenant ce mespris de Fortune?"—"Maintenant la Fortune est maistresse de moy") to the final verses ("Je les menois danser aux rayons de la Lune"—"Et les Muses de moy, comme estrangers, s'enfuyent") becomes an anatomy of melancholy based on a systematic opposition of every attractive illusion entertained in the past and the harsh realities of the present. With satirical intent the quatrains of the structurally complex sonnet 110 also develop line-by-line correspondences and elaborate consecutive *vers rapportés* on war and peace. In the sestet, chiasmus illustrates Du Bellay's insistence on seeing how opposites functionally define one another:

> Comparant Paule quart avec Jules troisieme.
> Aussi ne furent onq' deux siecles plus divers,
> Et ne se peult mieulx voir l'endroit par le revers
> Que mettant Jules tiers avec Paule quatrieme.

Aware of the important tonic stress on the final syllable in French verse, Du Bellay's interest in verbal position as a means of directing attention is further evinced by his careful handling of rhyme. Rhyme controls, supports and equates with the syntactical unit. The delayed verb at the end of sonnet 16, "Bien loing sur un estang trois cygnes lamenter," fits the myth of the poet's swan song signaling his death, establishes a connecting link with the following sonnet where the same verb recurs, and through its strong position equates with the final spondee in its probable source (loquacia *cycni: Aeneid,* IX, 458). Du Bellay's habitual marking of the hemistich with internal rhyme or near rhyme of masculine with feminine endings bespeaks the craftsman's concern for stressing key words and for balance both of words and of meaning.[24] The effect of such rhyme may be to punctuate an otherwise

[24] E.g., "N'estant de mes ennu*is* la fortune assouv*ie* . . . Donc l'eternelle nu*ic*t a ta clarté rav*ie*" (sonnet 41), "A qui mesmes les *Roys* ne peuvent donner *loy*" (sonnet 42), "Veult tousjours contred*ire* à son propre des*ir*" (sonnet 53), "Se tormente l'espr*it* des affaires d'autru*y*" (sonnet 54), "Que je veulx desorm*ais* Fortune despit*er*" (sonnet 56), "Qui, comme Jupit*er* tout le monde temp*ere*" (sonnet 119).

unrelieved series, "La douleur, le soucy, les regrets, les ennu*is*" (sonnet 35), or to unite meaning, "Rend les yeux esblou*is* & la teste eslourd*ie*" (sonnet 59). The *Regrets* are spared the linguistic virtuosity of the *rhétoriqueurs* because rhyme illuminates meaning instead of itself and because the procedure is subject to countless variations: internal rhyme between unpaired verses may accentuate the traveler's futile gesture of distress in sonnet 34, "Et quelqu'autre bien *loing,* au danger d'abysmer, / En vain tendre les *mains* vers le front du rivage," or by doubling rhyme it may contrast his fortune, "C'est qu'on dit que je n'*ay* ce malheur merit*é*" (sonnet 43) with his true merit "Quelque *bien* à la *fin,* car je l'*ay* merit*é*" (sonnet 46).

Directing the reader's attention to the poetic argument by controlling, modifying and correcting his attitude is rooted in Du Bellay's professed desire to discover and reveal unvarnished truth. He invites his prospective reader to separate reality from illusion through the realization "Que Rome n'est plus Rome, & que celuy en vain / Presume d'en juger, qui bien ne l'a comprise" (sonnet 131). Where the *Antiquitez* set out to commemorate the remnants of Rome's past glory and uncover the spirit that survived its historical decline, the *Regrets* informally but resolutely examine the internal structure of present-day Roman society to uncover the truth of its moral decline, "Ne voyant que l'orgueil de ces monceaux pierreux" (sonnet 19). Conjoining in his perspective the physical demise of the old Rome and the spiritual death of the new, Du Bellay sees funereal emptiness beneath the glittering surface: "Qui les void par dehors ne peult rien voir plus beau, / Mais le dedans resemble au dedans du tombeau" (sonnet 90). At the outset of his itinerary in sonnet 80, "Si je monte au Palais," his eye encompasses the pride and vice hidden by pontifical ceremony and descends through the social structure to usury, "Si je descens en banque," and finally prostitution. The "monceau pierreux" that closes the sonnet equates moral with physical ruin in this vanity of vanities. The separation of mask from reality which becomes one of the informing principles of his writing, "Je ne veulx deguiser ma simple poësie / Sous le masque emprunté d'une fable moisie" (sonnet 188), becomes equally one of the collection's leitmotifs. The theme of the masked ball, "Aller de nuict en masque, en masque deviser, / Se feindre à tous propos" (sonnet 92), thus assumes the proportions of a generalized commentary on the society Du Bellay surveys and intends to unmask: "Icy de mille fards la traïson se deguise" (sonnet 127).

It is this effort to predispose his reader's moral reaction that aligns the *Regrets* with the purpose of Horatian satire and the admonition to teach, please and move. At various moments in the sequence Du Bellay recalls that "on se plaist à mesdire: / Pource qu'en mesdisant on dit la verité" (sonnet 76) and shows "d'un art Horacien, / Comme il fault chastier le vice & l'ignorance" (sonnet 167) where his "vray mestier, c'est de n'espargner homme, / Mais les vices chanter d'une publique voix" (sonnet 108). Despite the occasional self-consciousness of his narrative and the frequency of individual names, his generalized conclusions accord with traditional and contemporary satire.[25] The specific example of Rome in the *Regrets* affords a broad lesson for humanity, and whoever reads the sonnets can find "Quelque chose du sien protrait en ce tableau" (sonnet 62). Rome's catholicity, seen from the double perspective of imperial glory and Renaissance achievement, gained widespread assent among sixteenth-century humanists.[26] As the microcosm containing "Tout ce qu'on void de bien & de mal en ce monde" (sonnet 78) Du Bellay's chronicle preaches "la leçon coustumiere" (sonnet 151) and "parle tousjours des vices en commun" (sonnet 142). His heavy reliance on extracting a generally apprehensible feeling from an intimate experience precludes the so-called romantic irony with which he is sometimes labeled.[27]

One of the principal means of effecting persuasion to a mood or idea in Renaissance literary composition was the informal logic of the commonplace. Discussions of satirical irony in Ciceronian rhetoric include use of the many kinds of *loci communes* (Quintilian VIII, vi, 57) while in the dialectic underlying this system *sententiae, exempla,* adages, proverbs and apophthegms fortified a work's cause and developed it through induction, reasoning from particular facts to a general con-

[25] Cf. Jean Bouchet: "Aultres poetes sont Satyres dictz, qui tous leurs metres font reprehensifz de tous pechez publiques," *Epistres morales et familieres du traverseur* (1545), I, 13. The kind of generalized satire we find in Du Bellay, moreover, was used in schools of the period as an aid to rhetorical instruction. Cf. *Pasquillorum tomi duo* (1554).

[26] Cf. Montaigne: "Les astres ont fatalement destiné l'estat de Romme pour exemplaire de ce qu'ils peuvent en ce genre. Il comprend en soy toutes les formes et avantures qui touchent un estat; tout ce que l'ordre y peut et le trouble, et l'heur et le malheur," III, 9, p. 937.

[27] Cf. sonnets 112 and 44. Rosemond Tuve's apt observation that the Renaissance poet's "subject was still 'his meaning'," overshadowing the stress on "himself-seeing-it" (*Elizabethan and Metaphysical Imagery* (1965), p. 43), finds its counterpart in Du Bellay's "subject, qui produict naïvement en moy / Ce que par art contraint les autres y font naistre" (sonnet 180) and "elle est de mes vers le plus louable object: / Car en louant (Gournay) si louable subject . . ." (sonnet 182). His remark in the "Patriae desiderium" that "Quique placet paucis, displicet ipse sibi" counters the romantic tendency toward self-directed analysis of feeling in disregard of the audience's assent. Cf. Weber's closing comment, p. 462 and René Wellek and Austin Warren, *Theory of Literature* (1962), p. 223.

clusion (Cicero, *De inventione,* I, xxxi, 51). The general conclusions in Du Bellay's sonnet capsulize its meaning. Instead of being realistic descriptions of actual events, the numerous nautical allusions in the *Regrets* are rather poetic imagery whose styling resembles the frequently imitated Erasmian adages.[28] The formulaic introduction to many of the commonplaces, "Et fault bien (comme on dit) bien dire en mesdisant" (sonnet 143), underlines not only its rhetorical nature but also stresses its traditional appeal and shared understanding. Rhetoricians and Renaissance commentators on poetry hold that commonplaces should illuminate the poems that contain them and should reinforce or complement one another when conjoined in one poem, as in the series of conclusions in sonnets 46 and 48. By examining the historical development of these triple series we can see that they formed part on the common classical heritage of the Renaissance and left the poet considerable latitude even when his choice of imagery was limited to the four elements. Catullus' "In vento et rapida scribere oportet aqua" (LXX, 4) returns in Petrarch's sonnet "Beato in sogno" as "solco onde e'n rena fondo e scrivo in vento," and is loosely arranged in a series in Erasmus' *Adagia* (I, iv, 52 and 60), a fountainhead of Renaissance commonplaces. Ronsard coordinated and variously altered these sources in widely divergent contexts to express the same idea of futility: "Tu bastiras sur l'incertain du sable / Et vainement tu peindras dans les cieulx," "Dans un sablon la semence j'épan, / Je sonde en vain les abymes d'un goufre," "Brevement tu respons que je perdois ma peine, / Que j'escrivois sur l'eau & semais dans l'areine," "C'est vouloir peindre en l'onde, & arrester le vent."[29] The series of proverbs that closes Du Bellay's sonnet 46, "Je cognois que je seme au rivage infertile, / Que je veulx cribler l'eau, & que je bas le vent," welds together an otherwise fragmented poem while maintaining its structure, and indicates a meaning of the separate components which would have been open to the collective conscience of his Renaissance audience.

Stated another way, numerous and similar sources of commonplaces

[28] Screech, for instance, traces "Ja vers le front du port je commence à ramer" to Erasmus' "In portu navigare," p. 204. Cf. Screech's p. 93 and Weber, pp. 430–434, 437.

[29] Ed. Laumoiner, IV, 23; V, 132: XII, 262; *Les Oewvres de Pierre de Ronsard, texte de 1587,* ed. Isidore Silver (1966), II, 311. Cf. Thomas Wyatt's "Whoso list to hunt": "Since in a net I seek to hold the wind." Although a later generation altered its meaning to express the vanity of vanities, "L'onde où nous batissons nos folles esperances, / L'air où nous escrivons l'orgueil de nos puissances" (Jean Auvray, *La Pourmenade de l'ame devote* [1633], p. 54), or the inconstancy of love, "Estant dessus le sable elle escrivoit sur l'onde" (Pierre de Marbeuf, *Recueil de vers,* Rouen, 1628 [1897], p. 181), the structure of the series is essentially retained.

were available to Du Bellay. Biblical phrases that had become proverbial, "Et l'arbre par le fruict se cognoit, comme on dict" (II, 210: Matthew VII, 16) and folk wisdom, "Il n'est rien (ce dit-on en proverbe vulgaire)" (sonnet 73) enter equally into his satire, but most often his commonplaces are the same as those we find in other Renaissance satirists. As usual, Erasmus is the source book. Rabelais' story of the cook who sold the smoke from his roast (III, 37) is a patchwork of Erasmus' adages (I, iii, 1; II, iii, 68; and II, ix, 64) and derives its plot line from the long "Fumos vendere," I, iii, 41. Among the meanings of this last adage Erasmus includes pandering favors at court, which is precisely the subject of sonnet 144 where Du Bellay disclaims ability to "Vendre de la fumee à quelque poursuivant."[30] Alongside other sources, proverbs from Erasmus and his colloquy "Naufragium" structure Rabelais' description of the storm in IV, 18–23. The beginning of Du Bellay's sonnet 26 which describes the hidden dangers in the "mer Romaine" appears to draw on the same colloquy and closes with an *exemplum,* "Pour Charybde eviter tu tomberas en Scylle," whose general meaning Erasmus discussed at length in *Adagia* I, v, 4. This sonnet, as well as sonnets 33 and 101, thus concludes with an Erasmian commonplace in order to pose the poet's indecision and moral dilemma in widely intelligible terms.

The vast majority of commonplaces, however, resolve all doubt and lead the reader to a single moral attitude in keeping with Du Bellay's satirical themes and intent. In developing the theme of the social mask, the commonplace defines his attack against those who "Sçavent, comme lon dit, faire d'un diable un ange" (sonnet 182). It clarifies the reason for his laughter, "Je ry de voir ainsi deguiser ces Seigneurs, / Desquelz (comme lon dit) ilz font comme de cire" (sonnet 183), and sets him apart from the courtiers who "se prennent à rire, & ne sçavent pourquoy" (sonnet 150). As commonplaces weave this theme through the collection the adages culled from Erasmus blend with the particular referents and personae of Du Bellay's own experience and yet prolong the function and meaning they have within the broader Renaissance tradition. Sonnet 150 inveighs against the "vieux Singes de Court" who can only feign the habits of princes and "se vestir, comme eulx, d'un

[30] See Erasmus, *Opera omnia* (1703), II, 128–130. Ronsard also says "Je ne suis Courtisan ni vendeur de fumées" (*Ronsard, poésies choisies,* ed. Pierre de Nolhac [1959], p. 505). Cf. the conclusion to sonnet 52. See also Pietro Toldo, "La Fumée du rôti et la divination des signes," *Revue des études rabelaisiennes,* I (1903), 13–14; Ernest Langlois, "La Fumée du rôti payé au son de l'argent," ibid., 222–224; L. Sozzi, "Rabelais, Philelphe et le 'fumet du rôti'," *Etudes rabelaisiennes,* V (1964), 197–205.

pompeux appareil." The language and meaning of the adage "Simia in purpura" (I, vii, 10) underlies the sonnet and informs our understanding of sonnet 105 as well where Du Bellay treats the scandalous Innocenzo del Monte, who was awarded the red hat for having cared for Julius III's monkey and was derided as the Cardinal Simia.[31] In the same way, the rhetorically-trained Erasmus discusses an adage about making a statue of Mercury from base wood (II, v, 47) as an allegory subject to the precepts of decorum, and Rabelais elaborates the sententious lesson of this allegory in a discursively reasoned passage (IV, 62).

> On ne fait de tout bois l'image de Mercure,
> Dit le proverbe vieil: mais nous voyons icy
> De tout bois faire Pape, & Cardinaux aussi,
> Et vestir en trois jours tout une autre figure. (sonnet 102)

Du Bellay's initiates and explains a traditional allegorical development in the octave that prepares the background for the contemporary scene he decries in the sestet. So the moral lesson claimed by the conclusion (itself adapted from Erasmus) to sonnet 90, "C'est vrayment de les voir le salut d'un jeune homme," gains greater credence because of the picture of degeneracy that precedes it, the inductive logic of the commonplace and the prestige of the tradition to which it belongs.

It is perhaps not accidental that, in addition to incorporating Erasmian language, proverbs used to conclude sonnets employ distinctively Ramist language and syntax. Sonnet 54 exploits the logical pivot "donc" in the octave-sestet structure and treats the theme of wealth and wisdom in the order and manner recommended by Ramus:[32] "Celuy vrayement est riche & vit heureusement . . . Celuy vit seulement, lequel vit aujourdhuy." Concern for thematic logic and progression is demonstrated by the way key words sustain and advance the poet's chain-sequence narrative, as in sonnet 95 which continues "le mal qui fait peler" from the previous sonnet and introduces the theme of "aller sur le bufle" of the following sonnet. Around the coordinating axis of the word "racine"—representing at once the metamorphosis of Astolfo, "mes piedz en racine," in sonnet 87 and the lotus of Ulysses in sonnet 88—divergent literary sources are closely interrelated. The figure of Ulysses itself unites the various moments of the *Regrets*. "Et je pensois aussi ce que pensoit Ulysse" (sonnet 130), by its conjunctive beginning and treatment of Du Bellay's return to France (Ithaca), complements

[31] See Gladys Dickinson, *Du Bellay in Rome* (1960), p. 83.

[32] *La Dialectique,* pp. 118–119, "Enonciation copulative" and "Enonciation relative." The section deals with the link between cause and judgment. Cf. sonnet 53.

the anticipated return in the famous "Heureux qui, comme Ulysse, a fait un beau voyage" (sonnet 31). At the end of this last sonnet, the opposition of "l'air marin" to "la doulceur Angevine" and their geography have inspired critical conjecture;[33] but rather than being a precise reference to Rome or Anjou the opposition is used as a correlative to sum up the poem and the whole unhappy odyssey to Rome. "L'air y est corrompu" is found again in sonnet 83, not as an evocation of sea spray, but as a general token of Roman vice and the displacement of Venus by Mars.

The too patent interest in establishing a logical basis for several sonnets through hypothesis and result, cause and effect encumbered by Ramist syntax, shows that Du Bellay occasionally learned the lessons of the teachers he studied and the poets he read not too wisely but too well:

> Est cause que je fais des autres moins d'estime (sonnet 64)
> Et de tout ce qu'on void les causes & l'effect,
> Celuy vrayement doit estre un homme contrefait,
> Lequel n'a rien d'humain, que la seule figure. (sonnet 155)[34]

Fortunately, when the poems are more central to the themes of the sequence, the derivation of attitude from experience is divested of obtrusive terminology and logic blends with poetry in the description of "les regrets qu'esprouve une vertu / Qui se void defrauder du loyer de sa peine" (sonnet 47):

> Par la bonne fortune on se trouve abusé,
> Par la fortune adverse on devient plus rusé:
> L'une esteint la vertu, l'autre la fait paroistre: (sonnet 51)

It is in these sonnets dealing with the subject and substance of satire that the skill and variety of his poetic logic stand out. Numerous poems follow the relaxed but unfailing, deductive pattern of the syllogism. In explaining the ironic coexistence of laughter and satire, Du Bellay proceeds from the major and minor premises,

> Je veulx toucher sans plus aux vices moins secretz.
> Mais tu diras que mal je nomme ces Regretz,
> Veu que le plus souvent j'use de mots pour rire: (sonnet 77)

to the conclusion, "Car je ry, comme on dit, d'un riz Sardonien." When he passes from theory to practice in sonnet 106 his argument is framed along the lines of a disjunctive syllogism, since Renaissance satirists

---

[33] Pierre Moreau sees "l'air marin" as the Italian or Mediterranean air: "En marge de trois vers latins des *Regrets*," *Mélanges Henri Chamard* (1951), p. 73.

[34] See Quintilian, V, x, 80 and 86; *Aeneid* IV, 13: "degeneres animos timor arguit." Magny's sonnets 74, 175 and 176 are plagued by the same transparency.

considered it the weapon par excellence; after elaborating the "judgment commun" on the similarity between the papal seat and Jupiter's Olympus, the last two verses separate the subjects and conclude: "Mais l'un hait les tyrans, l'autre les favorise: / Le mortel en cecy n'est semblable au divin." Never a flattering comparison, the implacable logic of these lines utterly destroys any vestige of papal dignity.

This bedrock logic beneath the sonnet's lambent cadence, which resolutely calibrates the descent from Olympus to the iron age, coincides poorly with the figure paronomasia of earlier sonnets when it is seen from the modern view as a mere verbal play on the names of Du Bellay's friends: "Comte, qui ne fis onc compte" (sonnet 21), "Maraud, qui n'es maraud que de nom seulement" (sonnet 54). Such a view would overlook the Renaissance belief that the forms and meanings of words were somehow connected, would slight the assumptions of traditional rhetoric on which this belief was based, and would neglect the role it plays in implying an opposition between the iron age of Italy, "Le peuple de Ferrare est un peuple de fer" (sonnet 132) and the supposed golden age of France, "Paris sans pair" (sonnet 138).[35] The device supports the sweeping opposition of "ce bon siecle d'or" (sonnet 147) of Vergil and Horace to "cest aage de fer de vices tout rouglé" (sonnet 179) and contributes to the moral reference point of Du Bellay's satire.

## The Lesson of Satire

Horatian satire explicitly or implicitly assumes a high standard of conduct, yet Du Bellay's experience both in Rome and in France confirms his belief that "Ces beaux noms de vertu, ce n'est rien que du vent" (sonnet 145). Although he speaks of virtue in the same absolute terms from one end of the sequence to the other, "la vrayë vertu, qui seule est immortelle" (sonnet 27), "la vertu, qui est de nature immortelle" (sonnet 177), when this value does come into view through the use of Ariosto's Logistilla, "je voy la belle Dame / Qui d'un heureux signal nous appelle à son port" (sonnet 89), she enters in the form of a distant literary allusion and disappears from sight. In the early sonnets and in the "Patriae desiderium" Du Bellay forswears the Petrarchan muse, for what is the value of poetry which treats of ideals and values nonexistent in tangible form? But he also speaks of a lost paradise he once knew in the presence of Madame Marguerite, "Inter mortales cui dedit esse

[35] See Quintilian, I, vi, 28 and 34 for the search for the relation between verbal form and substance and its use in satiric irony. Cf. Rabelais, "croye que guerre soit en Latin dicte belle . . . par raison qu'en guerre apparoisse toute espèce de bien et beau," III, prologue; Isidore, *Etymologiarum sive originum,* XVIII, i, 9; and Scaliger on definition and etymology, III, 55.

Deam," and her brother Henri II. The warm sunlight emanating from her "bel oeil divin" (sonnet 7) fades and he descends into the cruel Roman winter (sonnets 8 and 9), yet he retains the memory of her perfection as the standard of virtue. While faithfully rendering the picture of corruption he sees around him, he continues to praise her as the virtue nearest God on this earth (sonnet 186). He thus resolves his original paradox by attempting to illustrate virtue in its highest earthly sense without himself becoming unearthly and maintains his own veracity without yielding to an insurmountably unreal Parnassus. Du Bellay does not write of virtue as though it were around him, but tries to make his reader feel what it is by comparison with its tawdry opposite. Travelling "le chemin plus batu" of the satirist instead of "Ce penible sentier qui meine à la vertu" (sonnet 3), he does not let us forget "la penible montee" of Henri II where "Hercule se feit Dieu par la seule vertu" (sonnet 172). Like Des Autelz, Tahureau, Paschal and Ronsard who also compared Henri II to Hercules at the Crossroads, Du Bellay employs an allegorical persona in whom his Renaissance audience would have seen, among other things, the civilizing man whose example testifies to the real existence of moral values and whose struggle against evil clears the path for virtue's triumph.[36]

Of course Du Bellay stood to lose nothing by such honest praise of the king and his sister. Like satirists of other periods he wraps up his sonnet sequence in a witty but logical plea for his own fame. He claims to shift his praise to God and only lauds Marguerite incidentally, "Car en donnant de tout la gloire au Createur, / Il loue l'ouvrier mesme, en louant son ouvrage" (sonnet 178). With recognition of the king's power as the mightiest under God, he reasons, ought not the king aid the arts by aiding Du Bellay? By this aid Henri could show how great his power really is, for, like God, "de rien un grand Roy peult faire quelque chose" (sonnet 191). Since in other sonnets he despises the destruction of moral fiber by flattery, he realizes the same charge may be leveled at him: "Je ne craindrois (Melin) que la posterité / Appellast pour cela ma Muse flateresse" (sonnet 178). After complimenting Marguerite, he is satisfied to say that this is not flattery but praise well deserved, and "de la louer sa bonté me dispense" (sonnet 182). Marguerite is inimitable and therefore is left off the heights of Parnassus. Following his lengthy attack on sycophancy for eroding men's sense of the truth, he seems to have built his own truthfulness into a strong pillar on which he can

[36] See Marc-René Jung, *Hercule dans la littérature française du XVI*^e^ *siècle* (1966), p. 136.

rest his praise of the most praiseworthy persons he has found in the world: "l'unique Marguerite" and Henri II.

Judgment of the quality and sincerity of Du Bellay's kind words must remain a moot point. Their importance and literary justification lie in the standards they establish for satire and the thematic and structural cohesion they afford to the collection. Henri's deification, whose dominion is made to embrace "le celeste & l'infernal empire" (sonnet 186), starkly contrasts with the mock-serious comparisons between the pope and Jupiter. Moreover, by his triumphant virtue, sacred stature and ultimate ability to "reprendre aux cheveux la fortune de France" (sonnet 124)[37] the king comes to represent the source of Du Bellay's deliverance from the "maux au jeu de la Fortune" and the means of his elevation on her wheel. His quasi-religious fervor enables him to complete the sonnet cycle and regain the "plus haulte aile" he renounced at the start by linking Marguerite to his feeling that "L'amour de la vertu, ma seule et seure guide, / Comme un cygne nouveau me conduit vers les cieux" (sonnet 189). Until her reappearance, the desired return of the golden age is limited to an exhortation, "ce Siecle de fer reface encor' entree, / Et qu'on revoye encor' le beau Siecle doré" (sonnet 170). But the beginning of the series addressed to Marguerite allows Du Bellay to resume and complete the Vergilian theme of deliverance from hell which sonnet 17 traced and to fulfill the atonement in the dedication, "J'ay sur mon doz chargé la pauvreté":

Dans l'enfer de son corps mon esprit attaché
(Et cest enfer, Madame, a esté mon absence)
Quatre ans & d'avantage a fait la penitence
De tous les vieux forfaits dont il fut entaché.
Ores, graces aux Dieux, ore' il est relasché
De ce penible enfer, & par vostre presence
Reduit au premier poinct de sa divine essence,
A deschargé son doz du fardeau de peché:
Ores sous la faveur de voz graces prisees,
Il jouït du repos des beaux champs Elysees,
Et si n'a volonté d'en sortir jamais hors. (sonnet 174)

[37] Fortune is traditionally represented with a long forelock, while the back of her head is bald. To prevail on her before she escapes one must seize the forelock. Cf. *Orlando Furioso* XXX, 35 and XLVI, 135; Du Bellay, VI, 12 for Henri's triumph over Fortune.

# CONCLUSION

Du Bellay did not officially win his laurel crown in the ritual Coronation of the Poet, nor did he ever attain the elusive Golden Fleece. But since subsequent generations have been willing to crown his poetic achievement with praise and continual attention, it seems fitting that the modern critical eye should focus on his mastery of the Trivium which underlies at once the Coronation and much of his poetry as well. Indeed, close examination of literary borrowings that source-hunting scholars continue to uncover throughout Du Bellay's works attests increasingly to the central importance of imitating rhetorical themes and structures in his verse and to its necessary alliance with poetic recreation—the Renaissance equivalent to the modern concept of originality. These discoveries seem to argue the predominance of an Apollonian artistic conscience over Dionysian enchantment and refute both the Renaissance notion of *fureur poétique* and its modern counterparts that Du Bellay was at his best when he did not know what he was doing. Du Bellay was of course keenly aware of his craft and its requirements. Poetic ecstasy may afford the occasion, but expediency determines its form. As his awareness sharpened and matured so did the poetic diction, imagery, interpretive power and overall direction of his verse. The points of this study have been (1) to show how the Trivium guided this awareness, just as it taught Renaissance students throughout Europe to think, write and speak, (2) to show how the combined arts of grammar, dialectic and rhetoric introduced the student to the full range of verbal expression including the poetic, and (3) to suggest that studies of Du Bellay are incomplete insofar as they discount his awareness of and adherence to these arts.

Like many other intellectual institutions of the Renaissance, the endurance and popularity of the Trivium stemmed in part from its adaptability and its being more inclusive than exclusive. Not only was the province of each of the three arts considerably more extensive during the Renaissance than today, but, equally important, they cooperated and overlapped in the various phases of their application. The discipline of grammar studied the medium of communication from the simple word to names and qualities; dialectic explored the methods of communication with the reader or listener involving conjunction, subordination and choice or distinction of ideas; rhetoric treated the means of pleasurable and persuasive communication ranging from logos to ethos to pathos; collectively, they contributed to the creation and understanding of artistic structure, material and proportion. Attempts to limit their scope or dissolve their links risk a fragmentizing or diminution in our critical understanding of any poet schooled in the Trivium.

This syncretic scheme should not imply unfailing variation in the Trivium during its many centuries of dominance, nor should it imply a perfectly homogeneous acceptance during the Renaissance. We have seen the Pléiade modify and purify in the humanistic sense (but not reject) the tradition of rhetoric it inherited. And to be sure, part of the modern uneasiness over allowing dialectic and rhetoric in poetry reflects a historic fact of steady semantic and philosophical evolution and reduction since the Renaissance, more than an unreasoning prejudice. The *Discours de la méthode* signaled the ultimate breach between dialectic serving the communication of an individual's opinion, mood or emotion to a wider audience and dialectic serving the scientific and philosophical inquiry of the individual (pp. 62–63).[1] Although the works of Ramus anticipate this breach, he stressed the presence of good dialectic in good poetry and saw beyond the delicate contours of verbal texture into the syllogistic and logical arguments that structured them. We have seen how the procedure of invention-disposition was shared by dialectic and rhetoric alike and how dialectic, as it was made practicable by Ramus and other sixteenth-century philosophers, enabled the poet to combine the abstract and the concrete, the universal and the particular, philosophy and history, the True and the Real. While making them harmonious, dialectic enables the poet to preserve their differences and to organize fields of human experience by providing relations like exclusion and inclusion whose recognition constitutes the poetic point of view. Whereas the modern poet in the symbolist tradition seems more interested in qualities that are nuanced for his own contemplation, the Renaissance sonneteer strives more for relationships and definitions that are open for public scrutiny. He speaks from his own intelligence to another intelligence on matters of persistent human significance, so his discourse—which is the poem—is reasonable in its inception, pursuit and resolution. Invention, being the writer's personal discovery and judgment of preexisting, external reality, avoids equally the solipsist's pure fantasy and the scientific philosopher's dry recital of facts. It further enables the poet to maintain intense lyric control without an attendant brittleness of form.

As we now understand it, the word *invention* conjures up mechanical conveniences having no previously known existence; it impels man into a more complex and more scientifically advanced but unknown future. In its sixteenth-century understanding, invention entails an increas-

[1] *Discours de la Méthode.*

ingly known communication between the poet's present and his cultural past. In addition to downgrading the syllogism in rational discourse, Descartes' entry into "le grand livre du monde" heralded the rejection from invention of whatever was not empirically verifiable: common sense, general reason and especially traditional wisdom. The point of view in discovery had to become universal, not just individual and partial. But invention allowed the Renaissance poet to relate his individual vision to the established masters of the Augustan age, the trecento or the community of humanists in his own age—to associate the individual with the universal. It is perhaps no accident that Du Bellay relies on Platonic language in the *Deffence et Illustration* when, as he invites the would-be poet to relate his particular contribution to the generality of models, he says "tu scais ou tu en doibs trouver les archetypes." As he proceeded from theory into practice, he was aware of working within a community of poetic presences, living and dead. If another voice sounds within his own it is not there through ignorance, but with approval and as a momentary resonance of his own distinctive speech. We have seen time and again in *L'Olive* how Du Bellay skillfully incorporates verse fragments from Ariosto as a momentary reflection of his own point of view, yet not without significant modifications that imprint his own presence, or how he radically alters an image or theme borrowed from Petrarch, yet not without establishing some unity of spirit within that diversity. In the *Antiquitez* he works within a consummate appreciation of Vergil and within the Renaissance tradition of meditations on the broken beauty of Rome to present us with both crystalline and chiaroscuro reflections on the mingled glory and pathos of the spiritual and tangible world. The poet's mind works in terms of analogues and discovers thematic and structural parallels in basically different situations.

Point of view has been stressed because it is the nexus between speaker and listener, writer and audience in rhetorically-oriented literature which "demande Le theatre du peuple & la faveur des Roys," because it may be taken quite literally, at least in Du Bellay, and because it provides the key to the decision incumbent on us of how and why he effects his borrowing and with what success. Some of the sonnets of *L'Olive* which are too patently translations or unsuccessfully integrate the model into the poet's own unique view bespeak a lack of experience with poetic form and perhaps with life itself. But as we move through the *Antiquitez* to the *Regrets* the point of view sharpens with an accompanying precision of feeling exacted by pain, and sources become more naturally and more successfully ingredients of the vision. In the

*Regrets* his personality does not get lost in the welter of minutiae that people his poems. Viewing a world of mixed comedy and tragedy and pathos, he now gravely, now ironically observes the brief players on the stage and gives them the same due he accords himself as another player on the same stage.

The imposition of order on feeling and experience which was assigned to the rhetorical procedure of disposition had its logical counterpart in the act of judging. And, indeed, thought arrangement in itself implies a judgment of priorities and relationships. It can entail comparison through juxtaposition of a radically unique point of view against a background (or foreground) of communal attitudes. The general methods of organization that guide Renaissance rhetoric go far in classifying—which is another way of defining—the types of thought progression we find in, for instance, the *Regrets.* Du Bellay resorts to what was referred to as composite organizing, where one proceeds from the smallest unit to the largest, in those sonnets where he moves from his individual viewpoint to a categoric maxim or other such figure of thought; on the other hand, he employs what would commonly have been recognized as resolutive organizing when, as in the sonnets based on enumeration, he proceeds from the whole to the smallest, from the actions of others in thirteen verses to himself in the last verse.

Far from the modern definition of rhetoric as words without substance, in the Renaissance it taught him to give vivid form and tactile substance to his thought, in short to wed art and nature. Rhetoric makes use of the arts of grammar and logic to give coherent shape in sensory effect. Passions, feelings, thoughts, purposes—all can be grounded and strengthened in the sense and designs of sense. The poet's eye has to see what his brain formulates as he transforms words into pictures and rhythms into palpable surfaces. In the three collections studied here the poet often invites us to follow visually the cyclic design of his thought which implies respectively his attitudes toward the movements of passion, of history and of his own personal odyssey. This circularity, which exists in individual sonnets and in whole sequences, becomes better defined as we move from the edenic vagueness of *L'Olive* to the all-too-real fallen humanity of Rome. Rather than being an academic exercise, it becomes an ingredient of Du Bellay's outlook on life. As we follow him to Rome and back we see that his own point of view—and, ultimately, ours— is itself transformed precisely for having undergone the turn in Fortune's Wheel. The latter sonnets in the *Regrets* are frequently dismissed out of hand for their lack of vivid precision, but they are a necessary complement and conclusion to the earlier poetic experience. There the Platonist seeks the shadows on the wall of the cave and yearns to behold the original figure, in the guise of Marguerite, face to face. It is the poignant imprecision of things hoped for but not quite seen, as Saint Paul would say, of the search for a paradise lost or rumored or yet to be grasped.

Style, according to Du Bellay's poetic manifesto, was to be the primary means of elevating poetry from the imperfect shadows of the "nuict gothique" and rediscovering the pure forms of the Golden Age. At its highest level of perfection, style could ally music, plastic art and verbal expression, would incarnate the poet's thought, win over the readers and gain their assent to his point of view by the sheer mastery of his means. These means were furnished by the multitude of tropes, schemes and figures whose exemplary use he studied in writers the Pléiade anthologized through the winnowing process of common consent and sensitive opinion. In explaining and evaluating his use of these components we see that Du Bellay usually avoids the callowness of cookbook recipes and that when he does, his poems become organic units instead of paralyzed fragments. In utilizing figures like antithesis that suppose extremes and absolutes, Du Bellay's subtle alterations constitute his personal signature and the mutual triumph of art and nature. But mere idiosyncrasy or mastery of technique does not make an inimitable style, as he tells us in the second sonnet of the *Regrets:* "En vain travaillera, me voulant imiter." When we are reading well and fully responding to his best poems, our actual awareness of technique *qua* technique is unconscious, as the precepts of rhetoric would have it; we are conscious of the aesthetic result. This result lies in fundamental matters of coherence, perception and how we conceive the structure of space and time. More than phonetic recurrence, Du Bellay's internal and end rhymes, alliterations and rhythms are definitions of time and attitude.

So at the hands of the good Renaissance poet, when he is good, rhetoric becomes poeticized logic, logic revised by the creative and critical imagination recalling original ideas. The poetic parlor games of the *rhétoriqueurs* and their abstract moral lessons have entered the dusty footnotes of literary histories and have little to say to the modern reader. But successful rhetorical repetition is viscerally didactic. No mere brew of bookish learning and distilled sources, Du Bellay's frequent exhortations to virtue—both through the overt example of Marguerite and implicitly through the engaging description of vice—are filtered through the pangs of lived experience and the tribulations of a man who knew Fortune's caprice at first hand. The frequent repetitions of the Renaissance poet, like those of Cicero and Saint Paul, are communications of the passion that is not satisfied by simple statement, but that beats through the pulses. So finally, for the Renaissance poet, poetry is related to logic and rhetoric as these two are related to reality.

# BIBLIOGRAPHY

## Editions of Du Bellay's Works

*Les Antiquitez de Rome et les Regrets,* ed. Eugénie Droz (Paris, 1945).

*La Deffence et Illustration de la langue françoyse,* ed. Henri Chamard (Paris, 1961).

*Divers jeux rustiques,* ed. Verdun Saulnier (Paris and Geneva, 1965).

*Lettres de Joachim du Bellay,* ed. Pierre de Nolhac (Paris, 1883).

*Les Oeuvres francoises de Joachim du Bellay,* ed. Antoine de Harsy (Lyon, 1575).

*Joachim du Bellay, Oeuvres poétiques,* ed. Henri Chamard (Paris, 1908–1961). Quotations in the text are from vols. I and II (1961), vol. III (1912), vol. IV (1934), vol. V (1923) and both parts of vol. VI (1931).

*Poésies françaises et latines de Joachim du Bellay,* ed. Ernest Courbet (Paris, 1931), 2 vols.

*Joachim du Bellay, Les Regrets et autres oeuvres poëtiques,* eds. J. Jolliffe and M. A. Screech (Geneva, 1966).

*Les Regrets suivis des Antiquitez, ed.* Pierre Grimal (Paris, 1948).

## Other Works Cited

Adler, Alfred. "Du Bellay's *Antiquitez* XXXI, Structure and Ideology," *BHRen,* XIII (1951), 191–195.

Agricola, Rudolph. *De inventione dialectica* (Paris, 1534).

Agrippa von Nettesheim, Heinrich Cornelius. *Opera in duos tomos concinne digesta, et nunc denuò, sublatis omnibus mendis,* in Φιλομούσων gratiam accurantissimè recusa. . . . (Leyden, n.d.).

Alberti, Leone Battista. *Della pittura,* ed. Luigi Mallè (Florence, 1950).

———. *Opere volgari,* ed. Anicio Bonucci (Florence, 1844), vol. II.

Amboise, Michel d'. *Les Complainctes de l'esclave fortuné* (Paris, 1529).

Ambrière, Francis. *Joachim du Bellay* (Paris, 1930).

Aneau, Barthélemy. *Picta poesis* (Lyon, 1552).

Anonymous. *Mémoires pour servir à l'histoire des hommes illustres dans la république des lettres* (Paris, 1727–1745), vol. XVI.

Arendt, Hannah. *Between Past and Future* (New York, 1961).

Ariosto, Ludovico. *Opere minori,* ed. Cesare Segre (Milan and Naples, 1954).

———. *Orlando Furioso,* ed. Lanfranco Caretti (Milan and Naples, 1954).

Aristotle. *Works,* ed. W. D. Ross (Oxford, 1959), vol. XI.

Arnaud, Charles. *Quid de pueris instituendis senserit Ludovicus Vives* (Paris, 1887).

Aubigné, Agrippa d'. *Les Tragiques,* eds. J. Plattard and A. Garnier (Paris, 1932), 4 vols.

Auvray, Jean. *La Pourmenade de l'ame devote* (Rouen, 1633).

Bacon, Francis. *Works,* eds. James Spedding, Robert Ellis and Douglas Heath (Cambridge, Mass., 1863), vol. IX.

Baïf, Jean-Antoine de. *Euvres en rime,* ed. Charles Marty-Laveaux (Paris, 1881–1890), vols. I and V.

Baldwin, Charles S. *Medieval Rhetoric and Poetic* (New York, 1928).

———. *Rennaissance Literary Theory and Practice* (New York, 1939).

Berni, Francesco. *Rime, poesie latine,* ed. Antonio Virgili (Florence, 1885).

Béroalde de Verville, François. *Le Cabinet de Minerve* (Rouen, 1601).

Boileau. *L'Art poétique*, ed. Ferdinand Brunetière (Paris, 1907).
Bouchet, Jean. *Epistres morales et familieres du traverseur* (Poiters, 1545).
Boyer, Frédéric. *Joachim du Bellay* (Paris, 1958).
Bracciolini, Poggio. "De varietate fortunae," *Latin Writings of the Italian Humanists*, ed. F. A. Gragg (New York, 1927), pp. 112–116.
Bruno, Giordano. *Opera latine*, eds. F. Fiorentino, F. Tocco, H. Vitelli, V. Imbriani and C. M. Tallarigo (Naples, 1879–1891), vol. II, part 3.
Brunot, Ferdinand. *Histoire de la langue française* (Paris, 1927), vol. II.
Buffum, Imbrie. *Agrippa d'Aubigné's "Les Tragiques," A Study of the Baroque Style in Poetry* (New Haven, Conn., 1951).
Buisson, F. *Répertoire des ouvrages pédagogiques du XVIe siècle* (Paris, 1886).
Burchiello, Domenico. *Sonetti*, no. ed. (London, 1757).
Burckhardt, Jacob. *The Civilization of the Renaissance in Italy*, tr. S. G. C. Middlemore (New York, 1961).
Bush, Douglas. "The Isolation of the Renaissance Hero," *Prefaces to Renaissance Literature* (New York, 1965).
Caesar, Julius. *The Gallic War*, ed. H. J. Edwards (London and New York, 1917).
Caldarini, Ernesta. "Nuove fonti dell'*Olive*," *BHRen*, XXVII (1965), 395–434.
Calvin, Jean, *Institution de la religion chrestienne*, ed. Jean-Daniel Benoît (Paris, 1957), vol. I.
Cassius, Dion. *Des faitz et gestes insignes des romains*, tr. Claude Deroziers (Paris, 1542).
Castor, Grahame. *Pléiade Poetics* (Cambridge, 1964).
Chamard, Henri. *Histoire de la Pléiade* (Paris, 1961–1963), 4 vols.
———. *Joachim du Bellay* (Lille, 1900).
Chambers, Frank McMinn. "Lucan and the *Antiquitez de Rome*," *PMLA*, LX (Dec., 1945), 937–948.
Chocheyras, J. "En marge de la *Défense et illustration*, Pierre Saliat: une préface critique de 1537," *BHRen*, XXVIII (1966), 675–679.
Cicero. *De inventione, De optimo genere oratorum, Topica*, ed. H. M. Hubbell (Cambridge, Mass., and London, 1949).
———. *Orationes*, ed. Albert Curtis Clark (Oxford, 1951–1952), vols. I, II, and VI.
———. *Rhetorica*, ed. A. S. Wilkins (Oxford, 1950–1951), 2 vols.
[Cicero]. *Rhetorica ad Herennium* (London and Cambridge, Mass., 1954).
Clark, Donald Lemen. *Rhetoric and Poetry in the Renaissance: A Study of Rhetorical Terms in English Renaissance Literary Criticism* (New York, 1963).
Clements, Robert J. "Anti-Petrarchanism of the Pléiade," *Modern Philology*, XXXIX (Aug., 1941), 15–21.
———. *Critical Theory and Practice of the Pléiade* (Cambridge, Mass., 1942).
———. *The Peregrine Muse* (Chapel Hill, 1959).
———. *Picta Poesis, Literary and Humanistic Theory in Renaissance Emblem Books* (Rome, 1960).
*Conteurs français du XVIe siècle*, ed. Pierre Jourda (Paris, 1965).
Crane, William. *Wit and Rhetoric in the Renaissance* (Gloucester, Mass., 1964).
Curtius, Ernst Robert. *European Literature and the Latin Middle Ages* (New York and Evanston, 1963).
Dassonville, Michel. "La Collaboration de la Pléiade à la *Dialectique* de Pierre de la Ramée (1555)," *BHRen*, XXV (1963), 337–348.

———. "De l'unité de la *Deffence et Illustration de la langue francoyse,*" *BHRen,* XXVII (1965), 96–107.

Descartes, René. *Discours de la méthode,* ed. Etienne Gilson (Paris, 1962).

———. *Regulae ad directionem ingenii,* ed. Giovanni Crapulli (The Hague, 1966).

Deschamps, Eustache. *Oeuvres complètes,* eds. Auguste–H.–E. Queux de Saint-Hilaire and Gaston Raynaud (Paris, 1882), vol. VII.

Dickinson, Gladys. *Du Bellay in Rome* (Leyden, 1960).

Dolet, Etienne. *La Manière de bien traduire d'une langue en aultre* (Lyon, 1540).

Drayton, Michael. *The Works of Michael Drayton,* ed. J. William Hebel (Oxford, 1931–1941), vol. II.

Du Bartas, Guillaume de Salluste. *The Works of Guillaume de Salluste, Sieur Du Bartas,* eds. U. T. Holmes, Jr., J. C. Lyons and R. W. Linker (Chapel Hill, 1935–1940), vols. II and III.

Englehardt, George J. "Medieval Vestiges in the Rhetoric of Erasmus," *PMLA,* LXIII (June, 1948), 739–744.

Erasmus, Desiderius. *De duplici copia verborum ac rerum* (London, 1573).

———. *Opera omnia* (Leyden, 1703–1706), vol. II.

Everhardus, Nicholaus D. *Loci argumentorum legales* (Frankfurt, 1591).

Fabri, Pierre. *Le Grand et Vray Art de pleine rhétorique* (Rouen, 1889–1890), vol. II.

Faral, Edmond. *Les Arts poétiques du XII^e^ et du XIII^e^ siècles* (Paris, 1958).

Ficino, Marsilio. *Opera omnia* (Basel, 1561).

Foclin, Antoine. *La Rhetorique francoise* (Paris, 1555).

Foucault, Michel, *Les Mots et les choses* (Paris, 1966).

Fremy, Edouard. *L'Académie des derniers Valois* (Paris, 1887).

Frye, Northrop. *Anatomy of Criticism* (New York, 1966).

Gadoffre, Gilbert. *Ronsard par lui-même* (Paris, 1960).

———. "L'Université collégiale et la Pléiade," *French Studies,* XI (Oct., 1957), 293–304.

Galland, Pierre. *Contra novam academiam P. Rami oratio* (Paris, 1551).

Garnier, Robert. *Bradamante,* ed. Raymond Lebègue (Paris, 1949).

George Gascoigne, *The Complete Works of George Gascoigne,* ed. John W. Cunliffe (Cambridge, 1907), vol. I.

Gilbert, Neal. *Renaissance Concepts of Method* (New York, 1960).

Gilson, Etienne. *La Philosophie au moyen âge* (Paris, 1962).

Gombrich, E. H. "Icones Symbolicae," *Journal of the Warburg and Courtauld Institutes,* XI (1948), 168–176.

Gourmont, Remy de. *La Culture des idées* (Paris, 1964).

Griffiths, Richard. "The Influence of Formulary Rhetoric upon French Renaissance Tragedy," *Modern Language Review,* LIX (April, 1964), 201–208.

Harvey, Lawrence. *The Aesthetics of the Renaissance Love Sonnet* (Geneva, 1962).

Heinze, Richard. *Virgils epische Technik* (Leipzig, 1915).

Héroet, Antoine. *Oeuvres poétiques,* ed. Ferdinand Gohin (Paris, 1909).

Hill, Raymond T. "The Influence of the *Noie* on the Poetry of Joachim Du Bellay," *Essays in Honor of Albert Feuillerat* (New Haven, Conn., 1943). pp. 85–92.

Horace. *Satires, Epistles and Ars Poetica,* ed. H. Rushton Fairclough (Cambridge, Mass., 1947).

Hulubei, Alice. "Virgile en France au XVIe siècle," *Revue du seizième siècle,* XVIII (1931), 1–77.

Isidorus. *Isidori Hispalensis episcopi Etymologiarum sive Originum libri XX,* ed. W. M. Lindsay (Oxford, 1911), 2 vols.

Jasinski, Max. *Histoire du sonnet en France* (Paris, 1903).

Jodelle, Etienne. *Les Oeuvres et meslanges poetiques,* ed. Charles Marty-Laveaux (Paris, 1870), vol. II.

Jung, Marc-René *Hercule dans la littérature française du XVIe siècle* (Geneva, 1966).

Juvenal. *Ivenalis saturae,* ed. A. E. Housman (Cambridge, 1956).

Klein, Robert. "The Figurative Thought of the Renaissance," *Diogenes,* XXXII (1960), 107–123.

Krappe, Alexander Haggerty. "Une Source virgilienne de la *Défense et Illustration de la langue française,*" *Revue du seizième siècle,* XV (1928), 342–343.

Kristeller, Paul Oskar. *Renaissance Thought* (New York, Evanston and London, 1961).

La Ceppède, Jean de. *Les Théorèmes spirituels* (Toulouse, 1613).

Langlois, Ernest. "La Fumée du rôti payé au son de l'argent," *Revue des études rabelaisiennes,* I (1903), 222–223.

———. *Recueil d'arts de seconde rhétorique* (Paris, 1902).

Lapp, John C. "Mythological Imagery in Du Bellay," *Studies in Philology,* LXI (April, 1964), 109–127.

La Taille, Jean de. *De l'art de la tragédie,* ed. Frederick West (Manchester, England, 1939).

Laudun, Pierre de. *Art poétique françois* (Paris, 1598).

Laumonier, Paul. *Ronsard et sa province* (Paris, 1924).

———. *Ronsard, poète lyrique* (Paris, 1923).

———. *La Vie de P. de Ronsard de Claude Binet* (Paris, 1910).

Lechner, Sister Joan Marie. *Renaissance Concepts of the Commonplaces* (New York, 1962).

Lee, Sidney. *The French Renaissance in England* (Oxford, 1910).

Le Hir, Yves. *Rhétorique et stylistique de la pléiade au parnasse* (Paris, 1960).

Lemaire de Belges, Jean. *Oeuvres de Jean Lemaire de Belges,* ed. J. Stecher (Louvain, 1882–1891), 4 vols.

Lenient, C. F. *De ciceroniano bello apud recentiores* (Paris, 1885).

Leonardo da Vinci. *Scritti letterari di Leonardo da Vinci,* ed. J. P. Richter (London, 1883), vol. II.

Lucianus Samosatensis. *Lucian,* tr. A. M. Harmon (Cambridge, Mass., and London, 1947), vol. III.

Longinus. *On the Sublime,* ed. W. Rhys Roberts (Cambridge, 1935).

McFarlane, I.D. *The "Délie" of Maurice Scève* (Cambridge, 1966).

Magney, Olivier de. *Les Souspirs,* ed. Ernest Courbet (Paris, 1874).

Marbeuf, Pierre de. *Recueil de vers,* Rouen, 1628 (ed. A. Heron, Rouen, 1897).

Marot, Clément. *Oeuvres,* ed. Georges Guiffrey (Paris, 1881–1931), vols. III–V.

Maurat-Ballange, A. "Ramus et Dorat," *Extrait du bulletin de la société archéologique du Limousin,* LXIII (1913), 5–27.

Melanchthon, Philipp. *Elementorum rhetorices libri duo* (1572).

———. *Opera omnia,* ed. Karl Bretschneider (Halle, 1834–1860), vol. XIII.

Miller, Perry. *The New England Mind: From Colony to Province* (Cambridge, Mass., 1953).
———. *The New England Mind: The Seventeenth Century* (Boston, 1961).
Minturno, Antonio. *De poeta* (Venice, 1559).
———. *L'Arte poetica* (Naples, 1725).
Montaigne, Michel de. *Oeuvres complètes,* eds. Albert Thibaudet and Maurice Rat (Paris, 1962).
Moreau, Pierre. "En marge de trois vers latins des *Regrets,*" *Mélanges d'histoire littéraire de la renaissance offerts à Henri Chamard* (Paris, 1951), pp. 71–79.
Mornet, Daniel, *Histoire de la clarté française* (Paris, 1929).
Motin, Pierre. *Oeuvres inédites,* ed. Paul d'Estrée (Paris, 1882).
Muret, Marc-Antoine. *De philosophiae et eloquentiae conjunctione oratio IV* (Venice, 1557).
Nelson, C. E. "Enumeration and Irony in *Les Regrets* of Du Bellay," *French Review,* XXXVI (January, 1963), pp. 266–275.
Nichols, Stephen G., Jr. "Marot, Villon and the *Roman de la Rose,* A Study in the Language of Re-creation," *Studies in Philology,* LXIII (April, 1966) 135–143.
Nolhac, Pierre de. *Ronsard et l'humanisme* (Paris, 1966).
Ong, Father Walter J. *Ramus and Talon Inventory* (Cambridge, Mass., 1958).
———. *Ramus, Method and the Decay of Dialogue* (Cambridge, Mass., 1958).
Ovid. *Heroides and Amores,* ed. Grant Showerman (Cambridge, Mass., and London, 1947).
Ovid. *Opera omnia* (London, 1921), vol. III.
Panofsky, Erwin. "Et in Arcadia Ego: On the Conception of Transience in Poussin and Watteau," *Philosophy and History: Essays Presented to Ernst Cassirer* (New York, 1963), pp. 223–254.
———. *Meaning in the Visual Arts* (New York, 1955).
*Pasquillorum tomi duo* (Basel, 1554).
Patch, Howard R. *The Goddess Fortuna in Mediaeval Literature* (Cambridge, Mass., 1927).
Pater, Walter. *The Renaissance* (Portland, Maine, 1902).
Patterson, W. F. *Three Centuries of French Poetic Theory (1328–1630)* (New York, 1966), 3 vols.
Peacham, Henry. *The Garden of Eloquence,* facsimile reproduction of 1593 edition (Gainesville, Fla., 1954).
Peletier du Mans, Jacques. *Art pöetique* (1555), ed. André Boulanger (Paris, 1930).
Petrarca, Francesco. *Francesco Petrarca, prose,* eds. G. Martellotti, G. Ricci, E. Carrara, E. Bianchi (Milan and Naples, 1955).
———. *Francisci Petrarchae, Opera omnia* (Basel, 1581).
———. *Petrarca: Le Familiari,* eds. Vittorio Rossi and Umberto Bosco (Florence, 1933–1942).
———. *Rime, Trionfi e poesie latine,* eds. F. Neri, G. Martellotti, E. Bianchi and N. Sapegno (Milan and Naples, 1951).
———. *Scritti inediti di Francesco Petrarca,* ed. Attilio Hortis (Trieste, 1874).
Peyre, Henri. *Literature and Sincerity* (New Haven, Conn., and London, 1963).
Plato. *Oeuvres complètes,* trans. and ed. Léon Robin (Paris, 1961), vol. IV.
*Poètes du XVIe siècle,* ed. Albert-Marie Schmidt (Paris, 1953).
Pontano, Giovanni. *Carmina,* ed. Johannes Oeschger (Bari, 1948).

Puttenham, George. *The Arte of English Poesie,* eds. Gladys Willcock and Alice Walker (Cambridge, 1936).
Quintilian. *Institutio oratoria,* ed. H. E. Butler (Cambridge, Mass., and London, 1953), 4 vols.
Rabelais, François. *Oeuvres,* ed. Abel Lefranc (Paris, 1913–1955), 6 vols.
Rainolds, John. *Oratio in laudem artis poeticae 1572* (Princeton, 1940).
Ramus, Peter. (Pierre de la Ramée), *Petri Rami professoris regii et Audomari Talaei collectaneae praefationes, epistolae, orationes* (Paris, 1577).
———. *La Dialectique (1555)*, ed. Michel Dassonville (Geneva, 1964).
———. *Rhetoricae distinctiones in Quintilianum; oratio ejusdem de studiis philosophiae et eloquentiae conjugendis* (Paris, 1549).
Raymond, Marcel. *Baroque et renaissance poétique* (Paris, 1955).
———. *L'Influence de Ronsard sur la poésie française (1550–1585)* (Paris, 1927), 2 vols.
*Rhetorica ad Herennium,* ed. Harry Caplan (Cambridge, Mass., 1954).
Ronsard, Pierre de. *Oeuvres complètes,* ed. Paul Laumonier (Paris, 1914–1960), 17 vols.
———. *Les Oeuvres de P. de Ronsard,* ed. Marc-Antoine Muret (Paris, 1584).
———. *Les Oeuvres de Pierre de Ronsard, texte de 1587,* ed. Isidore Silver (Chicago, 1966), vol. II.
———. *Poésies choisies,* ed. Pierre de Nolhac (Paris, 1959).
Saba, Guido. *La Poesia di Joachim du Bellay* (Messina and Florence, 1962).
Sainte-Beuve, C. A. *Tableau historique et critique de la poésie française au XVIe siècle* (Paris, 1843).
Sannazaro, Jacopo. *Arcadia,* ed. Giambattista Corniani (Milan, 1806).
Satterthwaite, Alfred. "Moral Vision in Spenser, Du Bellay and Ronsard," *Comparative Literature,* IX (Spring, 1957), 136–149.
———. *Spenser, Ronsard and Du Bellay: A Renaissance Comparison* (Princeton, 1960).
Saulnier, Verdun. "Commentaires des *Antiquitez de Rome,*" *BHRen,* XII (1950), 114–143.
———. *Du Bellay* (Paris, 1963).
———. "Introduction à l'étude de Joachim du Bellay," *L'Information littéraire* (Jan.–Feb., 1950), 1–7.
———. "Joachim du Bellay et son Regret latin de la patrie," *Fin du moyen âge et renaissance* (Anvers, 1961), pp. 271–281.
Scaliger, Julius Caesar. *Poetices libri septem,* fifth edition (Heidelberg, 1617).
Scève, Maurice. *Oeuvres poétiques complètes de Maurice Scève,* ed. Bertrand Guégan (Paris, 1927).
Sebillet, Thomas. *Art poétique françoys,* ed. Félix Gaiffe (Paris, 1932).
Seneca. *Controverses et suasoires,* ed. Henri Borneque (Paris, 1902), 2 vols.
Seznec, Jean. *The Survival of the Pagan Gods* (New York, 1961).
Sherry, Richard. *Treatise on Schemes and Tropes* (London, 1550).
Silver, Isidore. "Du Bellay and Hellenic Poetry: A Cursory View," *PMLA,* LX (March, 1945), 66–80.
———. "Pindaric Parallelism in Du Bellay: A Proof of his Independent Imitation of Pindar," *French Review,* XIV (May, 1941), 461–472.

Six, André. "Explication française: Du Bellay, *Antiquités de Rome*-Sonnet III," *Romance Notes,* VIII (Spring, 1967), 281–284.

Sozzi, L. "Rabelais, Philelphe et le 'fumet du rôti'," *Etudes rabelaisiennes,* V (1964), 197–205.

Spingarn, Joel Elias. *A History of Literary Criticism in the Renaissance* (New York, 1949).

Spitzer, Leo. "The Poetic Treatment of a Platonic-Christian Theme (Du Bellay's Sonnet of the Idea," *Comparative Literature,* VI (Winter-Fall, 1954), 193–217.

Stone, Donald, Jr., *Ronsard's Sonnet Cycles, A Study of Tone and Vision* (New Haven, Conn., and London, 1966).

———. "The Sense and Significance of Ronsard's Seasonal Hymns," *Symposium,* XVIII (Winter, 1964), 321–331.

Tahureau, Jacques. *Odes, sonnets et autres poésies,* ed. Prosper Blanchemain (Geneva, 1869).

Tasso, Torquato. *Opere,* ed. G. Gherardini (Milan, 1824), vol. III.

Thibaudet, Albert. *Montaigne,* texte établi par Floyd Gray (Paris, 1963).

Toldo, Pietro. "La Fumée du rôti et la divination des signes," *Revue des études rabelaisiennes,* I (1903), 13–28.

*Tottel's Miscellany,* ed. Hyder Rollins (Cambridge, Mass., 1965).

Turberville, George. *Epigrams, Songs and Sonnets,* ed. J. P. Collier (London, 1869).

Tuve, Rosemond. *Elizabethan and Metaphysical Imagery* (Chicago and London, 1965).

———. "Imagery and Logic: Ramus and the Metaphysical Poets," *Journal of the History of Ideas,* III (Jan.–Oct., 1942), 365–400.

Tyard, Pontus de. *Discours philosophiques* (Paris, 1587).

———. *The Universe of Pontus de Tyard, A Critical Edition of "L'Univers,"* ed. John C. Lapp (New York, 1950).

*Variétés historiques et littéraires, recueil de pièces volantes et curieuses,* ed. Edouard Fournier (Paris, 1855–1863), vol. VI.

Vergil. *Works,* eds. John Conington and Henry Nettleship (Hildesheim, 1963), 3 vols.

Vianey, Joseph. "Origines du sonnet régulier," *Revue de la renaissance,* IV (1903), 74–93.

———. "La Part de l'imitation dans les *Regrets,*" *Bulletin Italien,* IV (1904), 30–48.

———. *Le Pétrarquisme en France au XVI^e siècle* (Montpellier, 1909).

———. *Les Regrets de Joachim du Bellay* (Paris, 1946).

Villey, Pierre. *Les Sources italiennes de la "Deffence et Illustration de la langue française"* (Paris, 1908).

Vipper, G. "La Poésie de Joachim du Bellay et sa portée historique," *Beiträge zur romanischen Philologie,* II (1963), 77–95.

Weber, Henri. *La Création poétique au XVI^e siècle en France* (Paris, 1956).

Weinberg, Bernard. *A History of Literary Criticism in the Italian Renaissance* (Chicago, 1961), 2 vols.

Wellek, René and Warren, Austin. *Theory of Literature* (New York, 1962).

Wilkins, Ernest H. "The Coronation of Petrarch," *Speculum,* XVIII (April, 1943), 155–197.

Yates, Frances. *The Art of Memory* (Chicago and London, 1966).

## GLOSSARY OF SPECIALIZED TERMS

The following list includes and defines some of the terminology of rhetorical devices, categories and faults mentioned in this book. The numbers refer to the pages on which the terms are discussed or appear in cited passages.

*aenigma*—obscure allegory: 50.

*aetiologia*—successive addition of explanations to a principal idea: 151 n.

amplification—attempt to strengthen or draw attention to anything the writer considers remarkable or noteworthy: 33, 46–47, 53, 61, 62.

anadiplosis—beginning a verse with the last word of the previous verse (a form of *reduplicatio*): 57, 58, 149, 153.

anaphora—repetition of one or several words at the beginning of consecutive verses: 56, 58 n., 60, 61, 63, 77, 106, 127.

antonomasia—use of an epithet or a common noun in place of a person's proper name, or the use of a proper name in place of a general idea: 51, 87, 92.

*articulus* (comma)—omission of coordinating conjunctions to create an impression of haste or perturbation: 53.

asyndeton—omission of coordinating conjunctions in a series: 38, 59, 93.

*barbarismus*—use of incorrect or shocking language to express the speaker's cultural deficiencies or to inspire an emotional reaction in the reader: 30.

battology—pointless and tiresome repetition: 69.

*chiasmus*—reversal of word order in the second of two consecutive and syntactically parallel verses: 56, 92, 156.

*communicatio*—consultation with the implied reader prior to making a decision: 63, 156.

*commutatio*—complete transposition of words with a corresponding interchange of their meanings: 129 n.

*compar* (isocolon)—balancing hemistichs by means of punctuation or word arrangement: 55, 77, 105, 128, 129.

*confessio*—narrator's admission of weakness, guilt or inferior stature: 63.

*correctio*—replacement of an expression by one which the narrator considers more apt to reveal his true thought. 63.

*deprecatio*—entreaty to grant a favor or to forgive the inferior stature of the narrator: 62.

*efficacia*—accomplishment of an intended result or establishment of a state of mind in the reader by means of logical but vivid expression: 13, 49 n., 57 n., 74 n.

enallage—decisive alteration in the grammatical function of words for a dramatic effect: 129.

*enargia*—use of embellished figures in vividly illustrating a subject for the mind's eye of the reader in order to make him feel he is actually witnessing an action or experiencing an emotion: 42 n., 73, 77, 79 n.

*energia*—use of vigorous language in conveying the intensity of the writer's thoughts: 48, 73, 74, 75, 79 n.

epanalepsis—beginning and ending a verse with the same word: 56, 129, 150.

epideictic—speech used on ceremonial occasions to eulogize or condemn: 46 n.

epizeuxis—emphatic repetition of one or several words: 53–54, 58 n., 105, 150.

*evidentia*—lively and descriptive enumeration of an object's properties: 42 n., 73.

*exordium, propositio, narratio, confirmatio, refutatio* and *peroratio*— the six sequential steps of rhetorical discourse: 37.

*expeditio*—summary dismissal of several supposedly considered alternatives: 54, 101.

figures, tropes, schemes—the three categories of rhetorical ornaments: 50, 52, 61, 77, 155.

*gradatio*—anadiplosis sustained for more than two verses so as to create a chain sequence: 58–59, 63, 134, 155.

hyperbaton—transposition of the customary or logical word order for emphasis: 53, 56, 125, 150.

*licentia*—admission or reproach addressed to an implied reader, which accentuates the speaker's honesty at the risk of his welfare: 156.

*merismus*—division and elaborated examination of a subject to amplify its properties: 61.

metonymy—replacement of the name of an object or person by one of its attributes or by a closely related term: 50, 51.

*oeconomia*—arrangement and division of the parts of a discourse or intellectual expression: 34 n., 40.

paronomasia (*adnominatio*)—play on similar sounds and/or etymological meanings of words: 52, 53, 164.

polyptoton—inflected repetition of a noun within a single thought: 136.

polysyndeton—repetition of conjunctions or other connecting words in close sequence for a cumulative effect (the opposite of *asyndeton*) : 59, 92–93, 104, 151.

*praeteritio*—narrator's feigned or genuine dismissal of subjects he does not wish to treat: 54–55, 57, 63.

*pragmatographia*—description of an extensive and animated scene: 20, 77.

prosopopoeia—speech of an absent, dead or imaginary person which conforms to his station in life and idiosyncrasies: 42 n., 44, 61–62.

*reduplicatio*—redoubling for emphasis: 57, 128.

*reticentia*—stopping oneself in the midst of a statement for fear of revealing one's true thoughts: 63.

sententia—maxim: 27–28, 31, 49, 52, 62, 72, 75, 78, 79, 80, 81, 82–83, 87, 159.

synecdoche—use of a part for a whole class, or the whole for a part: 50–51.

tapinosis—degradation of a subject by means of derisive vocabulary in an elevated style: 43.

*traductio*—progressive variations developed from the same linguistic root: 53, 77, 87, 125, 126 n., 129 n., 149, 155.

*translatio*—alteration of the meaning of a word by its unusual association with another word or idea (a form of metaphor): 42.

vivid portraiture—use of *enargia* and/or *energia:* 39, 74–75, 81, 106, 122.

zeugma—application of a grammatical modifier to a series of words in such a manner that it is logically connected only with the first word: 92 n., 125, 126 n.

# INDEX


Accolti, Bernardo, 101
Adler, Alfred, 119
Aesthetic principles: modern, 1, 2, 21, 26, 32, 34–35, 39, 60, 150, 164, 167, 168, 170; Renaissance, 10, 13, 16, 21, 25, 27, 28, 32, 38, 39–40, 41, 42, 48, 50, 60, 103, 150, 160, 167
Agricola, Rudolph, 9, 11, 38
Agrippa von Nettesheim, Heinrich Cornelius, 70
Alberti, Leone Battista, 75, 81
Allegory, 7, 24, 39, 43, 48, 50, 62, 75, 82, 88, 103, 121, 155, 162, 165
Amboise, Michel d', 114
Ambrière, Francis, 2
Aneau, Barthélemy, 13, 16, 18, 26, 34, 38, 39, 42, 43, 50, 69, 72, 75, 103
Aphthonius, 31, 80
Arendt, Hannah, 115
Argument: intrinsic (artificial), 11, 12, 18, 36, 82–83; extrinsic (inartificial), 12, 36, 62, 82
Ariosto, Ludovico, 21, 99, 102–103, 104, 108–109, 151, 164, 166, 169
Aristotle, 9, 10, 12, 17, 21, 31, 36, 37, 40, 41, 43, 73, 80, 146
Arnaud, Charles, 9
Art: and cause, 14; technique, 67; and nature, 67, 68–70, 71–72, 74, 75, 79, 85, 96, 124, 137, 155, 170; form, 97; Vergil's, 119; and point of view, 120; permanence of, 126; Horatian, 159; music, plastic and verbal, 171
Aubigné, Agrippa d', 14, 36, 59, 69, 74, 146
Augustan, 27, 88, 127, 133, 143
Augustus, Octavian, 38, 126
Auvray, Jean, 160

Baïf, Jean-Antoine de, 54, 57, 72
Baldwin, Charles Sears, 26, 152
Belleau, Rémy, 41
Berger, Bertrand, 46
Bergson, Henri, 146
Berni, Francesco, 8, 146
Béroalde de Verville, François, 13
Binet, Claude, 48
Boethius, 9
Boileau-Despréaux, Nicolas, 29, 31
Bouchet, Jean, 13, 159
Boyer, Frédéric, 2, 154
Bracciolini, Poggio, 115
Britannus, Jean, 143–144
Bruno, Giordano, 14, 75
Brunot, Ferdinand, 135
Buchanan, George, 115
Buffum, Imbrie, 59
Buisson, Ferdinand, 25
Burchiello, Domenico, 138
Burckhardt, Jacob, 116
Buridan, Jean, 21
Bush, Douglas, 116

Caesar, Julius, 12, 71, 119, 126, 129, 133
Caldarini, Ernesta, 99
Calvin, Jean, 115–116
Capilupi, Lelio, 100
Caracciol, Antoine, 35
Castiglione, Baldassare, 115, 122
Castor, Grahame, 34, 73
Catullus, 160
Cause, 12–14, 15, 16, 17, 19, 34, 39, 51, 57, 70–71, 74, 75, 81, 82, 103, 111, 120, 123, 126, 130, 139, 148, 156, 159, 162, 163
Chamard, Henri, 2, 7, 27, 30, 34, 50, 67, 73, 82, 84, 88, 92, 97, 98, 104, 116–117, 120, 129, 134, 143, 151
Chambers, Frank McMinn, 2, 119
Charles V, Holy Roman Emperor, 62, 123
Chateaubriand, François-René de, 3
Chaucer, Geoffrey, 118
Chocheyras, J., 78
Cicero, 7, 9, 10, 11, 12, 14, 21, 22, 28, 29, 30, 32, 35, 37, 41, 47, 48, 49, 63, 64, 69, 70, 78, 80, 85, 88, 129, 136, 143, 151, 159, 160, 172
Clark, Donald Lemen, 18, 29, 31, 73
Classicism, Graeco-Roman, 3, 7, 9, 10, 25, 29–30, 31, 39, 50, 54, 57, 64, 67, 79, 115, 127, 144, 146, 151, 160
Claudian, 39

Clements, Robert J., 45, 69, 74, 76, 142
Coligny, Gaspard de, 51–52
Copia, 33–35, 36–37, 40, 41–42, 47, 51, 52, 62, 73, 74, 78–79, 81, 85, 96, 155
Corneille, Pierre de, 54
Coronation of the poet, 7, 70, 167
Corso, A. G., 100
Crane, William, 13, 62
Curtius, Ernst Robert, 48, 104, 142

Daniello, Bernardino, 26, 106
Dante Alighieri, 54
Dassonville, Michel, 10
Della Torre, Battista, 104
Demosthenes, 7, 28, 88
Deroziers, Claude, 79
Des Autelz, Guillaume, 27, 42, 74, 165
Descartes, René, 17, 19, 20, 81, 151, 168, 169
Deschamps, Eustache, 58
Des Masures, Louis, 85, 95
Diane de Poitiers, 81
Dickinson, Gladys, 162
Dionysius of Halicarnassus, 73
Disposition, 9, 27, 30, 34, 35, 37–40, 52, 62, 156–157, 168, 170
Dolce, Ludovico, 107
Dolet, Etienne, 47, 86
Dorat, Jean, 7, 9
Drayton, Michael, 45
Droz, Eugénie, 84, 151
Du Bartas, Guillaume de Salluste, 31, 48, 59
Du Bellay, Jean, 33, 43, 75
Du Bellay, Joachim, critics of, 2–3, 18, 27, 38, 87–88, 94, 95, 96–97, 104, 116–117, 120, 139, 154, 163
Dulard, Jean, 21

Edoard, Nicolas, 41, 44, 62, 75
Education, 3, 7, 10, 16, 26, 84, 86, 151, 159, 163, 167, 170. *See also* Trivium
Effect, 12–14, 15, 16, 39, 40, 51, 57, 62, 70–71, 73, 75, 78, 82, 103, 122, 126, 128, 134, 139, 148, 156, 163
Englehardt, George J., 47
Erasmus, Desiderius, 12, 47, 57, 78, 80, 83, 160, 161, 162
Estienne, Henri, 39
Everhard, Nicholas, 53
Exercise, 11, 17, 45, 68, 70, 71–72, 81

Fabri, Pierre, 27, 31
Faguet, Emile, 79
Faral, Edmond, 29, 41, 47
Faustine, 89
Ficino, Marsilio, 14
Foclin, Antoine, 24, 26, 32, 50, 51, 52, 61, 63
Fortune, 13–15, 39, 52, 62, 75, 80–82, 107, 115, 123, 124, 129, 130, 137, 138–141, 142, 147, 149, 155, 157, 163, 166, 170, 172
Foucault, Michel, 24
Frye, Northrop, 27, 120

Gadoffre, Gilbert, 10
Galland, Peter, 10, 26
Gallus, Cornelius, 87
Garnier, Robert, 80
Gascoigne, George, 13, 47, 79, 139
Gilbert, Neal, 12
Gilson, Etienne, 115
Gombrich, E. H., 76
Goujet, Abbé Claude-Pierre, 88
Gourmont, Remy de, 1
Grévin, Jacques, 42
Griffiths, Richard, 1
Grimal, Pierre, 84, 97, 142, 151
Guidiccioni, Giovanni, 100
Guillet, Pernette du, 42, 63

Habert, François, 89
Harsy, Antoine de, 21, 39
Harvey, Lawrence, 17
Heinze, Richard, 93
Henri II, King of France, 15, 34, 38–39, 44–45, 47, 55, 82, 123, 165–166
Hermogenes, 31
Héroet, Antoine, 142
Hill, Raymond T., 151
History, 12, 20, 51, 76, 88, 107, 111, 116, 120, 121, 125, 132, 134, 135, 137, 138, 158, 170
Homer, 7, 68, 88

Horace, 8, 20, 21, 29, 35, 41, 45, 46, 67, 69, 70, 71–72, 83, 88, 104, 115, 129, 142, 143–145, 146, 147, 149, 152, 158–159, 164
Hugo, Victor, 30
Hulubei, Alice, 88

Illumination, 73, 74, 79, 160
Imagination, 1, 12, 16, 22, 27, 34, 50, 70, 73, 75, 82, 96, 154, 171
Imitation: of authors, 3, 7, 79, 87, 88–89, 98, 102, 106, 144; and translation, 4, 37, 46, 84–85, 95, 96, 152; of nature, 14, 48, 74, 77, 128; of language, 43
Induction and deduction, 9, 17, 19, 55, 80, 159, 162
Ingenium, 27, 70, 71, 75, 81, 82, 96
Invention, 8, 9, 16, 22, 23, 33–37, 42, 44, 78, 79, 85, 86, 96, 168–169
Irony, 54, 55, 62, 67, 119, 121, 125, 130, 133, 134, 135, 140, 145, 146–148, 149, 153, 155, 159, 164, 170
Isidore of Seville, 73

Jamyn, Amadis, 26, 69
Jasinski, Max, 97
Jeanne d'Albret, Queen of Navarre, 12
Jodelle, Etienne, 14, 78
Johannes Scotus Erigena, 128
Judgment, 8, 9, 16–17, 20, 23, 24, 33, 34, 40, 46, 70, 71, 81, 122, 126, 162, 164, 168, 170
Julius III, Pope, 157, 162
Jung, Marc-René, 165
Juvenal, 87, 139

Klein, Robert, 76
Krappe, Alexander Haggerty, 88
Kristeller, Paul Oskar, 3

Labé, Louise, 17
La Ceppède, Jean de, 148
Lambin, Denis, 10
Langlois, Ernest, 161
Lansac, Louis de, 32
Lapp, John C., 67, 119
La Taille, Jean de, 20
Laudun, Pierre de, 48
Laumonier, Paul, 58, 71
Le Blanc, Richard, 86
Le Caron, Louis, 76
Lechner, Sister Joan Marie, 23, 62
Lee, Sidney, 117
Lefèvre d'Etaples, Jacques, 11
Legrand, Jacques, 26
Le Hir, Yves, 34
Lemaire de Belges, Jean, 13, 20
Lenient, Charles F., 8
Leonardo da Vinci, 70
Le Queux, Regnaud, 27
Le Roy, Loys, 10, 86–87, 94, 152, 153
L'Hospital, Michel de, 38, 85
Logic: in composition, 1, 3, 15, 22; traditional, 9; distinguished from dialectic, 10–11; evolution of, 10–12, 168; method, 12–14, 55; enthymeme, 17, 83; poetic, 22, 43, 103, 126, 130–132, 133, 147, 156, 163–164, 165, 168, 171; thematic, 162. *See also* Argument, Cause, Effect, Induction and deduction, Judgment, Syllogism
Longinus, 31, 47, 72
Lucan, 123
Lucian, 39, 147

McFarlane, I. D., 1
Macrin, Salmon, 90, 104
Magny, Oliver de, 32, 146, 151, 155, 163
Mallarmé, Stéphane, 101
Manilius, 87, 95
Marbeuf, Pierre de, 160
Marcellus II, Pope, 153
Marguerite de France, Sister of Henri II, 152, 164–165, 171
Marguerite de Valois, Queen of Navarre, 46
Marot, Clément, 31, 39, 52, 58, 63, 84
Martial, 80, 81, 134
Marvell, Andrew, 18
Maurat-Ballange, Albert, 10
Melanchthon, Philipp, 12, 39, 82
Memory: in literary composition, 14, 85, 96, 111, 151, 153, 165; criticized, 17, 78; location of, 23; in rhetoric, 30, 34; artificial, 80, 165

Metaphor, 23, 28, 42–43, 48, 50, 51, 62, 74, 130, 131, 132, 155
Michel, Guillaume, 86
Michelangelo, 8
Miller, Perry, 11, 12, 24
Minard, Antoine, 48
Minturno, Antonio, 26, 45, 74
Molinet, Jean, 29
Molza, Francesco Maria, 101
Montaigne, Michel de, 8, 9, 12, 13, 14, 16, 17, 20, 22, 23, 31, 33, 45, 68, 69, 70, 72, 73, 75, 78, 79, 80, 81–82, 84, 151, 159
Moreau, Pierre, 163
Morel, Jean, 44, 149, 156
Mornet, Daniel, 21
Motin, Pierre, 76
Mozzarello, Giovanni, 98
Muret, Marc-Antoine, 10, 63, 78, 104, 128

Nature: and poem, 8; and reason, 11; imitation, 14, 37, 48, 73, 77, 86; in discourse, 15; natural judgment, 16; image, 19, 21; natural method, 20, 34, 38, 40, 62; and dialectic, 24; and art, 68–70, 71–72, 74, 75, 79, 82, 85, 96, 124, 137, 149–150, 170, 171; vague, 76; and fortune, 81; mental analogue, 107; fallen, 116; powers of, 118; elemental, 130–133, 139
Navagero, Andrea, 104
Nelson, C. E., 148
New Comedy, 146
Nichols, Stephen G., Jr., 84
Nolhac, Pierre de, 7, 10, 45

Olivier, François, 2
Ong, Father Walter J., 10, 11, 49
Ovid, 26, 91, 115, 129, 138

Panofsky, Erwin, 116
Paschal, Pierre de, 122, 165
Pasquier, Etienne, 9
Patch, Howard R., 81, 142
Pater, Walter, 117
Patterson, Warner Forrest, 2, 25, 30, 57, 74
Paul IV, Pope, 145, 157
Paul, Saint, 107, 111, 171, 172
Peacham, Henry, 146
Peletier du Mans, Jacques, 27, 29, 69, 70, 73, 124, 141
Persius, 140
Peter of Spain, 21
Petrarca, Francesco, 7, 11, 26, 50, 70, 81, 97, 98, 99, 101, 102–103, 104, 115, 124, 152, 160, 164, 169
Peyre, Henri, 2
Piccolomini, Alessandro, 141
Pindar, 87
Plato, 40, 70
Plutarch, 76
Poetic fury, 25, 32, 36, 41, 67, 140, 144, 148, 167
Point of view, 32–33, 54, 62, 72, 75, 76, 106, 120–122, 124, 132, 133, 137, 154, 155, 156, 168, 169, 170, 171
Pontano, Giovanni, 14, 87, 138
Puttenham, George, 57, 61, 77

Quadrivium, 11
Quintilian, 7, 10, 13, 18, 20, 21, 22, 30, 31, 32, 34, 35, 36, 37, 38, 39, 41, 43, 45, 47, 48, 49, 50, 51, 52, 53, 54, 55, 57, 58, 59, 61, 63, 64, 69, 70, 71, 73, 74, 78, 80, 83, 85, 88, 104, 122, 129, 136, 140

Rabelais, François, 17, 21, 23, 33, 50, 68, 71, 83, 115, 147, 161
Rainolds, John, 14
Ramus, Peter (Pierre de la Ramée), 9–13, 16, 17, 19, 20, 22, 24, 26, 33, 35, 40, 62, 68, 70, 82, 88, 103, 120, 162, 168
Raymond, Marcel, 2, 8, 17–18, 87
Rhetoric: traditional, 1, 62, 120; combined with logic, 1, 3, 8, 11, 13, 25, 28, 33, 49–50, 70, 71, 167, 172; criticized, 2; distinguished from logic, 11, 167; and poetry, 21, 25–27, 28, 29, 30, 70, 85, 104, 129, 130, 167; reformed, 29, 64; method, 35, 41, 55, 144, 147, 163
Riccoboni, Antonio, 18
Richardson, Alexander, 24
Romantic, 1, 2, 116, 120, 150, 154

Ronsard, Pierre de, 4, 7, 10, 14, 18, 19, 21, 22, 25, 26, 27, 30, 31, 32, 33, 34, 35, 36, 38, 39, 41, 42, 44, 46, 48, 49, 50, 51, 53, 54, 55, 56, 57, 58, 59, 60, 61, 62, 63, 68, 69, 71, 87, 97, 101, 102, 124, 126, 128, 129, 133, 142, 143, 146, 150, 151, 153, 156, 159, 160, 161, 165

Saba, Guido, 2, 104, 142, 154
Sainte-Beuve, Charles Augustin, 2, 97
Saint-Gelais, Mellin de, 42, 68, 165
Saint-Gelais, Octavien de, 84
Salanus, 27
Saliat, Pierre, 78
Sannazaro, Jacopo, 77, 99, 129, 138
Sansovino, Francesco, 99
Satire, 18, 26, 32, 36, 41, 52, 54, 57, 97, 122, 140, 141–147, 149, 151, 157, 158–159, 161, 163–165, 166
Satterthwaite, Alfred, 97, 119, 120, 154
Saulnier, Verdun, 2, 46, 50, 84, 93, 97, 120, 126, 139, 151
Scaliger, Julius Caesar, 8, 13, 19, 24, 26, 28, 40, 42, 49, 57, 73, 74, 80, 140
Scève, Maurice, 20, 52, 54, 55, 56, 59, 63, 125
Screech, M. A., 1, 143, 152, 160
Sebillet, Thomas, 17, 26, 29, 33, 40, 73, 84, 86, 96, 141
Seneca, 48
Seznec, Jean, 75
Shakespeare, William, 42
Sherry, Richard, 82
Sidney, Sir Philip, 73
Silver, Isidore, 87
Simonides, 76
Six, André, 125
Sozzi, L., 161
Spenser, Edmund, 45
Speroni, Sperone, 28
Spingarn, Joel Elias, 29
Spitzer, Leo, 106
Stone, Donald, Jr., 7, 69, 79
Sturm, Jean, 11
Style, 34, 35, 36, 37, 92, 157; elevated, 27, 88, 151; decorum, 31, 40–46, 69, 152, 162; levels of, 40–46; figures, schemes and tropes demonstrated, 50–64, 150, 151, 153–154, 155; amplification, 46–47; ornaments, 47–49; stressed, 64–85; low, 72, 141–144, 149, 151; figured, 73, 78–79; forceful, 104,; narrative and imitative, 122; conclusion, 171
Surrey, William Howard, Earl of, 47, 61
Syllogism, 17–19, 24, 163–164, 168–169

Tacitus, 30
Tahureau, Jacques, 74, 165
Talon, Omer, 50, 61
Tartaret, Pierre, 21
Tasso, Torquato, 22, 28, 37, 74
Teaching, pleasing, moving, 22, 31, 36, 41, 59–50, 74, 82, 121, 159
Theocritus, 46
Thibaudet, Albert, 24
Things and words (*res* and *verba*), 8, 21, 24, 34, 69, 71, 73, 78, 85, 89, 142
Tibullus, 115
Toldo, Pietro, 161
Tomitano, Bernardino, 101
Translation, 3, 4, 10, 25, 27, 55, 84–96, 123, 152–153, 169
Trivium, 1, 3, 10, 23, 103, 167–168. *See also* Education
Turberville, George, 18
Turnèbe, Adrien, 31, 46
Tuve, Rosemond, 14, 18, 32, 62, 76, 159
Tyard, Pontus de, 15, 63, 74, 76, 79

Valla, Lorenzo, 11
Vauquelin de la Fresnaye, Jean, 141
Vergil, 3, 37, 46, 50, 52, 54, 57, 68, 84–95, 102, 115, 119, 124, 134–135, 136–137, 151, 152, 153, 164, 169
Verlaine, Paul, 2, 79
Vianey, Joseph, 2, 46, 47, 84, 88, 97, 134, 139, 142, 151
Vida, Marco Girolamo, 86
Villey, Pierre, 28
Villon, François, 118
Vinsauf, Geoffroi de, 13
Vipper, G., 1
Virtue, 39, 44, 59, 69, 70, 71, 72, 75, 80–82, 98, 108, 123, 139–140, 150, 151, 156, 163, 164–166, 171

Volpe, Girolamo, 100

Warren, Austin, 159
Weber, Henri, 2–3, 33, 53, 88, 97, 120, 142, 146, 151, 154, 159, 160
Weinberg, Bernard, 13, 26, 37, 122
Wellek, René, 159
Wilkins, Ernest, 7
Wyatt, Sir Thomas, 160

Yates, Frances, 24